# Home Builder

## David Alan Rundle

Reading
BOROUGH

London: The Stationery Office

Applications for reproduction should be made in writing to The Stationery Office Limited, St Crispins, Duke Street, Norwich NR3 1PD

ISBN 0 11 701997 6

Cataloguing in Publication Data

A CIP catalogue record for this book is available from the British Library

Published by The Stationery Office and available from:

**The Publications Centre**
(mail, telephone and fax orders only)
PO Box 276, London SW8 5DT
General enquiries 0171 873 0011
Telephone orders 0171 873 9090
Fax orders 0171 873 8200

**The Stationery Office Bookshops**
59–60 Holborn Viaduct, London EC1A 2FD
temporary until mid 1998
(counter service and fax orders only)
Fax 0171 831 1326
68–69 Bull Street, Birmingham B4 6AD
0121 236 9696  Fax 0121 236 9699
33 Wine Street, Bristol BS1 2BQ
0117 9264306  Fax 0117 9294515
9–21 Princess Street, Manchester M60 8AS
0161 834 7201  Fax 0161 833 0634
16 Arthur Street, Belfast BT1 4GD
01232 238451  Fax 01232 235401
The Stationery Office Oriel Bookshop
The Friary, Cardiff CF1 4AA
01222 395548  Fax 01222 384347
71 Lothian Road, Edinburgh EH3 9AZ
(counter service only)

Customers in Scotland may
mail, telephone or fax their orders to:
Scottish Publications Sales
South Gyle Crescent, Edinburgh EH12 9EB
0131  228 4181  Fax 0131 622 7017

**The Stationery Office's Accredited Agents**
(see Yellow Pages)

*and through good booksellers*

Printed in the United Kingdom for TSO
J0028278 4/98 C50 10170

# Foreword

**Owen Luder CBE,**
Past President RIBA FRSA,
Vice-Chairman Architects Registration Board, Vice-Chairman Academy of Experts

One of the biggest problems facing us into the next millennium is the provision of sufficient and adequate housing to meet the demands of a growing and changing population.

A significant part of that demand will be met by adapting and extending existing homes to provide better and more spacious accommodation to meet the changing needs for existing occupiers.

*HomeBuilder* is here to help all involved in designing and building house extensions get it right from the start. It is important to avoid mistakes that will be difficult, expensive and heartrending to rectify later.

Do you need planning approval? If so, are you a special case? What are the special requirements if your house is listed? What do you have to do to meet the requirements of the building regulations? Again, which work is exempted and which is controlled? What about foundations and underpinning? Cavity wall infilling? Wiring and piping? What kind of roof?

Two experienced authors have put together this very practical guide through the maze of planning and building regulations and other building legislation that not only controls what you are allowed to do, but also ensure it is carried out properly in a way that will be a pleasure to you and your neighbours.

No building is successful unless it works properly. If the roof leaks, or the wind whistles through ill-fitting windows, the interior environment is uncomfortable or hostile to occupants and users and it has failed the user test.

This book helps the professional and the homeowner to design and construct the extension that meets the requirement that it must not only look good and work but also comply with the regulations.

Owen Luder CBE PPRIBA
November 1997

# Contents

# LIST OF DIAGRAMS

# LIST OF TABLES

# LIST OF TECHNICAL SPECIFICATIONS
Technical specifications describe means of construction

# Preface

**About *HomeBuilder***

**Keys and symbols**

**Controls**

**Standards**

# About *HomeBuilder*

There are numerous rules and regulations that govern what you can and cannot do if you plan to construct, extend, or alter a building.

In the UK, these rules and regulations have grown up over the years and include national and local legislation, the requirements of public and private bodies supplying water, heat, power and like services, the development of public health policies, the implications for environmental protection and so on. *HomeBuilder* is a guide through this sometimes complicated area, providing practical advice to those intending to commission, design, specify and carry out building work on domestic properties to meet the procedural and technical requirements of planning and building controls in England and Wales.

*HomeBuilder* gives guidance on:
- **alterations** to a house (there is a special section on loft conversions);
- **extensions** to a house at the front, back, side, etc.;
- the **addition of extra storeys** (but not to a house which has, or would have, more than three storeys);
- **detached buildings** for use with a house, such as garages, car ports, greenhouses and other small buildings;
- **access** to a house.

*HomeBuilder* does **not** give guidance to meet the requirements in Scotland or in Northern Ireland where different controls apply. And, it does **not** give specific guidance on converting a building or house or a part of a house to **separate** self-contained accommodation (such as flats), although these matters are touched upon when *HomeBuilder* gives guidance on:
- **converting a building to a house**;
- **converting a part of a house** to self-contained but not separate accommodation.

## Using *Homebuilder*

Building work can be complicated in that all operations are linked to others; for example, the building of a wall requires not only attention to the structure itself but also to the provision made for foundations, supporting structures, fire resistance, roofs, floors, heat conservation, windows, wiring, plumbing, sewage disposal and so on. Similarly, one planning requirement may apply to more than one part of a building, and a part of the building can be subject to more than one requirement. The guidance in *Homebuilder* helps readers understand this and presents the various operations and specifications in easily identifiable parts, arranged as described below.

### Part 1

The first step is to find out whether what you want to do is subject to any controls and, if so, what are the requirements. Sections are devoted to planning controls, to explanation of planning consent for any "development" (widely defined), to what you need to know about development permitted without consent, to what are your "permitted development rights", and to those special cases where such rights may be taken back so that you will, after all, need consent – perhaps with conditions attached. The rather different approach to building controls is explained – if what you intend is defined as "building work" or as a "material change of use" – and the likely limits on the application of the requirements. You have to be sure that the work which is carried out complies with these requirements.

## Part 2

If you find that you will need planning consent or have to meet the building control requirements you will inevitably have to deal with some paperwork. Sections give guidance on completing consent applications, documentation for planning control purposes and those other applications which you may have to make depending on circumstances. For the notices which will have to be given for building control purposes and the other information which you can deposit if you choose to do so (the "full plans" option) the procedures will obviously be somewhat different; explanations are given depending on whether you decide to deal with the local authority's building control department or with an approved inspector of your choice.

## Part 3

Because planning legislation requires consents to be given, it is not possible to give guidance that will ensure that your application is a success. However, *HomeBuilder* does give guidance that can increase your chances of success and discusses what to do if your plans are refused.

## Part 4

Building regulations usually set requirements that must be satisfied; here are explained the requirements which apply to the various operations and procedures involved in the work you are undertaking. Look out for **limits on the application** of some of the requirements. Guidance is given, sometimes using technical specifications, a table or a diagram, on what you can do to help meet them. Part 4 is divided into a number of detailed sections and is more fully explained later on (⇨ Using Part 4).

## Appendices

The Appendices A to H give additional information to support the main text. Sometimes several parts of the building have to be considered at the same time and it is convenient to deal with them together in one place. There are five sections in the Appendix that do this: B=Structural stability; C=Means of escape; D=Energy conservation; E=Ventilation; and G=Loft conversions.

# Sources

Much of *HomeBuilder* is based on, and occasionally quotes verbatim from, existing regulations specified by various authorities, both public and private. Sources used are:

**Building regulations**     (BR) Referred to throughout *HomeBuilder* and based on the *Building Regulations 1991, amended 1994* (unless otherwise stated). They are published by The Stationery Office. Where *HomeBuilder* quotes verbatim, the relevant reference is given: for example, "(BR B2)" after a reference means Requirement B2 of Schedule 1 of the building regulations.

**Approved documents**   (AD) Occasionally referred to, especially in diagrams and tables. The approved documents support – and have, over the years, grown out of – the building regulations. They are published by The Stationery Office. The approved documents give practical advice on meeting the requirements. If you follow this guidance, the planning authorities may well look on it as evidence tending to show that you are meeting the requirements. If you choose not to follow the guidance, then it becomes your responsibility to show that you are meeting the requirements by some other means.

**The Act**      Appears occasionally within the text and means the Building Act 1984.

**Alternative approaches**   There are occasional references in *HomeBuilder* to alternative approaches. These are usually references to codes of practice published by the British Standards Institution (BSI). The codes are recommendations written for experienced designers and, because they are more comprehensive, some of the provisions might go beyond the provisions needed to meet the regulations. You should consider whether a particular recommendation in a code is relevant, remembering that the building regulations do not require more to be done than is needed to secure reasonable standards of health, safety and energy conservation.

## Seek out the specialists

Professional advice should be taken from a registered architect, a chartered building surveyor or planning consultant especially if there are unusual circumstances. For example, when the site includes difficult ground or if it is an existing building in a conservation area, or is listed as of architectural or historic importance. The local authority can give advice in these situations.

You should also obtain advice if you plan to adopt technical specifications other than those given; also if work to any part of an adjoining building is involved.

## KeepIng a record

Although there is no requirement to do so, you might find it useful to keep a record, which could be passed on to any future owners. This might include drawings (preferably as built), specifications and building contracts, details of the location of pipework, electrical wiring and other services, cut off points and maintenance items, also any agreements you may have reached with neighbours.

Other information to record might include the manufacturers and colours of paints used and warranties, operating instructions and servicing instructions for mechanical and electrical equipment as such items as boilers, time clocks, pumps and motorised valves, shower units, unvented hot water systems, extract fans, electrical distribution boards and current breakers or fuse boxes.

# Keys and symbols

Throughout *HomeBuilder*, especially in Part 4 and the Appendices, keys and symbols are used to highlight and clarify the text. They are explained below and also in the opening pages of Part 4 (⇨ Using Part 4).

| | |
|---|---|
| ⇨ | Cross-references that appear throughout. |
| BR | The Building Regulations (⇨ Sources). |
| AD | Approved Documents (⇨ Sources). |
| 📖 | Brief explanations and definitions of terms used in the legislation. |
| ⚑ | Additional comment, not part of the BRs or ADs, etc. |
| ☞ | Exit sign: building matters outside the scope of *HomeBuilder*. |
| WBL | Water Byelaws |
| BS | British Standard |
| Checklist | Some sections, and sub-sections, of *HomeBuilder* include *CHECKLISTS*, provided to ensure that all work planned and/or carried out meets the necessary requirements. The reader is invited to tick-off the boxes accordingly. |

The Technical Specifications (TS) are shown thus:

---

**4.5–1: Roof coverings**

---

and are referred from the text by "TS" and the relevant number.

# Controls

If you construct, extend or alter a building you will probably need to take account of planning or building controls, sometimes both. These controls, which can also apply to the change of use of a building, have different purposes and are administered by separate departments of the local authority. *HomeBuilder* addresses this in more detail later on, but here general guidance is useful in understanding this often tricky matter.

## Who needs controls – and why?

Controls exist for a number of very sound reasons; to:
- prevent the proliferation of eyesores;
- avoid conflict with local site conditions and the interests of those in neighbouring properties;
- ensure that any alterations or extensions to buildings are properly constructed, safe, and fit for their intended purpose.

## What's the difference?

Planning and building controls can apply to:
- new buildings;
- extensions;
- alterations;
- changes of use.

## Planning control

Planning control is solely the responsibility of the local authority (fees are fixed). If planning controls do apply planning permission is discretionary although some building work and some changes of use are automatically permitted development.

## Building control

Building control is either the responsibility of the local authority (fees are fixed) or of an approved inspector – fees are negotiable. The choice is yours. If building controls do apply you must comply with the requirements. Some building work and changes are exempt. If you choose the local authority route you can give a building notice or you can deposit full plans – again the choice is yours. You must expect the work to be inspected.

## Other constraints

As well as the planning and building control authorities one or more of the following factors could have a bearing on what you intend to do:

- restrictive covenants;
- building society agreements;
- landlords;
- tenants;
- neighbours (party walls, right to light, access, etc.);
- housebuilder's warranty;
- insurers;
- Environmental Agency (liquid-waste disposal, etc.)
- water, electricity and gas authorities.

# Meeting control requirements

In order to have your plans accepted and to construct your building in a way that meets all the requirements you need to keep accurate records – at all stages of the process from design to completion. You may, too, choose to employ specialist help for all or part of the project.

**Keeping a record**    Although there is no requirement to do so, you might find it useful to keep a record, which could be passed on to any future owners. This might include drawings (preferably as built), specifications and building contracts, details of the location of pipework, electrical wiring and other services, cut-off points and maintenance items, also any agreements you may have reached with neighbours.

Other information to record might include the manufacturers and colours of paints used and warranties, operating instructions and servicing instructions for mechanical and electrical equipment and such items as boilers, time clocks, pumps and motorised valves, shower units, unvented hot-water systems, extract fans, electrical distribution boards and current breakers or fuse boxes.

**Seek out the specialists**    Professional advice should be taken from a registered architect, a chartered building surveyor or planning consultant especially if there are unusual circumstances. For example, when the site includes difficult ground or if it is an existing building in a conservation area, or is listed as of architectural or historic importance. The local authority can give advice in these situations.

You should also obtain advice if you plan to adopt technical specifications other than those given; also if work to any part of an adjoining building is involved.

# Standards

Standards are a complex subject. The readership of *HomeBuilder* will range from those who have never heard of (let alone read) a British Standard to those who are beginning to come to grips with the new European numbering system which has already given standards bodies much difficulty.

Further complications exist in that standards are in a state of flux as countries convert from their own national standards to those of European or international standards – for example, in the UK from those published by the British Standards Institution (BSI). The widely used DIN standard, too, is being replaced and (not surprisingly) does not always correspond one-for-one with the new EN standards.

In *HomeBuilder*, therefore, the standards used are numerous.
- **British standard**. Look for the Kitemark which shows that the product has been tested by the BSI and complies with the relevant standard.
- **Technical approvals**. Ask the supplier or manufacturer for a Certificate from one of the government-designated Technical Approval bodies. There are two – the British Board of Agrément and Wimpey Laboratories (WIMLAS) – and the Certificate shows that the product has been tested by one of them.
- **ISO standards**. The international standard now in use by more than 100 national bodies which make up the International Standards Organisation; for example, BS/ISO, DIN/ISO, EN/ISO and so on.
- Dimensions are given in metric.

# 1 What the law requires

**The guidance that follows is for**

**1.1 Planning control**

**1.2 Building control**

# 1.1
# Planning control

## INTRODUCTION

The rules and regulations embodied in planning control are designed to allow you to add to or alter your home while at the same time taking account of the likely impact on your neighbours, the public and the environment as a whole. They try to strike a balance between the householder's desire to alter his or her property as they wish and the needs of the community at large.

Many of the changes, in particular external changes, which you might wish to make to your home come within the scope of planning legislation. Certain changes in the way in which your home is used may also be affected by planning legislation. Therefore, if you intend to make any significant changes, you will need to consider whether you need to apply for planning permission.

In many cases, it will not be necessary to make a planning application, because either the works concerned are not **development** (⇨ 1.1.1) or because they are **permitted development** (⇨ 1.1.2).

> 📖 **Development** is the carrying-out of building, engineering, mining, or other operations, in, on, over or under land, or the making of any material change in the use of any building or land.
>
> **Permitted development** is where the government has, in effect, granted nationwide planning permission for certain works. However these rights may be modified in certain special cases (⇨ 1.1.3).

Even if the changes that you wish to make do require planning permission, this is not in itself a cause for concern. Most reasonable proposals are approved and there is much you can do to ensure that your proposal has the best possible chance of success.

## HOW TO PROCEED

If what you want to do will follow the guidance and advice, your planning application will probably be dealt with more quickly and is very likely to be approved. If, on the other hand, what you propose does not follow the guidance, your chances of success are slimmer. In all cases, the local planning authority will always take account of the impact of your particular development on your neighbours and the street scene. So there will be times when, even if your application complies with the guidelines, it will be unacceptable; likewise, times when proposals which do not comply fully with the guidelines will nevertheless be approved.

When you visit your local planning authority you should ask whether any similar proposals in your area have been approved recently. You will probably find that you have to collect some information about your property. Your local planning authority will be able to tell you whether:

- your permitted development rights have been taken up;
- any of the special cases apply;
- any trees are protected.

## Special cases

*HomeBuilder* gives specific guidance on your permitted development rights where your property is in a conservation area or on land subject to an Article 1(4). It can only give general guidance for the other special cases which you may find helpful before a planning application is made.

Lastly, you should refer to your deeds to see whether there are any covenants which restrict what you can do. If there are, these could mean that you cannot go ahead whether or not you would need planning permission.

> *In most cases, the local planning authority and the local authority will be one and the same. However, in some areas such as national parks which cover the area of more than one local authority they might be a separate body. If you are unsure, your local planning authority should be able to help you.*

When you have the information you need, there are three steps which you must now take:

- check whether what you want to do is development (⇨ 1.1.1) as defined by planning legislation. It is important to understand that this extends beyond actual building works and can include changes in the way in which your property is used;
- if what you want to do is development, check whether it is permitted development (⇨ 1.1.2) – that is, work for which you do not need to make a planning application after taking other special cases (⇨ 1.1.3) into account;
- finally, if you do need to make a planning application, before you do so consult Parts 2 and 3 of *HomeBuilder*.

# 1.1.1 Development

Improvements or alterations to a property which do not materially affect the external appearance of a building are specifically excluded from the definition of development with one exception. The exception is work which, although below ground, will provide additional space.

> *Whether work does materially affect the external appearance of a building can be a matter of dispute and is likely to be decided on a case-by-case basis. The decision is likely to depend on whether the work has a significant effect on the appearance rather than just on the materials to be used (or the way they are to be used). The higher the initial standard of appearance the more possible it becomes that it will be judged material. It has to be said that some alterations can, at best, be seen as insensitive.*

For most householders, there are four areas considered to be development. These areas are:

- alterations which materially affect the external appearance, such as forming new openings and closing others;
- additions, such as an extension, loft conversion, conservatory porch, garage, or their like;
- other works, such as erecting a garden shed, wall or fence, laying a drive, digging a swimming pool, and installing a satellite dish or radio transmitter aerial;
- a material change of use, such as using or letting your garage for business use. This may well include a hobby which expands beyond what could reasonably be considered as normal domestic use or allowing your property to be used for business, to the extent that the main use and overall character would no longer be typical of a private dwelling.

  *Whether some changes of use are regarded as material changes is a matter of degree – and whether or not they will need planning permission will depend on the amount of the change. Others are always material changes which will always need planning permission.*

These "other" material changes are outside the scope of *HomeBuilder* but will include the following:
- separating a house into flats or bedsits;
- subdividing a flat;
- providing a separate dwelling for an elderly relative or live-in help.

## 1.1.2 Permitted development

What is permitted development can be more easily understood if, first, its terms are defined and, second, a checklist is created which identifies the type of work affected.

### Definitions

Terms used in the legislation include those in the following panel.

> A **curtilage** is a yard, garden or field attached to and enclosed with a dwelling house.
>
> A **highway** is any road or footpath used by vehicles or pedestrians.
>
> An **original dwelling** is the house as it was built or stood on 1 July 1948, excluding any extension built since that date.
>
> A **terraced house** is any house in a block of three or more – and including end-of-terrace houses.
>
> **Volume** is the product of the height, width and depth – all measured externally.

*CHECKLIST*
- ☐ Extensions
- ☐ Conservatories
- ☐ Small porches
- ☐ Satellite dishes and aerials
- ☐ Painting

- ☐ Roof extensions and loft conversions
- ☐ Garages, car ports, hard-standings and drives
- ☐ Sheds, greenhouses, other outbuildings, swimming pools
- ☐ Fuel storage tanks
- ☐ Walls, fences and gates
- ☐ Means of access
- ☐ Trees
- ☐ Material change of use
- ☐ Demolition

If the works you wish to carry out are permitted development, you do not have to submit a planning application. It is important, however, to check that you have interpreted the regulations correctly, otherwise you could be at risk of enforcement action and may even have to remove your extension or shed, etc. Refer to your checklist.

Sales people will often give you general advice as to whether or not you need planning permission, but you must check that such information is correct insofar as it affects your home. It is you and not the sales people who will be liable for any breaches of the planning regulations.

## Special cases

This planning control section of *HomeBuilder* deals with permitted development as it affects most houses, including the two special cases of development within **conservation areas** and on **Article 1(5) land**. However, for explanation of these and other special cases ⇨ 1.1.3.

## Extensions

The term "extension" includes **conservatories**, but see also **small porches, roof extensions** and **loft conversions** in this section.

Any extension, no matter how small, to a property divided into flats requires planning permission, as will any extension that creates a separate dwelling, such as a granny flat. Unless your house is one of the special cases many extensions, in particular single-storey extensions to the rear of the property, do not require planning permission.

### Conditions

The size of the extension that you can build as permitted development depends on the **volume** of the **original dwelling** and the volume of any later extensions.

In the case of **terraced houses** you can extend by up to 50m³, or 10 per cent of its original volume if that is more.

In all other cases, you can extend by up to 70m³, or 15 per cent of its original volume if that is more.

However, in both cases:
- the additional volume, calculated as a percentage, should be no more than 115m³; and
- any garages, outbuildings or other structures within 5m of the house, or 5m of

the house as extended, are treated as an extension to the original house, and therefore their volume must be included in the permitted development allowance.

## Other conditions

Any extension built using your permitted development rights must also meet other strict conditions. These include the following:

- the extension must not be higher than the highest part of the roof of the original house; and
- with one **exception**, no part of the extension should be nearer the **highway** than 20m or no nearer the highway than the original dwelling if that is already less than 20m from the highway. The exception is a small **porch** (⇨ below);

  *For the vast majority of houses, this would not affect an extension to the rear or side of the property. However, in the case of a corner property, you will invariably need to apply for planning permission for a side extension. Likewise, where a house backs onto a road, rather than another property, if the proposed extension is less than 20m from the road and extends beyond the existing rear building-line, you will again need to apply for planning permission.*

- if the extension will be over 4m high, it must be at least 2m from the boundary;

  *In practice, this means that for most two-storey extensions to terraced properties and even many semi-detached properties you will need to apply for planning permission.*

- it must not cover more than 50 per cent of the area of **curtilage** excluding the area of original building.

## Special cases

If your house is in a **conservation area** or on **Article 1(5) land**, even if it is detached, then you:

- only can extend by up to 50m$^3$, or 10 per cent of the volume of the original dwelling if that is more up to a maximum of 115m$^3$; and
- you must not clad it with timber, stone, artificial stone, plastics or tiles.

# Conservatories

In terms of permitted development, a conservatory is an extension to the house and exactly the same rules apply.

# Small porches

A porch is also an extension to the house and – with one exception – the rules for permitted development apply. The **exception** is a small porch, even if it is in front of the existing building, if it is outside an external door, not more than 3m high above ground level, not more than 3m$^2$ in area measured externally, and not less than 2m from your boundary with the highway.

# Satellite dishes and aerials

Permitted development rights in respect of satellite dishes vary according to where your property is located, the size of the dish and where you want to install it. A second satellite dish will always need planning permission. In most situations, you can install a dish up to 70cm diameter (but only 45cm if it is to be placed on a chimney). The highest part of the antenna should be positioned below the highest part of the roof or, in the case of a dish attached to the chimney, below the highest part of the chimney.

You are also required, as far as is practicable, to locate the dish so as to minimise its effect on the external appearance of the building and to remove it when it is no longer required.

### Special cases

If your house is on **Article 1(4) land** you need planning permission to install a dish up to 90cm diameter on a chimney. Article 1(4) land is land in Cleveland, Cornwall, Cumbria, Devon, Durham, Dyfed, Greater Manchester, Gwynedd, Humberside, Lancashire, Merseyside, Northumberland, North Yorkshire, South Yorkshire, Tyne & Wear, West Glamorgan and West Yorkshire.

In **conservation areas** and **Article 1(5) land**, you need planning permission to locate a satellite dish on a chimney or on any wall or roof slope that fronts a highway (or in the case of the Norfolk Broads, a waterway), or on any building over 15m high, even in the Article 1(4) areas above.

Ordinary television aerials do not generally require planning permission, unless they are restricted by an Article 4 direction (⇨ 1.1.3). Other aerials, for example those used by amateur radio enthusiasts, may require planning permission, depending on their precise size and location. Seek advice from your local planning authority.

## Painting

Planning permission is not required for painting your property, provided it is not an advertisement.

### Special cases

You will need to apply for planning permission if the property is a listed building (⇨ 1.1.3) and you intend to change the colour.

## Roof extensions and loft conversions

If you simply wish to install sloping roof lights or convert your existing loft to make usable floor space without altering the roof slope then planning permission will not be required, provided you do not create a separate dwelling. If, however, you wish to alter the existing roof slope by, for example, adding a dormer window or a loft extension, then you will need to apply for planning permission if the roof slope that you wish to alter fronts any highway (this would include the side roof slope, in the case of a corner property).

### Conditions

Certain conditions apply:

*   the roof extension should not be higher than the highest part of the original roof;
    *   📖 *Therefore, if your extension involves raising the ridge of the existing roof, you will require planning permission.*
*   the volume of the permitted roof extension or dormer is restricted to 40m³ in the case of a terraced house and to 50m³ in other cases;
    *   📖 *In practice, few extensions and alterations are likely to exceed these limits.*

- the volume of the extension when taken together with any other extensions should not increase the volume of the original house by more than 50m³ (or 10 per cent of its original volume if that is more) in the case of a terraced house or by 70m³ (or 15 per cent of its original volume if that is more) in all other cases.

### Special cases

You will always need to apply for planning permission if you live within a **conservation area** or on **Article 1(5) land**.

## Garages, car ports, hard-standings and drives

Garages and car ports which would be less than 5m from the existing house (including any extensions) are treated as an extension to the house (⇨ above). If they are positioned more than 5m away from the house, then they are treated as a shed or outbuilding (⇨ below).

Regardless of the location of the garage, it can only be used for purposes incidental to the enjoyment of a dwelling house and cannot be used for commercial purposes.

For hard-standings and drives you do not, with one exception, need to apply for planning permission to provide a hard-standing on which to park your car, or to form a drive. The **exception** is forming a drive which requires extensive excavation.

### Special cases

If your house is in a **conservation area** or on **Article 1(5) land**, then a garage or car port wherever it is sited, is treated as an **extension** to the original house (⇨ above).

## Sheds, greenhouses, other outbuildings, swimming pools

Any structure less than 5m from the house – even in its extended form – is treated as an extension. In such circumstances it may be worth siting your building more than 5m from the house if this will avoid making a planning application.

> 📖 *You can erect a building or enclosure for a "purpose incidental to the enjoyment of a dwelling house", subject to certain conditions. The range of buildings/structure is quite wide and includes sheds, greenhouses, gazebos, aviaries and enclosures for pets, including bees. In fact, almost anything that you or your family may do for recreational purposes or as a hobby; it does not, however, include the creation of a separate dwelling.*

### Conditions

There are conditions that you must comply with:

- the building should be no more than 4m high in the case of a ridged (sloping) roof and 3m in other cases;
- the total area of the original garden covered by building or enclosures must be less than 50 per cent;
- no part of the building should be nearer the highway than 20m or no nearer the highway than the original dwelling if that is already less than 20m from the highway.

HomeBuilder                                                    Part 1: What the law requires

### *Special cases*

If you live within a **conservation area** or on **Article 1(5) land**, any building which is larger than 10m³ is treated as an extension to the house (⇨ above).

> *This volume is, in fact, very small; many separate buildings, including modest garden sheds, could come into this category.*

## Fuel storage tanks

Planning permission is required for all fuel storage tanks with one exception. The **exception** is a tank used for heating oil, smaller than 3,500 litres, no more than 3m above ground and no nearer the highway than 20m – or no nearer the highway than the original dwelling if that is already less than 20m from the highway.

## Walls, fences and gates

You do not need planning permission to erect a wall, fence or gate up to 2m high above ground level with one exception. If your property is higher than that of your neighbour's, the height is measured above the ground level on your property.

The **exception** is that if the wall or fence is next to a road used by motor vehicles then you will need planning permission if the height will be more than 1m above ground level at any point even if, for example, only the piers to a gate or wall would be higher.

> *If the height of your existing wall, fence or gate is already more than the heights given above, you can still repair it or alter it – but not replace it – that is, provided you do not increase its existing height.*

## Means of access

If your new access is part of some other development that is permitted development, such as a garage or a hard-standing for a car, then, with one exception, you do not require planning permission for it or for the opening in the boundary.

The **exception** is that if your house is on a trunk-road or other classified road, you will always require planning permission to form a new access, even if it is only for pedestrians.

> *If you want the roadside kerb dropped, you will need to apply to the highway authority, which will usually carry out the works but at your expense.*

## Trees

There are three circumstances in which you may require consent from the local planning authority to remove or prune a protected tree even if the work is permitted development.

1  If the protected tree is covered by a tree preservation order.
2  If it is in a conservation area.
3  If it is part of a landscaping scheme.

> *In practice you can prune a protected tree if you use secateurs – but beware of using a saw. Do not remove any roots or branches without checking with the local authority first and note that you will be responsible for ensuring that anyone else carrying out the work for you is aware of these constraints.*

**10**    HomeBuilder

However, if you have planning permission for the work, even if it will involve the complete removal of a protected tree, you do not have to make another application for its removal. This does not apply if the work is carried out as permitted development.

### Tree preservation orders

If you wish to lop or fell a tree which is protected by a tree preservation order, you will need to make an application to the local planning authority six weeks in advance and, with one exception, wait for the decision before carrying out the work. The **exception** is if the tree is dangerous when you can fell or lop it without consent.

> *You will probably be required to plant a replacement tree of a size and species agreed with the authority, usually in the same spot.*

### Trees protected by landscaping conditions

The original planning consent of your house, particularly for newer properties, may require you to retain and maintain particular trees and shrubs for a specified period and even obtain consent before pruning.

### Special cases

If the tree is in a **conservation area** (and is not already covered by a tree preservation order or part of a landscaping scheme) you must give the local authority notice before doing any work with three exceptions.

1   You can take the tree out or lop it if its diameter is less than 75mm at a height of 1.5m above the ground.
2   You can take the tree out if its diameter is less than 100mm at a height of 1.5m above the ground but not lop it.
3   You can take the tree out (or lop it) if it is a fruit tree (however large).

> *The notice gives the authority time to make a tree preservation order if it wishes to do so. If it has not done so after six weeks you can carry on.*

## Material change of use

If you are forming a separate flat or bedsit, even if it is for a relative, you will require planning permission, but this is outside the scope of *HomeBuilder*.

You can use your home, garden and any building within the garden, for any "purpose incidental to the enjoyment of a dwelling house" without planning permission.

> *In essence, this means that anything that can reasonably be considered to be a reasonable activity for a householder is acceptable.*

For instance, you want to change the garage to a dining room or use a room or building specifically for a hobby. If you are considering altering or changing the use of your garage, you will need to check that there is not a planning condition requiring you to keep it available for parking.

Breeding pets, restoring or repairing your own car, using a room as a games room all come within the scope of permitted development. The scale of any hobby needs to be reasonable and, when it exceeds what can reasonably be expected for a residential property, you have probably reached the point where planning permission is required.

The use of your home for business purposes is slightly more complex; it is a matter of degree. For instance, if you wish to use a single room of your home as an office, you only have the occasional caller and delivery, and you are not employing anyone else, you are unlikely to need planning permission.

> *If, however, the use is more intensive and you employ people to work from your home, you will almost certainly require planning permission. One consideration may be whether or not the business use will predominate.*

Similarly, if you wish to work as a childminder using your own home you do not need planning permission. On the other hand, if you want to run a nursery from home, even if it involves only one or two rooms, you will need planning permission because the use is much more intensive.

## Demolition

Planning permission is not required:

- to demolish a building such as a shed or garage provided that it is less than 50cm³;
- to demolish a wall or fence;
- to demolish a building for health or safety reasons;
- if you have planning permission for redevelopment.

In all other cases, you will need a **prior approval consent**.

> *This gives the local planning authority the opportunity to approve details of the demolition and restoration of the site, if it so wishes.*

### Special cases

In a **conservation area** you will need a **prior approval consent** to demolish a building with a volume of more than 50m³ and a **conservation area consent** to demolish any of the following:

- a part of a building (even if small);
- a complete building if the volume is more than 115m³;
- in England, a gate, wall or fence over 1m high next to the highway or a public open space – over 2m high elsewhere;
- in Wales, a gate, wall or fence over 1m high next to a road used by vehicles; over 2m high elsewhere.

If the land is **Article 1(5) land** you do not also need to apply for **conservation area consent** for demolition.

## If you're still unsure

The golden rule is: if in doubt, check with the local planning authority first. Most authorities will be happy to give you informal advice, either by telephone or in person at the office. If you are told that planning permission is not required, it is generally best to ensure you get written confirmation.

Where cases are less clear-cut, or marginal, some authorities may ask you to apply for a **certificate of lawful development** (⇨ 2.1.6). The certificate will tell you whether the work which you wish to carry out is lawful, or whether you need to apply for planning permission. However, it will relate only to the work as shown on your application; if you subsequently change your mind and you wish to do something different, you must check again.

## If things go wrong

If you have followed the advice above, you should not find yourself in any conflict with the local planning authority.

Sometimes, however, even though the work you are carrying out is permitted development, a neighbour or passer-by might contact the local authority, which is then obliged to follow up any complaint. In this instance, it is best to provide any information requested so that the matter can be cleared up quickly. If there is any doubt, you should stop work while the matter is resolved.

If you do not respond to the authority's initial inquiries, even if it transpires that you do not need planning permission, you may find yourself receiving a **planning contravention notice** and you are required by law to respond to it. Failure to do so can lead to a substantial fine.

> *If you have carried out works that do require planning permission, and you have not obtained it, your are at risk of enforcement action. Most local planning authorities will give you the opportunity to remedy the problem. If you find yourself in this situation you would be well advised to seek professional advice.*

## 1.1.3  Other special cases

Guidance has been given in 1.1.2 regarding **Article 1(5) land** and **conservation areas**, but guidance has not been given in 1.1.2 regarding Article 4 directions, listed buildings, previous planning consents, and previous permitted developments.

Permitted development rights (⇨ 1.1.2) can be removed in special cases. Guidance for two of the special cases – Article 1(5) land and conservation areas – was given earlier with the guidance on permitted development (⇨ 1.1.2).

For the rest, local considerations can play a larger part and *HomeBuilder* can offer only general comments.

## Article 1(5) land

This is land in a National Park, an Area of Outstanding Natural Beauty (AONB), the Norfolk Broads, or an area designated under the Wild Life and Countryside Act. The local authority will tell you whether your property is in Article 1(5) land.

> *Some permitted development rights have been taken away and more stringent requirements are likely to be imposed.*

## Conservation areas

These are areas with clearly defined boundaries designated under the Planning Acts. The local authority will tell you whether your property is in a Conservation Area (⇨ Article 4 directions below).

> *Some permitted development rights have been taken away and more stringent requirements are likely to be imposed.*

## Article 4 directions

The directions known as Article 4 can remove some, or all, of a property's permitted development rights.

Article 4 directions usually cover a distinctive group of properties within a conservation area which have various common features that tie them together. If your property is covered by an Article 4 direction, you will need to check with the local planning authority precisely what can and cannot be done. There may even be different restrictions on your property, compared with that of your neighbour.

## Listed buildings

Since 1947, buildings which have been judged to be of special architectural and/or historic interest have been registered and are given statutory protection. The protection applies not only to the building but also to any other buildings and other structures, boundary walls and fences within the curtilage which will include the garden.

So, even if you do not need planning permission because the work is not development or is permitted development, you will need **listed building consent** for demolition or partial demolition and for any work which could affect the character of the building, such as internal and external alterations (which may include painting the outside).

> *The planning authority keeps a copy of the register of listed buildings. This tells you which buildings are protected, whether the building is listed Grade I (very rare), Grade II\* or Grade II and the reasons why. Remember that even if the building is not listed it may still attract special attention if it is located in a conservation area. If you own a listed building you must keep it in a good state of repair (grants may be available to help you meet the cost). If you do not the local authority can carry out any essential work – at your expense – and even compulsorily purchase the property.*

## Previous planning consents

Conditions attached to planning consents may impose restrictions and these will take precedence over permitted development rights.

## Previous permitted development

Some of the permitted development rights may have been taken up since the original house was built, either as rights or with the benefit of a planning permission, and with one exception these must be taken into account when calculating any remaining rights.

The **exception** is a small porch which meets certain conditions (⇨ 1.1.2).

# 1.2
# Building control

## INTRODUCTION

Building control regulations are necessary to ensure reasonable standards of health, safety and energy conservation in the public interest. What they require to be done is what it is reasonable to do, not what it is possible to do, so that the benefits justify the costs.

## EXEMPTIONS AND LIMITATIONS

The Building Act exempts some kinds of buildings from the Building Regulations but many of these are outside the scope of *HomeBuilder*. However, the regulations also exempt further kinds of buildings, define building work in some detail, and exempt some kinds of work. The definition of building work and the various exemptions are given below. If the regulations have not exempted a building or building work from a requirement, they may still do so if the work is an alteration. These exemptions are also given below. Even if the work is not exempt from a requirement there may be a limit on its application if certain conditions are met. These limits with each requirement are given in Part 4 of *HomeBuilder*.

Some kinds of protection fall outside the scope of the regulations altogether. These include the protection of property and contents against fire and theft. Both might require additional measures and more demanding provisions. The sometimes conflicting demands of escape and security should be thought through at the beginning and, if necessary, discussed with your local fire authority and your insurance company.

On the other hand, it might not be appropriate to follow the guidance where work is being done to a building that is listed as of historic or architectural importance (the local authority will tell you if your property is listed). Considerations of health, safety and energy conservation should then be balanced with the conservation interest, according to the circumstances of a particular case.

## 1.2.1  Exemptions

### CHECKLIST
- ☐ Exempt buildings
- ☐ Exempt building work
- ☐ Exempt change of use

You may find that what you intend to do is exempt. If it is not consult the later pages of this section.

The term "temporary" in **temporary buildings** means less than 28 days but what is a building in an age of mobile homes and portable buildings? The small caravan towed behind a car is clearly not a building; neither is a motor caravan.

> 📖 **A building** is any permanent or temporary building but not any other kind of structure or erection.

The problem arises with the large caravan or "mobile home", perhaps winched off a trailer and skids, possibly in two parts linked together on site, never to be moved again. Are these buildings and, if so, are they erected?

A rule of thumb might be that large caravans and mobile homes which can be lawfully driven or towed behind a vehicle on the public road are vehicles (and subject to the Caravans Act). Those which cannot, and have to be carried – even if they are not erected in the usual sense and may be moved to another site – are nevertheless and therefore subject to the Building Regulations and the 28-day rule.

## Exempt buildings

Exempt buildings will include greenhouses and agricultural buildings. Also the following.

### Detached buildings

These are buildings into which people do not normally go or go from time-to-time only to inspect or maintain fixed plant or machinery. Detached buildings are exempt if every point of the building is at least one-and-a-half times its height from both:

- the nearest point on the boundary of its curtilage; and
- any part of another building into which people can normally go.

> 📖 The **height** of a building is measured to half the height of the roof or wall (or the parapet, if there is one) whichever is the higher.
> A **curtilage** is a yard, garden or field attached to and enclosed with a dwelling house.
> The **floor area** of a building is measured between the inside faces of the outside walls and to the outer edge of the floor where there is no outside wall. The area is the total area of all the floors, if there is more than one.

### Small detached buildings

- buildings that are single storey, have a **floor area** of no more than 30m$^2$, contain no sleeping accommodation, are more than 1m from the boundary of their curtilage and are constructed substantially of **non-combustible materials**;
- buildings that have a floor area of no more than 15m$^2$ and contain no sleeping accommodation.

### Temporary buildings

Buildings that are not intended to remain where they are erected for more than 28 days.

> 📖 A **non-combustible material** – the highest level of reaction to fire performance. Examples include concrete and concrete bricks and blocks, fired clay, ceramics, metals, plaster and masonry, also products classified under British Standard 476.

## Exempt building work

This is defined as:

- the erection of an exempt building;
- the extension of an exempt building, provided that the building will remain exempt after it is extended;
- the extension of any building, whether or not the building is an exempt building, provided that the extension has an area of no more than 30m², is at ground level and is either: a **conservatory**, porch, covered yard or covered way, or a car port open on at least two sides.

> 📖 A **conservatory** has at least threequarters of the area of its roof and at least one half of the area of its external walls made of translucent material.

## Exempt change of use

Although the regulations define exempt buildings and exempt building work, they do not define exempt changes of use. However, a change will be exempt if either the building is an exempt building (and will remain so after the change), or the change is not a material change of use.

A change is a **material change of use** if, after the change, the building:

- is not presently being used as a **dwelling** but will be so;
- does not contain a **flat**, but will do so; or
- is an exempt **building**, but will no longer be one.

> 📖 A **dwelling** includes a dwelling house and a flat.
> A **flat** is separate and self-contained premises constructed or adapted for residential use and forming part of a building from some other part of which it is divided horizontally.

> 📑 *If the change of use is not exempt the building will have to comply with certain requirements (⇨ 1.2.2). Note that a loft conversion to provide additional accommodation for the dwelling is not a material change of use.*

## 1.2.2 Controlled work

### CHECKLIST

- ☐ Building work
- ☐ Services and fittings
- ☐ Insulation material (cavity walls)

☐   Underpinning

☐   Material change of use

If after reading 1.2.1 you find that the work you intend to carry out is not exempt you must now check whether it is **controlled work**. Controlled work is defined as the:

- erection of a **building** or the extension of a building, horizontally or vertically;
- provision or extension of a **controlled service** or **fitting**;
- material alteration of a building or a controlled service or fitting;
- insertion of **insulating material** into the cavity wall of a building;
- **underpinning** of a building.

> 📖   A **controlled service** or **fitting** is one on which parts of Schedule 1 of the Building Regulations imposes requirements concerning hygiene (Part G), drainage and water disposal (Part H) or heat-producing appliances (Part J).
>
> **Underpinning** involves supporting a building from underneath by excavating below an existing foundation, constructing a new foundation and supporting the existing foundation on the new one  (⇨ Appendix A2).

## Building work

Controlled work:

- the erection of a building;
- the horizontal or vertical extension of a building;
- a material alteration of a building
- a material change of use of a building.

> 📝 *Remember that a temporary building is exempt.*

### Erection or extension

> 📝 *Part 4 tells you the requirements which apply to each part of the building. You will see that there are limits, and also exceptions, to the application of some of the requirements. Read Appendix H1 to find out to which parts of the building the regulations apply.*

### Material alteration

> 📖   A **material alteration** is one which would, at any stage, result in the building or any part of it  (including a controlled service or fitting) which now complies with a relevant requirement no longer complying with it or, if it does not comply now, complying with it to any lesser extent.
>
> A **relevant requirement** is one in relation to which Part A of Schedule 1 of the Building Regulations imposes a requirement concerning the structure and Part B of the Schedule imposes a requirement concerning the means of escape, internal fire spread (structure), external fire spread or access and facilities for the fire service.

> 📝 *The reason for defining an alteration as "material" is to catch only those which, if they are not done properly, could present a significant risk to health or safety.*

*The reason for requiring compliance "at any stage" is to catch those which could present a risk while the work is being done, such as making a large opening in a wall. (The relevant requirements are listed in Appendix H1.)*

## Services and fittings

Controlled work:

* the provision or extension of a **controlled service** or **fitting**;
* a material alteration of a controlled service or fitting.

> 📖 The **passage of sound** is a complicated subject with many possibilities. It is therefore outside the scope of *HomeBuilder* and you should refer to the Approved Document E supporting the Building Regulations. Guidance particularly concerned with existing buildings is also available from the Building Research Establishment (⇨ Useful addresses).

### Provision or extension

*You will see (⇨ Appendix H2) that there are limits, and also exceptions, to the application of some of the requirements.*

### Material alteration

*None of the requirements listed in this building work section applies directly to an alteration to a controlled service or fitting. However, if, in carrying out the alteration, any of the requirements would be adversely affected, then the alteration becomes a material alteration and the same compliance rules will therefore apply.*

## Insulation material (cavity walls)

Controlled work:

* the insertion of cavity fill into the cavity wall of a building.
  *The insertion of insulation material in the cavity of an existing wall is deemed not to be a material alteration as defined in the regulations. Therefore, because cavity filling which is unsatisfactory or unsuited to the exposure conditions could prejudice a reasonable standard of health, it is now defined as building work, is subject to control and will be treated in the same way as the insertion of insulation in a new wall (⇨ 4.3.1).*

## Underpinning

Controlled work:

* the insertion of a new foundation to support an existing foundation.
  *It might be unwise to underpin only the settled part of a building because it can lead to more differential movement.*

It has been argued that underpinning an existing foundation is an addition and not strictly an alteration. Therefore, because unsatisfactory or inappropriate work could prejudice a reasonable standard of health or safety, underpinning is now defined as building work, is subject to control and will treated in the same way as new work (⇨ Appendices and also 4.1.5).

> 🕮 *Underpinning should not be undertaken without specialist advice. Partial underpinning is likely to be judged counter-productive.*

## Material change of use

> 🕮 *If the change of use is defined as a material change, the building will have to comply with the relevant requirements.*

If the work is controlled work, you should now turn to the information on the necessary paperwork (⇨ 2.2). Then go to Part 4 to find out which of the requirements apply to the various parts of the building and what you can do to meet them.

All the work must be carried out using proper materials and be conducted in a workmanlike manner (BR 7). However, only the requirements concerning energy conservation and provisions for disabled people require anything more to be done than is needed to secure reasonable standards of health and safety (BR 8).

## 1.2.3   Other legislation

The Gas (Safety) Regulations, the Water Byelaws and the Electricity Act will apply to alterations or extensions to the **gas**, **water** and **electricity** installations and the work must not contravene their requirements.

☛ There is insufficient space in *HomeBuilder* to offer technical guidance on meeting these requirements but they are dealt with in a general manner later on (⇨ 4.7 and 4.8).

The Construction (Design and Management) Regulations apply to the carrying out of construction and maintenance work.

If the work is for a "domestic" client – for example, a householder who lives in, or will live in, the premises during or after construction – the client and the designer (if there is one) must avoid creating hazards which can be foreseen and also must warn those who will carry out the work and could be affected by the hazards where they cannot.

If the work is not for a domestic client, a planning supervisor must be appointed. Your local authority or the Association of Planning Supervisors (⇨ Useful addresses) should be able to supply you with some names.

# 2 Dealing with the paperwork

**The guidance that follows is for**

**2.1 Planning control**
**2.2 Building control**

# 2.1
# Planning control

## INTRODUCTION

If, after reading Section 1.1, you do decide that the building work you plan does require planning permission, then you will have to submit a **planning application** which will be considered by the local planning authority.

The authority will take into account the policies in its Development Plan and also any comments received from your neighbours and others with an interest. The authority will then either approve the application, with or without conditions, or refuse it. If the conditions are unacceptable or the application is refused outright you can appeal to the Secretary of State (⇨ 2.2.1). The application itself comprises the forms, appropriate plans, site plan and the requisite fee.

In this section of *HomeBuilder* you will find help in understanding and completing the necessary application forms and information to ensure that you will have all the correct documentation and plans when the time comes. See also Part 3, where guidance is given on preparing the proposal which will be the subject of your planning application.

> As well as applying for planning permission you may have to deposit plans for building regulations purposes and these are separate procedures, each with their own time limits. There is a dilemma here – you may not wish to commit yourself to the cost of preparing the (usually more detailed) plans needed for the building regulations deposit until you know that you have planning permission. This may mean that the start of the work is delayed but you can save some time by preparing a basic set of plans which you can then supplement with the information which is relevant for each purpose. You can add this to the plans or attach it to them.

## 2.1.1  Before starting work

If you have found that the work that you wish to do will need planning permission it is a good idea to visit or contact your local planning office for advice. Many authorities operate design guides for householder developments and also more specific guidance for conservation areas (⇨ 3.1).

## 2.1.2  Preparing the application

A number of steps are necessary to ensure that your planning application is as accurate as it can be. Time taken at this stage will pay for itself later and avoid delays and queries from the planning authority.

## The plans required

You will need a **site plan** or a map of the area to a scale of at least 1:2500 (preferably 1:1250) with the boundaries of your property clearly outlined in red. If you own any adjoining land it should be outlined in blue. If you are submitting the application yourself, rather than using an agent, most local planning authorities will provide you with an extract from the Ordnance Survey map but you will have to pay a fee for it.

If you are extending your house or erecting an additional building on the site, a block plan and detailed building plans will be required.

The **block plan** should be to a scale of not less than 1:500 – for many smaller sites 1:200 would be more appropriate. It should show the existing buildings, boundaries and access, together with the proposal shown in hatching or some other distinctive form. The extent of any tree canopies should also be shown, especially in the case of those trees protected by a tree preservation order.

The detailed **building plans** are basically floor plans and elevations. These should be provided to a scale of 1:100 or 1:50. It is important that the elevations show all the external walls of the extension/new building, not just the most prominent ones.

With more complex proposals, you may also need **sections** through the building and enlargements of any **details**. It is important that your building plans are easily comparable, therefore you must not, for example, provide a block plan in Imperial measurements and the more detailed building plans in metric dimensions. These plans should also indicate the materials you wish to use and any trees that may need to be lopped or removed as a result of your proposal.

Whoever prepares the plans, it is essential that you or someone with the appropriate skills checks them for errors, preferably on-site and before submitting the application. Ask questions, such as the following:

*   have all existing windows been show correctly on the plans?;
*   are your neighbours' properties – including windows where shown – depicted correctly?;
*   are the windows on the elevations shown correctly on the floor plans and vice versa?

    *Mistakes in plans can cause your neighbours a great deal of concern; they may even object unnecessarily or misinterpret the plans and, in doing so, delay the determination of your application by the local authority. So, the time spent in getting plans right at this stage is time well spent.*

## Filling in the forms

Your should now decide whether you are going to deal with the planning application yourself or appoint an agent such as an architect, a building surveyor or a town-planner to act on your behalf. If your property is a listed building or you are proposing a significant alteration to a building within a conservation area, you will generally be well advised to appoint a competent person to advise you. This is also worthwhile, at least with larger projects, although many straightforward proposals can be dealt with by the applicant with some guidance from the planning officer.

### Choosing a professional

Often the best way to appoint a professional is to ask neighbours and friends who have had similar work done to recommend someone. It is generally preferable to choose an architect recommended by the Royal Institute of British Architects (RIBA) or a building surveyor recommended by the Royal Institution of Chartered Surveyors (RICS). If you choose a town-planner, he or she should be a member of the Royal Town Planning Institute (RTPI) (⇨ Useful addresses). It might be a good idea to ask this individual to show you work he or she has carried out in your area.

Remember that if you choose this route, all correspondence/decisions will go to your agent. This means that the local authority planning officer will not discuss matters with you as well as your agent. To do otherwise becomes time consuming and can lead to misunderstandings. If your agent is not local it is useful to provide a daytime telephone number for yourself, so that you can arrange a site visit directly with the officer, rather than through a third party.

The precise format of planning application forms varies from authority to authority; many of them have **application forms** specifically for householders. In addition to the application forms, you will be given guidance notes to help you complete them. If you have any difficulty with the forms, the staff at the local planning office will usually be happy to help you, in which case you will probably find it much easier to call into the office.

The application form will require the following information:

- your address and telephone number (it is useful to include a daytime number as well);
- the address and telephone number of your agent, if you appoint one;
- details of your proposal, for example a two-storey side extension, or erection of a detached garage;
- the type of application, whether or not it is full – in the case of most domestic applications – or outline.
- additional information about your proposal – does it require a new access for vehicles or people? Does it involve the felling of any trees? Will there be any alteration to the existing drainage? What materials do you propose to use?

## Certificates of ownership

The application form has to be signed in two places: the first signature relates solely to the information on the application form itself, the second to the ownership of the land. This often gives rise to confusion.

If you own the property – either outright or by virtue of a mortgage – and there is no freeholder, you complete the certificate which confirms that you are the sole owner of the application site and you do not have any agricultural tenants. This is known usually as **Certificate A**.

If you are not the sole owner of the land – for instance, if you live in a flat or a leasehold house, you own the property in common with someone else, or it is a property that you hope to buy should your planning application be successful – you need to notify the other owner(s) and occupiers in writing, 21 days before you submit your application.

It is a good idea to send a copy of the plans and application with your letter notifying them of the application. You must then sign a certificate (usually **Certificate B**) to say that you have done this.

> *If you are not sure who the owner of the land is, you need to follow a different procedure; the planning authority will advise you. If your proposal involves a party wall or an extension up to the boundary some planning authorities, following the passing of the Party Wall Act, are asking you to notify your neighbour of the proposal and to complete a Certificate B. It is doubtful if this is necessary (it will not affect the outcome of the application) but it may be simpler to comply with the request.*

## 2.1.3  Fees

With most planning applications, a fee is payable. As a guide, for an extension to one existing dwelling the fee is £90, but is liable to increase. The fee for a very small development, such as erecting a satellite dish or a fence over 2m high, is the same as for a substantial extension, even one including a garage. Fees may also be payable for other purposes. Where this is the case, *HomeBuilder* identifies them in the text which follows.

### Exemptions

There are a few categories of development which are exempt from fees. These will include, for example, adaptations to a downstairs bathroom or bedroom used by a disabled person. Also, the list may include those alterations which otherwise would be categorised as permitted development but where the permitted development rights have been removed either by conditions or by an Article 4 direction (⇨ 1.1.3).

## 2.1.4 Submitting the application

Planning offices usually require four copies of the application and plans. However, some authorities may require more to enable copies to be circulated both within the authority itself and to the various outside bodies such as parish councils and amenity groups which may have an interest in your proposal. These extra copies may well permit your application to be dealt with more quickly. Before submitting your application, ensure that you have the following (the best way is to make a checklist).

### CHECKLIST

- ☐ Planning application form, with all the necessary questions answered, and signed
- ☐ Appropriate ownership certificate, completed and signed
- ☐ Site plan
- ☐ Plans of the proposed development
- ☐ Planning application fee
- ☐ Any other information specifically requested by the authority, such as photographs, adjacent properties, etc., shown on the block plan
- ☐ Covering letter detailing any special factors or further information which you would like the authority to take into account
- ☐ A copy of everything submitted – for your own file

> If you can, it is a good idea to take your application into the planning office.
> The staff will check that you have completed the forms correctly and have the
> appropriate documentation. You may well be able to correct any minor
> mistakes there and then and you will at least be clear about what is required.
> Otherwise, if all the necessary information and the fee are not included, the
> planning office will not be able to register your application. If you have
> forgotten something, it can delay matters considerably, resulting in further
> correspondence.

The local planning authority will check your application and plans. The fee paid for the application will not be returned if the application is refused. However, you do have a right of appeal against the refusal itself (⇨ 2.2).

# 2.1.5 Consultation

Once the application is registered, your neighbours and others, including council departments and parish councils, where appropriate, will be notified. By law, the planning authority must consult people in adjoining properties (even if your proposal is unlikely to affect a property at the rear), other public bodies (depending on the precise nature of your application), as well as other council departments. Such consultation is designed to avoid any conflicts later. Those consulted are usually given 21 days to make their comments but the council is required to take account of all comments received up until the time at which it determines the application.

You are not required to notify your neighbours before you submit a planning application, but it is often a good idea to do so. At very least, let them know that you are making an application.

Where **conservation areas** and **listed buildings** are concerned, the application must be advertised by way of a **site notice** (which you must display) and a **public notice** (which the planning authority will place in the local press). These notices can increase the time taken to deal with the application.

## What will the council take into account?

Among other things, the local planning authority will look at:
- the effect of your proposal on your neighbours;
- how well your proposal fits into the street scene or surrounding area;
- whether your proposal is in accordance with their policies and various guidelines;
- any comments received.

A report will be prepared on your application by the planning office and forwarded to the planning committee for a decision.

> Many householder applications are dealt with under delegated powers,
> particularly where there are no objections from the neighbours and no complex
> issues raised. How precisely this is done depends on the authority, so it is a
> good idea to check whether your application will be dealt with by this process
> or whether it will go to committee. The committee route will take longer. The
> report will be available for inspection at least three working days before the

*planning committee meet and you and anyone else with an interest will be
able to study it. If you think it is incorrect or that some important information
has not been included, you should contact the planning officer to discuss it;
there may be a straightforward explanation.*

The committee will usually approve your application with **conditions** (⇨ 2.1.8), or
refuse planning permission altogether (⇨ 2.1.9). You must comply with the conditions
in order for the planning permission to be valid. If you are unsure as to what some of
the conditions may mean, you should ask. If you want to carry out the works differently to those shown on the approved plans you will need to go back to the planning
office to check if it wants a further application. Its decision will depend on how different your revised proposal is, also whether there will be any different effect on the
neighbours. Further guidance on following the progress of your application is provided
later (⇨ 3.1.4).

## 2.1.6  Special cases

Applications for **conservation area consent** and **listed building consent** are made, as
with planning permission, to the local planning authority. However, these applications
are forwarded to English Heritage – or to Cadw in Wales – (⇨ Useful addresses) for its
view and it can, if it is not happy with the proposal, instruct the local planning authority to refuse it. The law also requires that the application must be advertised in the press
and on the site and all of this can considerably extend the time needed for the application to be dealt with. It is very important, therefore, that you do not start work in
anticipation of such consent being granted and that you allow plenty of time for your
application to be dealt with.

### Conservation area consent

If your house lies within a conservation area and your planning application involves the
demolition of any part of the existing building, you will need to apply for conservation
area consent as well. The procedure is very similar to that outlined above for planning
permission. Further guidance on preparing the application for conservation area consent is discussed more fully later on (⇨ 3.1.6).

#### Plans
In addition to the plans required for planning permission, you will need plans of any
existing building that you propose to demolish, even partially. The part of the building
which you wish to demolish should be outlined in red. The plans of what you wish to
build should be well detailed with enlargements of specific details.

> *Partial demolition is likely to be decided on a case-by-case basis with attention
> being paid to features which, if lost, would adversely affect the character of the
> remaining structure.*

#### Filling in the forms
There is a separate form if you are applying for conservation area consent. As explained
earlier (⇨ 1.1.3), there may be circumstances where what you wish to build is actually
permitted development but you nevertheless need conservation area consent for demo-

lition. In such circumstances, consent is unlikely to be forthcoming unless what you wish to replace it with is acceptable.

The information required on the forms is very similar to the planning application. You need to make sure that the project is clearly explained in a covering letter and that the before and after plans are clearly identifiable.

### Fees

No fee is payable for an application for conservation area consent.

## Listed building consent

Again, you need to complete a separate form and to provide more detailed plans than those submitted with an application for planning permission. If you are altering the existing building you will probably be asked to provide details of how the work is to be carried out. These details must reveal internal alterations proposed, particularly if these affect in any way features in the building which were reasons for listing it. Guidance on preparing the application is discussed more fully later on (⇨ 3.1.7).

> You will probably save yourself time and trouble by discussing with the local planning authority what information is required before you submit your application.

### Fees

No fee is payable for an application for listed building consent.

> It may be worth your while to enquire whether any grants are available towards the cost of the work: for example, to re-roof with stone roof instead of tiles; to match existing windows and the detail of decorative features; or to remove paint from brickwork, and so on.

## Certificate of lawful development

As explained earlier (⇨ 1.1.2), if you think that the works you wish to carry out do not need planning permission or are permitted development, you can apply for a certificate of lawful development. The Certificate will provide you with immunity from enforcememt action. It is also useful if you are buying a house and you want to be sure that the work carried out by a previous occupier did not require planning permission.

### Plans

You will need to provide a site plan and, as with a planning application, detailed plans, although fewer copies will usually be required.

> You must be sure that all your plans show precisely what you wish to do because the Certificate relates solely to the plans submitted with your application and only in relation to your property as it is at the time of the application. Therefore, if your property is located in an area which is later declared to be a conservation area, and you have not carried out the work, you will need to check whether the work the Certificate related to is still lawful. For instance, if it related to a roof extension, this would now need planning permission; similarly, it would do so if it related to an extension and in the meantime you had built another extension and together they would exceed the permitted development rights.

*Fees*

A fee is payable for the application for the Certificate.

## 2.1.7 The decision

The majority of planning applications made by householders are dealt with under powers delegated to the chief planning officer by your local authority, although the scope of these powers and the procedures vary from authority to authority. The planning officer should be able to tell you under which procedure you application will be dealt with.

Other planning applications, usually the more contentious ones, are dealt with by a committee. In this situation, you can inspect the report three days before the meeting, or you may even be sent a copy.

You should read the report carefully, and ensure that:
*    there are no factual errors or omissions; and that
*    the comments made by the planning officer are fair.

The report will include details of comments received from neighbours; this does not mean that the planning officer necessarily agrees with the views expressed. Again, read the report carefully:
*    are there any matters in favour of your proposal which the report does not mention?;
*    do you wish to comment on anything raised by your neighbours?

   *If you have any comments regarding these matters, you should write to the planning officer as soon as possible, making sure that a copy is received by the planning committee secretary.*

## 2.1.8 Planning permission

Hopefully, at the end of this, you will receive approval for what you want to do. You will be required to start work within five years; if you fail to do so, you will have to re-apply.

### Conditions

The planning permission will usually include a number of conditions that you must satisfy. You may be required to submit certain details, such as samples of the materials you intend to use, before you start work. These details must be formally submitted to the planning authority in order to comply with your permission. Any other conditions, such as putting obscured glass in particular windows, or putting up a fence around your trees while the work is being carried out, must also be complied with.

If you don't comply, you may find yourself both in receipt of a **breach of condition notice** and a fine to prove it!

Many of the conditions will be fairly straightforward, such as requiring you to use materials to match the existing building, or preventing you from inserting any windows other than those shown on the plans considered by the council.

*It is your responsibility to ensure that your development is built in accordance with the planning permission. Similarly, if you are unsure about the meaning of any of the conditions, ask the planning officer for an explanation. Your planning permission is valid only if you comply with the conditions.*

In circumstances where you would find it difficult to comply with any of the conditions, discuss it with the planning officer before you start work. Ultimately, you might need to make a formal application to have the conditions altered or removed, but this course is preferable to receiving a breach of condition notice or an enforcement notice.

If your application is granted with conditions attached to it you have the right to appeal against any or all of the conditions.

*The decision letter will give the reasons for the conditions, and only when you are clear as to why they were attached will you be in a position to decide whether an appeal is really the best way forward. It is important to remember that the planning process is separate from building control so, if there is a conflict between the requirements of the planning permission and what the building control officer asks you to do, it must be resolved before you start work. If necessary, arrange a meeting with both the planning officer and the building control officer present. They will have different concerns but a compromise can usually be found.*

## 2.1.9  Refusal

If your application is refused you have the right to appeal. The decision letter will give the reasons for refusal, but these are not always easy to understand and are often worded in rather vague terms, such as "loss of residential amenity" to the neighbours, or "detrimental effect" on the street scene. Far more appeals are lost rather than won and only when you are clear as to why permission was refused will you be in a position to decide whether an appeal is really the best way forward.

*Before you decide to go to appeal, it is a good idea to discuss the refusal with the planning officer and to see if you can do anything to overcome the objections – perhaps a compromise is possible.*

Amending your proposal is one way of meeting planning objections. Perhaps you can re-think your proposal so that it will:
- not require planning permission because it is permitted development;
- overcome the local planning authority objections.

If you can reach an agreement without the need for appeal it is often better to do so (and there is no fee for a similar application submitted within 12 months). Although the planning officer will not be able to say that a revised proposal will definitely be approved, you should at least discover whether your changes will overcome the reasons for refusal.

Nonetheless, it may become clear that, after you have discussed your refusal with the planning officer, there is no scope for compromise. If so you might choose to:
- appeal against the decision to the Secretary of State for the Environment; or
- simply give up the project.

## 2.1.10 Appeals

Although there are no fees for lodging an appeal, your chances of success are increased if you employ someone with substantial experience of planning appeals, such as a chartered town-planner, to help you, although obviously you will have to meet the costs of such help.

If you wish to appeal against a planning refusal or condition, you must do so within six months of the decision. A planning appeal is heard by an inspector representing the Secretary of State for the Environment or the Secretary of State for Wales. The inspector will hear the evidence from both sides and will make a decision in respect of the case.

There are three different procedures for appeals.

1   Most are dealt with by **written representation**, which is cheapest and quickest. This essentially involves the preparation of a written statement challenging the council's reason for refusal, with appropriate photographs, plans and supporting documents. A planning inspector visits the site (accompanied by both parties), but neither party is allowed to make representations to the inspector.

2   If you want to address the inspector, you may opt for an **informal hearing**. In this procedure, the inspector receives written statements from both parties three weeks before the hearing and, at the hearing, identifies the aspects that he or she would like to discuss in more detail. Both parties are given the opportunity to raise other relevant points, as are any members of the public attending the hearing. It usually takes several months longer to be heard, compared with a written appeal.

3   Finally, you could choose a **public inquiry** – a much more formal procedure than a hearing and much more expensive because it is usual for both parties to be legally represented. Not only is the cost greater but so is the time taken to deal with the appeal and it is seldom appropriate for the average householder.

## 2.1.11 Enforcement

You are only likely to encounter enforcement proceedings if you have carried out work which required planning permission without first obtaining such permission. It might be that you thought that the works were permitted development, or you built your extension differently to that shown on the approved plans. Even in these circumstances, the local planning authority will only start enforcement proceedings if what has been built is unacceptable and you are unwilling to remedy the situation. They will certainly be willing to discuss other ways of resolving the matter first.

Should you find yourself threatened with enforcement action, it is a good idea to get advice from someone familiar with the planning system.

# 2.2
# Building control

## INTRODUCTION

If, after reading Section 1.2 on building legislation, you decide that what you intend to do is controlled building work and/or a material change of use then, with one exception, you will have to choose whether to use the local authority's building control services (⇨ 2.2.1) or to appoint an independent approved inspector (⇨ 2.2.2). The one **exception** is the installation of a **gas appliance** by a person or the employee of a person approved by the Council of Registered Gas Installers (CORGI) in accordance with the Gas Safety (Installation and Use) Regulations (⇨ Useful addresses).

If you decide to follow the local authority route (⇨ 2.2.1) you, or someone acting on your behalf, will have to prepare the necessary documentation – usually plans and a specification – and send off the necessary notices. The local authority will examine the plans and it will inspect the work on-site.

If you decide to follow the approved inspector route (⇨ 2.2.2) you, or someone acting on your behalf, will still have to prepare the necessary documentation and then appoint the approved inspector who will then send off the necessary notices, examine the plans and inspect the work.

Fees will be payable in either case. The fee payable to the local authority is laid down in Fees Regulations. The fee payable to the approved inspector is negotiable.

The Construction Industry Council, which is responsible for approving inspectors, maintains the Register of Approved Inspectors (⇨ Useful addresses).

## 2.2.1  The local authority route

At various times notices will have to be given to the local authority. These must be given by "the person who intends to carry out the building work". You may give the notices yourself but, if you do not, be sure to delegate the responsibility to someone. It is usual for the professional adviser, where there is one, to give the building notice and for the builder to give the commencement and other notices.

> *If, after three years, the controlled work has not been started or the material change of use made the local authority can cancel the building notice.*

### Before starting work

You must give the local authority a **building notice** and a **commencement notice**.

### Building notice

The local authority usually provides a form for you to complete and return. Depending on the type of work you intend to do, the form will ask you for certain information.

Make a checklist as, in all cases, you will be asked for the following.

## CHECKLIST

- ☐ Your name and address
- ☐ A description of the proposed building work or material change of use
- ☐ The location of the building and its present and intended use
- ☐ A statement of whether or not you are giving only a building notice or are depositing full plans

Before you decide which statement you want to make, read the full plans information provided in *HomeBuilder*.

> *The description of the proposed work required by the building notice need not be in the form of plans but the local authority can ask for "such plans as are necessary, in the particular case, for the discharge of their functions". It can specify the plans and when they are to be given. Be warned: these are not "deposited plans" and do not provide the same protection.*

If you are **erecting** or **extending** a building, you must include a plan. This should be to the scale of 1:1250 and must show further information – which also should appear in your checklist.

## CHECKLIST

- ☐ The size and position of the building or the building as extended and its relation to the adjoining boundaries
- ☐ The boundaries of its curtilage
- ☐ The size, position and use of every other building or proposed building within the curtilage
- ☐ The width and position of streets on or within the boundaries of the curtilage of the building or extended building

> *For the plan, you can use an extract from the Ordnance Survey; you will usually be able to obtain up to three copies of the extract from the local authority, for which there will be a charge.*

You must also give the following information which, again, add to your checklist.

## CHECKLIST

- ☐ The number of storeys, including basement storeys
- ☐ The provision you intend to make for drainage and the precautions you intend to take if you will be building over a drain or sewer

> *The local authority maintains a sewer map, which can be seen during normal office hours.*

- ☐ The steps you will be taking to comply with any local act that applies

> *The local authority must tell you if a local act does apply, which is unlikely.*

If the work involves the insertion of **insulating material** into cavity walls, in addition to the above information, you must state (add to your checklist) further information.

## CHECKLIST

- ☐ The name and type of insulation to be used
- ☐ If the insulation is approved by the British Board of Agrément, or complies with a British Standard specification

☐   Whether the installer holds a registration certificate from the British Standards Institution (BSI) or has been approved by the British Board of Agrément for the insertion of the material.

If the work involves the provision of an **unvented hot-water system**, to which the Building Regulations Schedule 1 G3 (hot-water storage) applies, you must give details (and add to your checklist).

## CHECKLIST

☐   The name, make, model and type of hot-water system

☐   The name of the body, if any, which has approved or certified that the system meets the G3 requirement

☐   The name of the body, if any, which has issued a current registered operative identity card to the installer or proposed installer of the system

   *Requirement G3 applies to systems which are not vented to atmosphere, have a capacity of more than 1.5 litres and do not supply hot water for space heating for an industrial process.*

# Depositing full plans

The building and commencement notices will satisfy the minimum legal obligations but you can, if you wish, deposit full plans with the building notice. Your right to deposit plans – and have them passed or rejected within a time limit – was introduced in 1936. It has several advantages:

*   you have the right to ask the Secretary of State to decide the matter if you should have a disagreement with the local authority;

*   you have the right to know, before you commit yourself to the expense of the work, whether what you say you intend to do will meet the requirements;

*   if your work is found not to have met the requirements then, if the work was shown on the plans, the plans have been passed (or not rejected by the time limit), and you have followed the plans, the local authority cannot give you a notice requiring you to alter what you have done and, if a court gives an injunction requiring you to do so, it can order the local authority to compensate you;

*   you have the right to ask for a completion certificate;

*   last, but not least, plans make the building control authority's task of inspection easier and reduce the chances of misunderstanding.

## What are full plans?

The Building Act says that "plans" include drawings, specifications or other information in any form, such as calculations. The regulations say that "full plans" consist of a description of the proposed work or material change of use, the plans, particulars and statements to be given with a building notice and "any other plans which are necessary to show that the work would meet the regulations".

   *These "other plans" can be a cause of disagreements because it is not usual for every part of the work to be shown on the drawings, for every detail of the materials and construction to be specified or for every part to be calculated. That said, the more information you give, the more certain you can be that the work is going to meet the regulations.*

If you do choose to deposit full plans, you must provide duplicate copies – the local authority will keep one set and return the other – and you also must:

- say in the building notice that you are depositing full plans;
- give the additional information.

If any of the fire safety requirements of the Building Regulations apply, you may be asked to send two additional copies of any plans that concern compliance. The fire authority can look at your plans at the same time as the building control authority.

> *Some time after you have deposited your plans you can expect a "snag sheet" telling you where the local authority believes that you have contravened the regulations. The intention is to give you an opportunity to change your mind but you may have to act quickly if the time left to run is limited. It is usual to delay starting work until you receive the notice telling you whether or not your plans have been passed. You do not want to have to alter work which the local authority might reject when it makes its inspections on-site. If your plans have been rejected, the notice must give the reason. This will help if you dispute the grounds for rejection.*

### Some more decisions

If you have chosen to submit full plans you should consider the following:

**Conditions**     You can tell the local authority (in writing) that, rather than have the plans rejected if they show any contraventions, you agree to having them passed subject to conditions. The local authority itself may suggest this (but it must get your consent).

**Depositing plans in stages**     You can tell the local authority that you will be depositing incomplete plans to start with, followed by further plans in one or more stages. For example, it might be that although your plans are nearly complete you still need some information, perhaps from a subcontractor or supplier who is withholding calculations until you have placed an order.

**Completion certificate**    The time to tell the local authority that you will want the certificate is when you deposit the plans. It will be too late afterwards.

## Fees

Fees will be payable according to the Building (Prescribed Fees) Regulations and will vary with the type and estimated cost of the work. The estimated cost is a reasonable estimate of how much a professional builder would charge excluding professional fees and VAT. While you may sometimes be asked to explain it, the cost bands are quite wide so that no great accuracy is called for. If you are doing work yourself you will be expected to include this.

With one exception the fee is payable in two parts: that is, 25 per cent when you give the building notice and 75 per cent after the first inspection. The fee will be the same whether you give only a building notice or deposit full plans but, if you deposit full plans, the first part of the fee is returnable if the local authority does not pass or reject them within the time allowed. The one **exception** is that the total fee is payable with the building notice if the estimated cost is below a minimum which changes from time to time.

> *The local authority will tell you how to calculate the fee when it gives you the building notice forms. If you still have any doubt about how much you should pay, ask.*

## Changing the rules

If circumstances dictate, the requirements of the Building Regulations can be dispensed with or relaxed. You can apply to the local authority to do this at any time.

> *A dispensation is rare: you would be asking that some requirement should not apply at all. For instance, you might think of asking for the fire safety requirements to be dispensed with because you live next to the fire station (you are unlikely to be successful). The regulations already contain many exemptions and the application of some of the requirements is also limited. A relaxation is not very different. Although you agree that some requirement applies, you believe that some specific provision in it should be relaxed to allow you to provide the necessary level of protection in some other way. In practice, the need for a relaxation is rare because few requirements now include specific provisions: most are written in functional terms and state only that adequate or reasonable provision must be made, which is not unreasonable.*

If you do apply for a requirement to be dispensed with or relaxed and the building control authority refuses your application you can appeal to the Secretary of State for the Environment under Section 39 of the Building Act.

It is far more likely that your problem lies with the guidance in one of the Approved Documents supporting the regulations. However, the question which then has to be decided is not whether you are following the guidance but whether you are meeting the requirements and that is a matter for a determination.

## Determinations

If you cannot reach agreement with the local authority over your plans – for example, there is some dispute over whether your plans meet the requirements in showing what is adequate or reasonable in relation to the particular case – you can apply directly for a determination to the Secretary of State for the Environment under Section 16(10) of the Building Act.

> *The application, for which a fee is charged, can only be made after you have deposited your plans and, because the determination is tied to your plans, before you have done the part of the work to which it relates. Summarise the point to be determined, show that you understand the requirements and present a concise and well argued case for your own proposal.*

## Passing plans

If you give a valid notice, the local authority must accept it. If you deposit plans, it must pass them, unless they are defective or show a contravention, in which case it can issue a rejection or pass the plans subject to conditions.

> *Plans are defective if they do not comply with some procedure; perhaps they are incomplete. They will show a contravention if they indicate that what you intend to do will not meet some technical requirement.*

The local authority must also reject the plans if they conflict with certain sections of the Building Act linked with the deposit of plans. The local authority should give its decision in writing before the relevant period from deposit expires and, if it fails to do so, it must return the fee paid.

> 📖 The **relevant period** is five weeks or the agreed extended period (not longer than two months).

However, you can agree with the local authority to extend the period to up to two months. This is usual; it give you time to deal with the "snag sheet" that a hard-pressed authority may send out only shortly before the five-week period ends. By avoiding a rejection you avoid the trouble of going round the course again.

## Rejecting plans

If the plans are rejected and you did not ask the local authority to pass them subject to conditions, it is still not too late to do so. You can still deposit further, amended, plans and meanwhile you can start the work.

> 📖 *If you cannot agree with the rejection or the conditions (⇨ Determinations) you should first discuss them with the local authority, but only if you have not started the part of the work.*

### Linked powers

Before the privatisation of the water and sewerage systems the local authority had to reject plans you deposited for building regulations purposes unless the plans also showed that requirements linked directly to the Building Act would be satisfied. The authority would discuss your proposal directly with you.

Following privatisation you still deposit your plans with the local authority but there are now two possibilities. If your local authority has agency powers it will still discuss your proposals directly with you. If it has not it will advise the water or sewerage undertaker (as the case may be) so that it can do so.

**Provision of drainage**     Your plans must be rejected unless they show that satisfactory provision will be made for drainage, or it agrees that no provision need be made (drainage includes both foul water and surface water).

> 📖 *Linked powers may be invoked where there is a drainage system which might be affected by the proposed works. The authority will want to ensure that the method of disposal is satisfactory. Perhaps you want to install a septic tank or even a cesspool, or connect a drain or sewer that might in some way be unsuitable: possibly overloaded or in poor condition. Remember that the Building Regulations apply only to the adequacy of the system itself, if any, that you propose to install.*

**Sewer connection**       You can only be required to connect to a sewer if:
* it is within 30.5m and at a level that makes it reasonably practical to connect to it;
* you are connecting into an existing drain or sewer; and
* you have the right to use it.

The requirement only applies if you are building a new drain to make the connection and have the right to build across any intervening land which you do not own.

**Building over a sewer**    If you intend to build or extend over a sewer or drain that is shown on the undertaker's sewer map, your plans must be rejected unless your proposal can be agreed unconditionally, or subject to conditions. This is to ensure that the drain or sewer will not be damaged by the work, or as a later result of it; also that access for maintenance and repair will be possible.

> *The local authority holds a copy of the sewer map and you can see it during normal office hours.*

> A **drain** serves the buildings within one curtilage.
> A **sewer** serves buildings in more than one.

**Provision of water supply**    Your plans must be rejected unless satisfactory provision is shown on the plans for a supply of wholesome water to domestic premises. A direct connection to a piped water supply – or, more usually, piped from a statutory water supply – will be deemed satisfactory.

## Commencement notice

You must give the local authority at least two days' notice that you intend to start work. Once you have let the two days pass, you can start the work. However, it is usual to wait for the local authority's confirmation that it has accepted your building notice: you do not want to find that you have started without having given a valid notice (some people forget to enclose the cheque).

## After starting work

After work has begun you must give the local authority some more notices so that it has an opportunity to inspect the work if it wishes to.

### Notices

Before you **cover up** any excavation for a foundation, or any foundation, damp-proof course, concrete or other material laid over a site, or cover in any way a drain or sewer to which Part H of the Building Regulations apply, you must give one day's notice.

> One **day** means any 24-hour period starting at midnight, but excluding Saturdays, Sundays and public holidays.

After **laying**, **haunching** or **covering** any drain or sewer you must give notice within no more than five days.

> **Haunching** is providing support, usually concrete, to the sides of a pipe.

> *If you fail to give these notices, the local authority can ask you to open up the work for inspection at your own expense. However, it is for the local authority to decide whether it does inspect and you can carry on with the work, once the period of notice has passed. Nevertheless, the local authority can, in the 12 months from completion, still give a notice requiring a breach of the regulations which comes to its attention to be made good.*

## Notice of contravention

It is possible that under Section 36 of the Building Act the building control authority may, if it finds a contravention of the building regulations, be able to give you a **notice of contravention** requiring you to pull down (or put right) the offending work.

> *The notice of contravention – usually called a "Section 36 notice" – is hedged around with conditions and, therefore, if you are unfortunate enough to receive one you should make it your business to read Sections 36 and 37 of the Building Act.*

If you have done work to comply with the notice of contravention then you must, within a reasonable time, give a notice that you have completed the work.

## Testing and sampling

The regulations say that you must use "proper materials which are appropriate to the circumstances in which they are used". The local authority can sample and test any materials (and products) which are **going to be used** in the work to satisfy itself that they will be appropriate.

> *The local authority should take and test samples itself but it would not be unknown for you to be asked for written evidence that a material or product is appropriate. In most cases it will be sufficient to provide a statement from your supplier that the material or product conforms to an appropriate British Standard, or has a certificate from a Technical Approval body, or is CE-marked, or has the level of performance which wll provide an equivalent level of protection. Remember that there may be more than one level of performance and be sure to choose the right one. A drainpipe which is suitable for carrying rainwater may not be suitable for carrying foul water (and will not be suitable for anything if it is cracked or broken). That said, these products should be (and CE-marked products must be) accepted if they are used appropriately and are in a satisfactory condition.*

If you are asked for test evidence, then:

- for **British Standards** (BS) look for the Kitemark which shows that the material or product has already been tested by the British Standards Institution and complies with the relevant standard; or
- for **technical approvals** ask the supplier or manufacturer for a certificate from one of the government designated Technical Approval bodies. There are two such bodies, the British Board of Agrément (BBA) and Wimpey Laboratories (WIMLAS), and the certificate shows that the material or product has already been evaluated and tested by one of them; or
- for **CE-marked** products look for the mark CE which shows that the product complies with the relevant European standard (it will be identified as BS/EN) and has already been tested by the corresponding European procedure. We are used to seeing the CE mark on some products, such as toys, and we shall soon begin to see it on construction products; or
- for an **equivalent level of protection** be aware that in the case of other materials and products you could be faced with a paperchase (and even wasted expense) unless you first agree what levels of protection and performance will be accepted as equivalent and what kind of test evidence you are being asked for.

## Notice of completion

You must give a notice of completion within five days of completing the work. Also, if you are erecting a building, or part of a building that you intend to occupy before completion, you must give at least five days' notice before you occupy it.

### Certificate of completion

People who have an interest in your property – such as a building society, bank or prospective purchaser – may ask to be satisfied that controlled building work and material changes of use have complied with the regulations. This is where the completion certificate is relevant.

> *In the past, a notice of passing of plans might have been taken to show that the work did comply; a rejection as indicating that it did not. Neither is necessarily so; what matters is what has been built, not what has been shown on the plans.*

If, when you deposited your plans, you requested a certificate of completion and if you have given a notice of completion, then the local authority must give you a certificate to show that the work complies with the regulations.

If you have given a notice of occupation before completion, the authority must give you a certificate to indicate that the requirements specified in the certificate – and only those requirements – have been complied with.

However, while certificates are evidence that the requirements, or those specified in the certificate, have been satisfied, they are not, unfortunately, conclusive.

## 2.2.2 The approved inspector route

Before starting the work on-site, and at completion of the work, notices will have to be given to the local authority. These will be provided by the approved inspector.

> *The documentation describing the work – usually plans and a specification – will have to be prepared by you, or by someone you employ for the purpose, and sent to the approved inspector and you should agree just what plans will be necessary in your particular case.*

## Before starting work

Some of the actions you or the approved inspector need to take before starting work are discussed below.

### Initial notice

This replaces the building notice and must be given to the local authority by the approved inspector who will then take over the responsibility for examining the plans and inspecting the work.

> *If, after three years, the controlled work has not been started or the material change of use made the local authority can cancel the initial notice.*

### Linked powers

On receipt of the initial notice the local authority will tell the approved inspector if any linked powers are involved but you will have to negotiate any necessary arrangements.

### Changing the rules

If you want a requirement of the regulations dispensed with or relaxed you (not the approved inspector) have to apply to the local authority for a dispensation or relaxation.

### Determinations

If you cannot agree with the approved inspector whether or not what your plans show meets the requirements you (not the approved inspector) can apply to the Secretary of State for a Determination (⇨ 2.2.1).

### Passing plans

The approved inspector will, on request, provide you with a **plans certificate** stating (if it is so) that the plans are not defective and do not show any contraventions of the Building Regulations.

## After starting work

The next notice will be at completion.

### Testing and sampling

The approved inspector can ask for evidence to show the suitability of the materials and products being used but must accept a CE-marked product if it is being used appropriately and is in a satisfactory condition.

## At completion

When work is completed you must submit a final certificate.

### Final certificate

The final certificate replaces the completion certificate and must be given to the local authority by the approved inspector who will then give up responsibility for the work. The final certificate will state that the work which has been carried out satisfies Regulation 4 (requirements relating to building work) and Regulation 6 (requirements relating to material change of use) of the Building Regulations but only to the best of the inspector's knowledge.

As with the completion certificate issued by the local authority, the final certificate is not conclusive.

You must be provided with a copy of the certificate.

# 3 Meeting the planning requirements

**The guidance that follows is for**

**3.1 Submitting a proposal**

# 3.1
# Submitting a proposal

## INTRODUCTION

This section provides you with guidance enabling you to submit a proposal that will have a greater chance of success: it also explains the planning and appeal process in slightly more detail.

## 3.1.1 Preparatory work

It is advisable to discuss your proposal with a planning officer at an early stage, after making an appointment. Notice of your visit will give the planning office the chance to check any relevant background information, such as the original planning permission, the planning history and the local plan policies.

You should make a sketch of your proposal and take this with you, along with a few photographs. You will then be able to gauge whether there is any conflict with the development plan, or any other of the local authority's guidelines.

The planning officer can only give an initial opinion; the planning authority is not bound by his or her advice. It may be that a change of policy is subsequently introduced or that other factors become apparent when the application is formally considered. You should never start work assuming that, on the basis of your discussions with the officer, the proposal is likely to receive planning permission.

> *You might be advised that your proposal – adding a dormer window to the front of your house, for example – is unacceptable, even though a neighbour may have already done something similar. This could be because the works were previously permitted development and planning permission was not required, or that there had been a change of policy in later years. It is always worth asking about similar proposals, but you must remember that the officer will advise you on the basis of the local authority's policies as they currently stand.*

## 3.1.2 Further guidance

When you visit or contact your local planning office, you should ask if there is any agreed policy or informal guidance which could affect your particular proposal. Each authority responds in a different way and the advice available will depend on where you live. Some authorities have produced guides for particular types of development such as roof extensions and side extensions to semi-detached properties, while others have produced guides for conservation areas.

> *While these guides may give you an idea of what will be readily acceptable (or what will not) do not be discouraged if you want something diffferent but do be sure to explain why in a covering letter; keep it brief. If you live in a special*

*area such as a green belt, an area of outstanding natural beauty or a national park, you must expect to be subject to more stringent controls.*

### 3.1.3 Neighbours

Local planning authorities have a legal duty to notify neighbours of planning applications (⇨ 2.1.5).

On the other hand, you are under no obligation to tell neighbours about your proposals before you submit your application, although it might be prudent to let them know your intention. By showing neighbours your plans, you are giving them the opportunity to raise any concerns, so that you can either reassure them, avoid any misunderstandings, or perhaps alter your proposal to take account of their views.

Even if you are unable to satisfy them, you will at least know the likely grounds for their objection and will be able to address the particular problem in your covering letter.

### 3.1.4 Consideration of your application

Government guidance on planning applications tends to favour granting planning permission. If the local planning authority refuses your application, there must be clear reasons for doing so. Therefore, most reasonable planning applications submitted by householders stand a very good chance of success.

Once your application has been with the local planning authority for three or four weeks, it is worth contacting the planning officer dealing with your application to see if any further information is required, and to arrange a date for a site visit if this has not already been done. At this point, you might be given an indication as to when your application will be decided and whether it will be either a delegated decision or referred to the planning committee.

You can ask whether there have been any objections to your application and, if possible, arrange to have a look at them. It may be that your neighbour's comments are based on a misunderstanding of your proposal or that you could amend your application to overcome their concerns. You might also feel that you need to comment on what they have said in their letters, in which case confine yourself to planning matters and do not get drawn into arguments unrelated to your application.

> *The policy on inspecting letters of objection varies, but with applications that will be dealt with by committee you are entitled to inspect letters of objection at least three working days before the meeting.*

It might well be that the planning officer will contact you, or your agent, for further information, confirmation of a particular matter, or to suggest a revision that would overcome objections to your proposal. You should respond to such requests as soon as possible because it is probable that no further action will be taken on your application until you have responded.

> *If the amendments suggested by the planning officer are either impractical or are unacceptable to you for some other reasons, you should let the planning officer know and, if possible, arrange a meeting to discuss the problem with*

*him or her. By doing so, you might be able to reach a compromise and at least you should understand, if not agree with, each other's point of view.*

On the other hand, some authorities may simply refuse your planning application if it is unacceptable. It is a good idea to let them know in your covering letter that you would welcome the opportunity of discussing any problems with your application, and that you would be willing to consider amending your proposal to overcome any objections. If you know that your application does not comply with the council's guidance in one or more respects – but you have good reasons for not doing so – it is important that you explain the reasons for this in your covering letter.

## 3.1.5 What are planning matters?

The local planning authority's consideration of your application will be based on what are known as "material planning considerations".

### Considerations

In order to assess your application, some planning authorities may raise a number of questions. Possible questions are discussed below.

#### *Does the application comply with the local planning authority's design guidance and the policies in the development plan?*

If not, it does not mean that it will automatically be refused, but you will need to demonstrate why other considerations outweigh those in the development plan in this instance. For example, if roof terraces and balconies are generally unacceptable, you will need to show that your particular roof terrace will not result in overlooking because of the large trees around the boundary of your garden, or the relationship between your house and that of your neighbour.

#### *Does your extension, building or wall design fit that of the neighbourhood?*

This will be of more importance where the extension, or whatever, can be seen from the road and within conservation areas and Article 1(5) land. Some local planning authorities have **architects' advisory panels** and their advice may be sought together with the advice of specialist interest groups.

#### *Will your development cause a loss of daylight or sunlight to your neighbours?*

A single-storey extension is unlikely to cause such problems unless, due to a change in levels, it is significantly higher than your neighbour's property.

If there is a problem, the planning officer will look at the existing situation and what the situation would be after your development had been built, and their judgement will be based on whether the amount of change is acceptable or not. Obviously, loss of daylight or sunlight to a living room or bedroom will be taken more seriously than loss of light to a bathroom or staircase.

*The tendency is to attach more importance to daylight than to sunlight and to base decisions on the amount of light remaining, not on amount lost. A rule of thumb has been that the light to a window should not be obstructed above a line drawn upwards from the bottom of the window at an angle of 45 degrees.*

### *Will your proposal result in a loss of privacy or amenity to your neighbours?*

Again, the planning officer will look at the situation as it is currently and how your proposal will change it. Therefore, if the overlooking from a new window at first-floor level would not add to the overlooking from existing windows, it will probably be acceptable. On the other hand, if it would allow views of the house and garden which would reduce your neighbour's privacy and enjoyment of their home, it would be unlikely to be acceptable.

> *In the case of overlooking, if particular windows (such as those in a bathroom) will have frosted glass or similar, make sure that this specification is clearly marked on the plans. It will save time and perhaps even avoid objections from your neighbours. In the case of the obstruction of views currently enjoyed from a neighbour's property the tendency is to hold that continued enjoyment is not a right.*

### *Will it interfere with traffic flows or limit pedestrian or driver visibility?*

Often, proposals involving new vehicular access onto busy roads are unacceptable, because they would slow down traffic, possibly resulting in accidents. Similarly, walls or fences over 1m high along the back edge of the pavement, which involve cars waiting on the road or footpath while the gates are opened, are unlikely to be acceptable. This can usually be overcome by setting the gates back far enough for the car to wait off the highway. In such cases, it is a good idea to discuss your application with the planning officer and the highway engineer before submitting it, to see if you can overcome the problems.

### *Will it affect any protected trees?*

The application will have to be free of any tree preservation orders or the likelihood of existing trees being destroyed.

If any trees on the site are protected by a **tree preservation order** you should show that neither they nor their roots will be adversely affected by your proposals or that the benefits of removing a tree will outweigh the harm caused by its loss. Make sure that your plans accurately show the position of each tree and its canopy and that space around will be left for working, scaffolding and access.

### *Do you have a particular reason for your application?*

If a member of your family needs ground-floor accommodation, or you want to give increased privacy to an elderly relative, you should explain this when you submit your application. Although it will not tip the balance in the case of an unacceptable application, most planning authorities are sympathetic to such problems and will try to find a solution to suit both parties.

You might also wish to write to all the planning committee members explaining why, in your opinion, your planning application should be approved. In this case, you should do so early enough for them to discuss it with you and perhaps even visit you.

## 3.1.6 Conservation areas

Local planning authorities have a statutory duty to preserve or enhance the quality of conservation areas. The way this is approached depends on the authority. Many authorities carry out special environmental works, operate a more restrictive code concerning advertisements, and generally require a higher-quality design than usual.

Other points to note are:

- your proposal does not have to mimic the older, original, buildings in the conservation area. An innovative, high-quality design that reflects some of the characteristics of the area will often stand a good chance of success, although this will depend to some degree on the character and homogeneity of the existing area;

- anything other than the more minor applications within conservation areas are likely to benefit from professional help. When selecting a professional, try to choose someone who has experience of making planning applications in conservation areas in your locality. Good-quality plans can speed up the application process and might well avoid unnecessary meetings;

- the application process is slightly different and it is realistic to expect your application to take longer to deal with, compared with one outside a conservation area. Notifying applications in the press and on-site can add to the time;

- generally, the planning authority must forward details of applications within conservation areas to the Historic Buildings and Monuments Commission for its views. While the Commission has the power to direct the planning authority to refuse the application, in practice it is more likely to request revisions. In recent years, a few authorities have agreed that some of the minor planning applications within conservation areas do not have to be referred on, which has cut the time needed to deal with them;

- many local planning authorities also have **conservation-area advisory committees**. The committees are made up of councillors and members of local amenity groups whose views must be taken into account when deciding applications. Some authorities seek the advice of specialist interest groups. Again, this can extend the time taken to process applications.

## 3.1.7 Listed buildings

Even more so than with conservation areas, it is a good idea to retain professional help when making alterations to listed buildings, particularly where the law in relation to them is concerned. As with conservation areas, the application must be advertised on-site and in the press and referred to the Historic Buildings and Monuments Commission (⇨ Useful addresses).

> *The planning authority will provide you with notices to display on the site. It will also place the advertisement in the press and refer your application to the Commission.*

# 4 Meeting the building requirements

**The guidance that follows is for**

# Using Part 4

## INTRODUCTION

The technical requirements of the Building Regulations and similar legislation may apply to more than one part of a building (⇨ Preface), so that a part can be subject to more than one requirement. For example, the requirements of fire safety, structural support, energy conservation (heat loss) and so on may all apply to the same external wall and have to be satisfied.

Part 4 tells you which requirements apply to each part of a building and summarises them. It uses re-wordings of the legal text employed in, and is an abbreviated version of, the legislation applicable to building works. It also directs you to the relevant legislation by means of cross-references.

In making your application to a building control authority you can use the legalistic approach of the regulations themselves. However, you might invite a legalistic response from the authority which could involve you in further cost and delay.

To explain these cross-references more fully:

| | |
|---|---|
| BR | refers to the Building Regulations 1991, amended 1994. |
| BR 7 | relates to the full text of a regulation. |
| BR B2 | means Requirement B2 of Schedule 1 of the Building Regulations. |
| BA | refers to sections of the Building Act 1984. |
| WBL | refers to the Water Byelaws. |

## The requirements

These tell you what function the building or some part of it must serve – but they do not tell you how to achieve it. For example, the requirement might say that the foul-water drainage system must be adequate but not what you should do to satisfy the requirement.

The technical requirements are usually re-wordings of the legal text, which you must read if you want to know exactly what the legislation says. An abbreviated reference is given after each requirement so that you can find it easily.

### *Meeting the requirements*

The guidance given in Part 4 tells you how you can meet each requirement; to aid comprehension the opening page of some of the sections shows a plan of the building with a blacked-in portion giving the location of the relevant planned works or parts of works.

The guidance is taken from the practical guidance approved by the Secretary of State for the Environment (⇨ Approved Documents). The authors' comments given in italics after the ⚐ symbol are not part of this guidance.

## Exemptions and limitations

In some cases, the regulations exempt some kinds of buildings, building work, and changes of use (⇨ 1.2). In other cases the requirements may be subject to limits on their application.

## Alternative approaches

This heading occasionally appears within the sections discussed in Part 4. The alternative approaches are usually references to codes of practice published by the British Standards Institution (⇨ Useful addresses). These references are written for experienced designers and, because they are more comprehensive, some of the provisions might go beyond the provisions needed to meet the regulations. You should consider, therefore, whether a particular recommendation in a code is relevant to the work that you want to do, remembering that the building regulations do not require more to be done than is needed to secure reasonable standards of health, safety, energy conservation, and provisions for disabled people (BR 8).

## Approved documents

The Building Regulations are supported by Approved Documents (ADs). These give practical guidance on meeting the requirements. If you follow the guidance provided by the ADs, then this will be evidence tending to show the building control authorities that you are meeting the requirements. However, should you choose not to follow the guidance, then it is your responsibility to show that you are meeting the requirements by some other means. The guidance in this section is, then, a re-wording of the ADs guidance.

## Guidance

**Headings**    The section headings in Part 4 refer to the main parts of the building, for example "4.2 Drainage". Under the heading a contents list gives more detail.

**Checklist**    The above-mentioned contents list is generally followed by a *CHECKLIST* of features that you will probably have to consider. You can, if you wish, tick each box when you are satisfied that you have made the necessary decisions after you have read the guidance, which may be in the form of a table, a diagram or a technical specification (⇨ below).

**The Basics**    The boxed text either describes briefly the most used provisions or, where this is not practicable, summarises the main features of the provisions that follow in the text.

&#x1F4D5;    This open book symbol in a tinted panel defines some of the terms used which have a special meaning.

&#x261E;    This additional comment is for information and is not part of the guidance itself.

☛ You might be shown this symbol if the information you need is lengthy, or is of specialised interest, in which case you are either advised to refer to the Approved Documents or offered an alternative approach. The symbol also appears where it is recommended that you seek professional advice.

**Technical specifications**    Describe forms of construction, materials which can be used, and may also describe design features. (⇨ Keys and symbols in the Preface.)

**Numbering**          The numbering of diagrams, tables and technical specifications (TS) relates them as closely as possible to their relevant text. They are each numbered according to the section into which Part 4 is divided: for example, "Diagram 4.2–1, Table 4.2–1, TS 4.2–1" and so on.

# 4.1
# Site and foundations

## INTRODUCTION

In this section the guidance is for:

4.1.1    Solid waste storage (access)
4.1.2    Fire service access
4.1.3    Guarding sunken areas
4.1.4    Site preparation
4.1.5    Foundations
4.1.6    Ground-supported floors

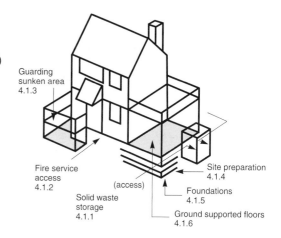

Guarding
sunken area
4.1.3

Fire service
access
4.1.2

(access)

Solid waste
storage
4.1.1

Site preparation
4.1.4

Foundations
4.1.5

Ground supported floors
4.1.6

## 4.1.1  Solid waste storage (access)

---

**THE BASICS**

Site the storage within 30m of the back door and 25m of the highway. If the distance is already more do not increase it. Where the local authority uses wheeled bins you should discuss the siting with them.

**For storage capacity:** ⇨ 4.9.4

---

*CHECKLIST*

☐   Access

## Requirements

There must be adequate access from the building to the storage place and from the storage place to the street (BR H4).

### Meeting the requirements

The storage should be within 30m of the dwelling and 25m of a street. If you are altering or extending the building and either distance is already greater, it should be made no greater than at present.

> 🕮 *The local authority is responsible for maintaining a collection service which it may contract out to others. With the increasing use of wheeled bins, however, the local authority may require these to be sited on the boundary of the curtilage of the property.*

## 4.1.2 Fire service access

> **THE BASICS**
> The whole building should be within 45m of the highway, or there should be access up to a door into the building. If the distance is already greater, don't increase it.

*CHECKLIST*
- ☐ Access

### Requirements

The access will meet the requirements if **provision** is made within the site to enable fire appliances to gain access to the building (BR B5[2]).

### *Meeting the requirements*

There should be access **either** to within 45m of every part of the building or to a length of external wall which is at least 15 per cent of the total length and has a door into the building. If you are altering or extending the building, it should be made no less accessible than it is at present.

> *The Building Regulations do not require work to be done outside the site of the works shown on the building notice or deposited plans (⇨ 2.2.1).*

## 4.1.3 Guarding sunken areas

> **THE BASICS**
> Guard areas next to a building if they are more than 380mm (or two risers if there are steps) below ground level. The guarding should be at least 1100mm high.

*CHECKLIST*
- ☐ Barriers

### Requirements

Barriers must be provided where there is a risk of people falling from the edge of any light-well, basement or other sunken area next to a building (BR K2). **Limit on application:** the requirement does not apply to areas where people approach the sunken area only to carry out repair or maintenance.

> *The requirement also does not apply where a barrier would restrict normal use.*

### *Meeting the requirements*

Barriers should also be provided where there is a risk of people falling more than 380mm – or if there are steps the height of more than two risers – from the edge of any light-well, basement or other sunken area next to a building (⇨ 4.4.2).

## 4.1.4 Site preparation

**THE BASICS**

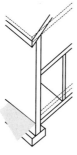

Clear away vegetable material from the site of the building to prevent its re-growth. If you think you have found any contaminants, tell the local authority's environmental health officer. If you find any foul-water or rainwater drainage, be sure that it is unused before you break it up. Be alert to any subsoil drainage running under the building (⇨ 4.2.3).

*CHECKLIST*
- ☐ Vegetable matter
- ☐ Contaminants

## Requirements

The preparation of the site will meet the requirements if:
- the ground to be covered by the building is reasonably free from **vegetable matter** (BR C1);
- the building and those inside it are protected from the danger of **contaminants** found either on or in the ground to be covered by the building (BR C2).

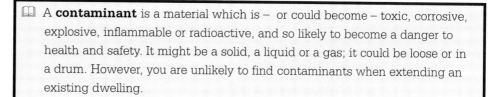

A **contaminant** is a material which is – or could become – toxic, corrosive, explosive, inflammable or radioactive, and so likely to become a danger to health and safety. It might be a solid, a liquid or a gas; it could be loose or in a drum. However, you are unlikely to find contaminants when extending an existing dwelling.

### Meeting the requirements
Where vegetable matter and/or contaminants are found, the planning authority will be concerned to ensure that no danger to public health and safety arises.

## Vegetable matter

You should always remove turf, roots and other vegetable matter from the ground to be covered by the building and its foundations to a depth that will prevent its later growth. You should also remove all compressible material which could affect the stability of the building.

## Contaminants

**Warning:** The Building Regulations do not require you to investigate the site as a whole, only to deal with contaminants that are found under the area to be covered by the building, but liquid and gaseous contaminants are mobile and can spread under a building from adjoining ground.

The first step, before you start work, is to recognise the problem if it exists. Check whether the site has a history which suggests there may be contaminants. Table 1 of Approved Document C contains a list of sites which are likely to contain contaminants. Table 2 of the document lists signs of possible contaminants. Check for patches of ground which are bare or an unnatural colour, and whether there is unusual vegetation.

The next step – when excavating starts – is to watch for any evidence of contaminants such as discoloured soil, drums or other containers. If there is evidence that the site of the building either contains or is affected by contaminants you should get in touch with the local authority's environmental health officer. In many cases, the remedy is to remove obvious contaminants and lay at least 100mm of concrete under the building, the normal construction for a ground-supported floor.

### Solid and liquid contaminants

The best course of action to take depends on the type and quantity of contaminants but it might be enough to cover the contaminant with a concrete ground-floor slab. In other cases it might be advisable to remove, say, 1m of ground and back-fill with suitable material to restore the levels before laying the (minimum) 100mm concrete slab.

### Gaseous contaminants

If the contaminant is in gaseous form, such as methane or radon, the remedy might be more elaborate, requiring ventilation and monitoring. Methane is a product of rotted organic landfill and many, but not all, landfill sites are known to the local authority. Radon is a naturally occurring radioactive, colourless and odourless gas and some parts of the country have higher levels than others. (The highest levels are in Cornwall, Devon and parts of Somerset, Northamptonshire and Derbyshire.). The British Geological Survey (⇨ Useful addresses) maintains a database of landfill sites and can gauge the risks from methane gas.

## 4.1.5 Foundations

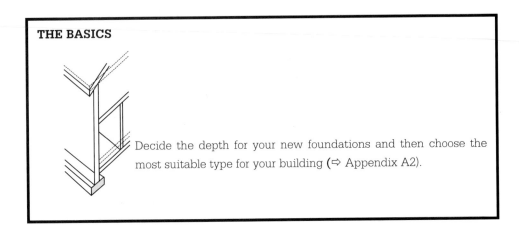

**THE BASICS**

Decide the depth for your new foundations and then choose the most suitable type for your building (⇨ Appendix A2).

*CHECKLIST*
- ☐ Stability
- ☐ Support
- ☐ Moisture

## Requirements

The **stability** of the building must not be impaired by ground movement due either to swelling, shrinking or freezing of the subsoil or due – insofar as the risk can be reasonably foreseen – to land-slip or subsidence (BR A2).

The foundations must be **constructed** to bear the combined dead-, imposed- and wind-loads and safely transmit them to the ground (BR A1).

The foundations must not be damaged by **moisture** from the ground and not carry moisture to any other part of the building which it would damage, and they must prevent moisture from reaching the upper surface of the floor (BR [C4]).

### Meeting the requirements

The Building Regulations are concerned only with damage which threatens health and safety. It is rare for damage due to ground movement to be a threat to health – even rarer for it to be an imminent threat to safety – as there are usually warning signs. The regulations are not concerned with cosmetic damage, although this might have a significant effect on property values.

## Stability

The long-term stability of the building depends on spreading the load evenly over ground that can be relied on not to move to any significant extent and is strong enough to bear the load. The main types of ground movement and their causes will include swelling and shrinking due to moisture changes and frost-heave; other less common causes of movement include landfill sites, compressible soils, land-slips and subsidence (⇨ Appendix A1).

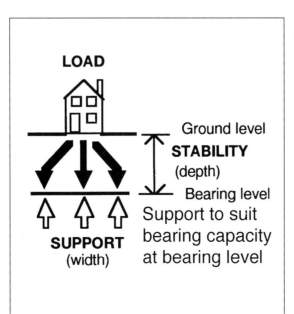

*Diagram 4.1–1:*
**Foundations – summary**

## Support

When you have considered the possible movement, you are ready to choose a type of foundation to suit the conditions (⇨ Appendix A). The most used type of foundation is the conventional strip-footing which, if properly used, is suitable for a wide range of situations. If you choose a concrete strip foundation, you will need guidance on raising on and extending existing foundations (⇨ Appendix A).

> 📖 HomeBuilder *gives guidance only on the traditional form of foundation – sometimes called a footing – which has a plain concrete base laid flat supporting a dwarf masonry wall finished slightly above ground level to take a damp-proof course. This form, if properly used, is suitable for a wide range of situations but there are other forms that can have advantages in some circumstances and also involve extending, raising on and underpinning existing foundations (⇨ Appendix A).*

## Moisture

Concrete and masonry below ground will not be adversely affected by moisture but on some sites the building authority may ask for sulphate-resisting cement to be used. Bricks and blocks should be chosen for their frost resistance and laid in cement mortar and the walls should be finished to receive a damp-proof course at least 150mm above the final ground level (⇨ 4.3.1).

# 4.1.6 Ground-supported floors

### THE BASICS

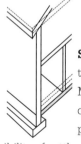

**Stability and structural support:** excavate the ground below the floor to a firm bearing level (probably a depth of about 250mm). Make up the level with non-compressible material (hardcore). If the depth would be more than 1m you should seriously consider a suspended floor (⇨ 4.4.1) to limit the expense and avoid the possibility of settlement. Lay a 100mm concrete slab (if there are any loadbearing internal walls).

**Moisture**: provide a damp-proof membrane of 1200-gauge polythene laid below the slab (difficult on a windy day) or three coats of cold-applied bitumen on the slab. Make the membrane continuous with the damp-proof courses in the walls and protect it with a floor screed.

**Heat loss**: unless the building is unheated, or heated but non-residential and with a floor area of no more than 30m², or a conservatory extension you need to limit heat losses. To limit the heat losses through the floor, start with the basic thickness (⇨ Table 4.1–1). These thicknesses depend on the performance of the insulating material you choose (thermal conductivity) and the ratio between the perimeter of the floor and its area (the P/A ratio).

**Ventilation**: if you build a ground-supported floor next to a suspended ground floor make sure that you do not obstruct any existing ventilation.

*CHECKLIST*
- ☐ Stability
- ☐ Structural support
- ☐ Moisture
- ☐ Heat loss

---

📖 A **ground floor** is the lowest surface of any storey and includes finishes that are laid as part of the permanent construction.

**Moisture damage** is serious enough to produce deterioration in a material or structure to the point that it would present an imminent danger to health or safety or, if it is an insulating material, would permanently reduce its performance.

---

📖 *Gound-supported floors are supported by the ground below. Other floors are suspended between supporting walls (⇨ 4.4.1).*

## Requirements

A ground-supported floor will meet the Building Regulations if:
- its **stability** will not be impaired by ground movement due either to swelling, shrinkage or freezing of the subsoil (BR A2);
- it will not be damaged by **moisture** from the ground, will not carry moisture to any other part of the building which it would damage, and will prevent moisture from reaching the upper surface of the floor (BR C4); **Limit on application:** requirement C4 does not apply where it will not increase health and safety – also where ground moisture will not damage the floor;
- it will be **constructed** to carry the combined dead- and imposed-loads to the ground safely and without either deformation or deflection of the building (BR A1);
- it will limit the **heat loss** to the ground (BR L1).

### Meeting the requirements

The building itself will normally protect the ground supporting the floor from major changes in moisture content and from freezing. However, where the building is exposed and unheated, and if movement could give rise to an imminent danger to health and safety, you should consider a suspended floor (⇨ 4.4.1) because it takes its support from the foundation level.

You should also consider a suspended ground floor where the depth of hardcore will be more than 1m and liable to settle.

## Stability

You can consider a suspended floor. This floor takes its support from the walls and foundations of the building. It is applicable, but only where the depth of the hardcore foundations will be more than 1m, the ground is liable to settle and the absence of landfill or radon gases has been confirmed.

## Structural support

A 100mm concrete slab should provide enough support for normal floor loads, with a thickening below non-loadbearing walls. However, this minimum thickness of slab may need increasing as it might not provide enough support for a loadbearing wall (⇨ TS 4.1–1).

---

### 4.1–1: Structural support

For the bed, lay a minimum 100mm of clean hardcore, which can be made up of broken brick or similar material. The depth of the hardcore can be more if needed to raise the slab to the required level but it should not be more than 1m and then only if non-compressible material is used, placed in layers and rolled.

For the slab (⇨ Diagram 4.1–2) lay at least 100mm of ready mixed concrete ST2 or *in situ* concrete composed of 50kg of cement to no more than 0.11m³ of fine aggregate and 0.16m³ of coarse aggregate or impervious material.

If the ground is chemically aggressive take precautions as for contaminated ground (⇨ 4.1.4). Also, if the slab is below the waterproof membrane and there are significant amounts of sulphates in the ground, use sulphate-resisting cement.

If the slab is lightly loaded, such as by a non-loadbearing masonry wall, the slab should be thickened to 200mm for a width of 200mm and the sides of the thickened part splayed out at 45 degrees. If the wall is loadbearing, it should be carried down through the slab to its own foundations.

*Diagram 4.1–2: Ground-supported floor – structural support*

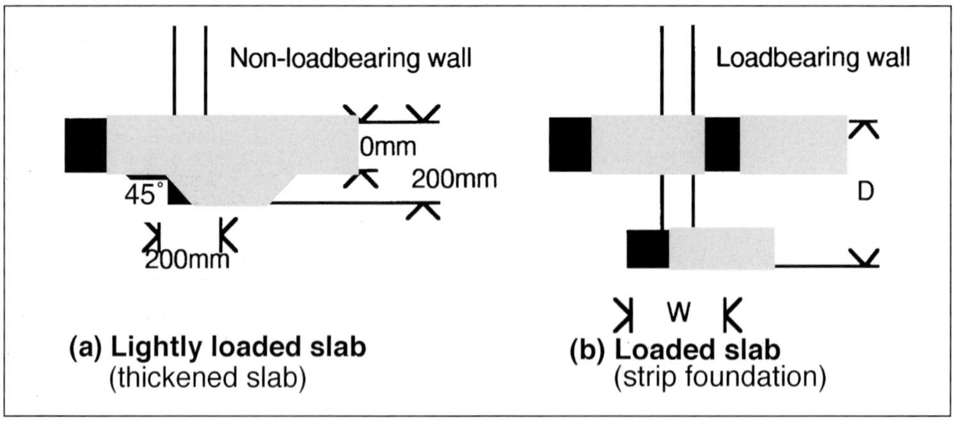

**(a) Lightly loaded slab**
(thickened slab)

**(b) Loaded slab**
(strip foundation)

## Moisture

Where a drain runs under the floor and where there may be implications for foul-water drainage and building settlement take an alternative approach (⇨ 4.2.1).

## 4.1–2: Damp-proof membrane (floor-beds)

A **damp-proof membrane** (floor-beds) may be laid **either** above **or** below the concrete slab. If it is laid **below** the concrete, use 1200-gauge (at least) polythene laid on a bed of material, such as sand, which will not damage the membrane, and with the joints sealed.

If the membrane is laid **above** the concrete, use **either** 1200-gauge polythene (poly-ethylene) sheet, **or** three coats of cold-applied bitumen solution, **or** a similar moisture-proof and vapour-proof material protected with either a screed or suitable floor finish.

Whether the membrane is laid below or above the concrete, make sure that it is continuous with the damp-proof courses in the walls.

Where contaminants have been found in the ground under the floor-bed it might be advisable to lay the damp-proof membrane below the slab, not above it, to protect the concrete.

*If any floor could be subject to water pressure you must take alternative action. The requirement can be met by following the recommendations in Clause 11 of CP 102: 1990 which gives recommendations for floors subject to water pressure.*

## Heat loss

To find the thickness of insulation material work out the ratio of floor perimeter (m) to floor area  (m²) (the P/A ratio) and find the thermal conductivity value (the "k" value) of the material you intend to you use (⇨ Table 4.1–1).

*The insulation can be placed above or below the slab. Choose a type that will not be compressed and, if it is below the damp-proof membrane, a type which will not be affected by moisture. In neither case should you rely on it to act as a damp-proof membrane.*

**Table 4.1–1:  *Insulation thickness: ground-supported floor (U-value 0.35 W/m²K)***

| P/A | Thermal conductivity (k) | | | | | | |
|---|---|---|---|---|---|---|---|
| | 0.02 | 0.025 | 0.03 | 0.035 | 0.04 | 0.045 | 0.05 |
| | Insulation thickness (mm) | | | | | | |
| 1.00 | 39 | 49 | 58 | 68 | 78 | 88 | 97 |
| 0.90 | 38 | 48 | 57 | 67 | 76 | 86 | 95 |
| 0.80 | 37 | 46 | 55 | 65 | 74 | 83 | 92 |
| 0.70 | 35 | 44 | 53 | 62 | 70 | 79 | 88 |
| 0.60 | 33 | 41 | 49 | 58 | 66 | 74 | 82 |
| 0.50 | 30 | 37 | 44 | 52 | 59 | 67 | 74 |
| 0.40 | 25 | 31 | 37 | 43 | 49 | 55 | 61 |
| 0.30 | 16 | 21 | 25 | 29 | 33 | 37 | 41 |
| 0.20 | 1 | 1 | 1 | 2 | 2 | 2 | 2 |

# 4.2
# Drainage

## INTRODUCTION

In this section the guidance is for:

4.2.1     Foul-water drainage
4.2.2     Rainwater drainage
4.2.3     Groundwater drainage

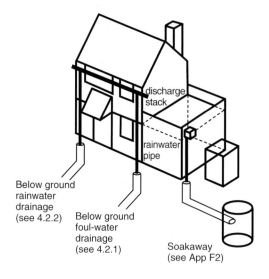

## 4.2.1 Foul-water drainage

---

**THE BASICS**

**Layout and construction**: use 100mm diameter pipes of flexible plastics or rigid stoneware with flexible joints. Lay the pipes at a gradient of 1:40 in suitable bedding. Lay flexible pipes at a depth of at least 0.9m under a drive and 0.6m in fields and gardens. Lay rigid pipes at a depth of between 0.4–7.4m under a drive and between 0.3–7.4m in fields and gardens (the actual depths depending on the type of bedding) or protect the pipes. Provide access points for clearing blockages. Ventilate the system by connecting it to a ventilating stack but only connect the stack to the sanitary pipework through water seals (⇨ 4.7.1).

**Disposal**: connect to a gravity foul-water drainage system if you can (⇨ Appendix F1).

---

### CHECKLIST

    ☐  Construction
    ☐  Watertightness and testing
    ☐  Ventilation and foul air
    ☐  Blockages and clearance
    ☐  Special precautions
    ☐  Final disposal (foul water)

    *The guidance in this section deals only with the requirements for drainage below ground. Foul-water drainage above ground is discussed elsewhere (⇨ 4.7.1). The Building Regulations do not require a system to be provided, only to be adequate if it is provided. However, where plans are deposited in accordance with the Building Regulations, the Building Act gives the local authority power to reject the plans unless they show that satisfactory provision will be made for the conveyance of foul water. The means of disposal must be agreed with the local authority and possibly also with the Environmental Agency (⇨ Useful addresses).*

> 📖 **Foul water** means waste water which consists of, or includes, waste water that has been used for cooking or washing

## Requirements

The foul-water drainage system must be adequate to carry the flow of foul water from the appliances within the building to a sewer, cesspool or a septic or settlement tank (BR H1).

### Meeting the requirements

The foul-water drainage system will be adequate if it is:

* constructed to carry the flow of foul water from the sanitary pipework to a suitable outfall (a foul or combined sewer, a cesspool or a sewage works);
* ventilated.

It must also:

* **prevent foul air** from the drainage system entering the building under working conditions;
* minimise the risk of **blockages** and be accessible for clearing them (BR H1).

> 📝 *Special precautions may be necessary. In some cases, you will have to consider one or more of the following: building settlement, surcharging, rodent control and ground loads.*

## Construction

When constructing drainage (⇨ TS 4.2–1 to TS 4.2–5), changes in direction and gradient should be as few as possible and as easy as practicable and, at the same time, allow for easy access wherever practicable (⇨ Diagram 4.2–1).

---

### 4.2–1: Layout

Drain runs should be laid in straight lines but slight curves are acceptable as long as they can be cleared of blockages. Other changes of direction will need access points. Only use bends close to the foot of discharge and ventilating stacks and in or close to inspection chambers and manholes; bends should have as large a radius as is possible.

Connections to an existing sewer/drain should be oblique or in the direction of flow. Special fittings – say, threequarter section branch bends, or "slippers" – can be used to turn an incoming drain into the direction of the flow in the chamber.

> 📝 *The simpler the layout, the better.*

## 4.2–2: Pipe sizes and gradients

Drains should have enough capacity (⇨ Table 4.2–1) to carry the flow and be laid to falls. The flow depends on the appliances connected (⇨ Table 4.7–1) and the capacity (⇨ Diagram 4.2–1)depends on the size and gradient of the pipes. A drain carrying only waste water should have a diameter of at least 75mm and a drain carrying soil water or waste water containing trade effluent a diameter of at least 100mm.

📖 *A short length at the head of a drain may be laid at a steeper gradient, giving the flow a "kick-start". But if a run of drain is laid on a steep gradient there is a risk that any solids may be stranded. Where the levels are likely to produce a steep gradient, then a steep drop is preferable. This should be in a vertical pipe (tumble-pipe) – close to, but outside, a manhole. You will run the risk of blockages if you use a drain with a larger capacity than the expected flow rate requires, simply with the idea of laying it at a lower gradient.*

***Diagram 4.2–1: Discharge capacity of foul drains running threequarters full***

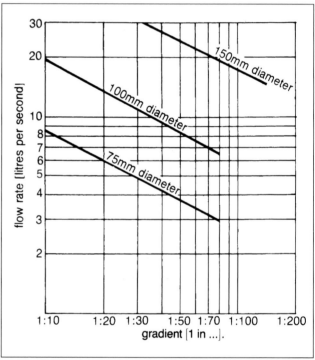

**Table 4.2–1:** *Foul drains – minimum gradients*

| Peak flow (litres/sec) | Pipe size (mm) | Minmum gradient (1 in . . .) | Maximum capacity (litres/sec) |
|---|---|---|---|
| < 1 | 75 | 1:40 | 4.1 |
|  | 100 | 1:40 | 9.2 |
| > 1 | 75 | 1:80 | 2.8 |
|  | 100 | 1:80* | 6.3 |
|  | 150 | 1:150† | 15.0 |

Notes

\* Minimum of 1 wc.

† Minimum of 5 wcs.

## 4.2–3: Depth of pipe cover

The depth of cover usually depends on the levels of the entries and exits of the system and the gradients and ground levels between. However, pipes must be protected where, for example, they could be damaged by digging or being driven over. Normally, the necessary protection will be provided by a suitable combination of cover, pipe and bedding. Where pipes are laid with less cover, special protection might be needed for ground loads.

## 4.2–4: Materials for pipes and joints

Care must be taken to match the materials used with appropriate joints (⇨ Table 4.2.2). Pipes, whether they are rigid or flexible, should have flexible joints to minimise the effect of differential settlement and nothing should project into the pipeline or cause an obstruction. All joints should remain watertight under both test conditions and working conditions.

📖 *Given the variety of materials and techniques available today, you should follow the manufacturer's instructions precisely. But special precautions may be required against rodent infestation.*

**Table 4.2–2: *Materials for below-ground gravity drainage***

| Material | British Standard |
|---|---|
| **Rigid pipes** | |
| asbestos | BS 3656 |
| vitrified clay | BS 65, BSEN 295 |
| concrete | BS 5911 |
| grey iron | BS 437, BS 6087 |
| **Flexible pipes** | |
| uPVC | BS 4660 |
| | BS 5481 |

Note
Some of these materials may not be suitable for conveying trade effluent

### *Bedding and back-filling*

In providing bedding and back-filling (⇨ TS 4.2–5) the depth should be at least 0.9m under any road and 0.6m in fields and gardens, but can be less if the pipes are protected.

Flexible pipes might not crack under load but they can flatten. The maximum depth of any drain should be 30m. This sounds very deep but is possible where a connection has to be made to a drain or sewer in hilly country. Again, a tumble-pipe provides the answer and reduces the amount of excavation.

If the drain or trench has to be excavated lower than the foundations of any building nearby, there are special regulations.

---

## 4.2–5: Bedding and back-filling

The choice of bedding and back-filling depends on the size and strength of pipes and the depths at which they are to be laid.

The following applies:

*Rigid pipes*: for bedding and back-fill (⇨ Diagram 4.2–2). For minimum and maximum depth (⇨ Table 4.2–3).

*Flexible pipes*: for bedding and back-fill (⇨ Diagram 4.2–3). The minimum depth should be 0.9m under roads and 0.6m in gardens and fields. The maximum depth should be 10m.

*Depth*: the depth of rigid and flexible pipes can be reduced if the pipes are protected (⇨ Special precautions, later in this section).

## Watertightness and testing

After laying, surrounding and back-filling, gravity drains and sewers up to a diameter of 300mm should withstand either a water-test or an air-test (⇨ TS 4.2–6).

   *Pumped systems will need testing to higher pressures.*

*Water-test*: Drains should pass a water-test to a pressure equal to 1.5m head of water

---

## 4.2–6: Watertightness and testing

measured above the invert of the drain. The drain can most easily be tested using a standpipe of the same diameter as the drain length to be tested, then filling the system, leaving it for two hours and topping it up. The drop in water level in the following 30 minutes should not be more than 6.5mm for each metre run of 100mm drain (4.5mm for a 150mm drain). To prevent damage to the drain, the head of water should not be more than 4m and it might be necessary to test the drain in sections.

*Air-test*: Drains should pass an air-test, such that if the system is pressurised the loss of head on a water-filled transparent U-tube (a manometer) after five minutes is not more than 25mm for 100mm-gauge and 12mm for 50mm-gauge.

   *Where the drain being tested runs into an open channel, remember to use a drain stop to seal the open end of the length of pipe under test.*

## Ventilation and foul air

*Diagram 4.2–2:* **Bedding for rigid pipes**

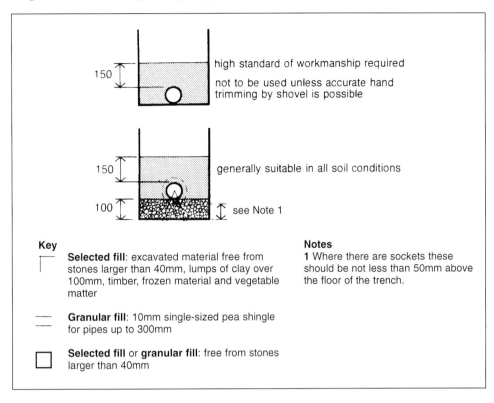

150      high standard of workmanship required

not to be used unless accurate hand
trimming by shovel is possible

150      generally suitable in all soil conditions

100      ⬍ see Note 1

**Key**

┌──  **Selected fill**: excavated material free from
│    stones larger than 40mm, lumps of clay over
│    100mm, timber, frozen material and vegetable
     matter

──   **Granular fill**: 10mm single-sized pea shingle
──   for pipes up to 300mm

☐    **Selected fill** or **granular fill**: free from stones
     larger than 40mm

**Notes**
**1** Where there are sockets these
should be not less than 50mm above
the floor of the trench.

*Diagram 4.2–3:* **Bedding for flexible pipes**

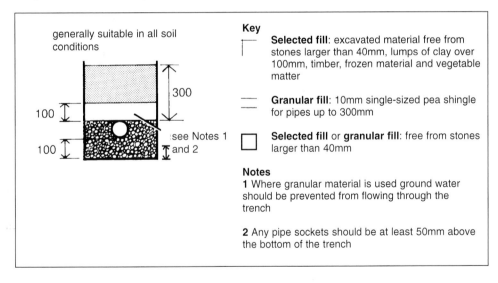

generally suitable in all soil
conditions

300

100

100      see Notes 1
         and 2

**Key**

┌──  **Selected fill**: excavated material free from
│    stones larger than 40mm, lumps of clay over
│    100mm, timber, frozen material and vegetable
     matter

──   **Granular fill**: 10mm single-sized pea shingle
──   for pipes up to 300mm

☐    **Selected fill** or **granular fill**: free from stones
     larger than 40mm

**Notes**
**1** Where granular material is used ground water
should be prevented from flowing through the
trench

**2** Any pipe sockets should be at least 50mm above
the bottom of the trench

**Table 4.2–3:** *Limits of cover for standard-strength rigid pipes*

| Pipe bore | Bedding class | Fields and gardens | | Light traffic roads | | Heavy traffic roads | |
|---|---|---|---|---|---|---|---|
| | | Min | Max | Min | Max | Min | Max |
| | D or N | 0.4 | 4.2 | 0.7 | 4.1 | 0.7 | 3.7 |
| 100 | F | 0.3 | 5.8 | 0.5 | 5.8 | 0.5 | 5.6 |
| | B | 0.3 | 7.4 | 0.4 | 7.4 | 0.4 | 7.2 |
| | D or N | 0.6 | 2.7 | 1.1 | 2.5 | – | – |
| 150 | F | 0.6 | 3.9 | 0.7 | 3.8 | 0.7 | 3.3 |
| | B | 0.6 | 5.0 | 0.6 | 5.0 | 0.6 | 4.6 |

Water seals (traps) on each appliance (⇨ 4.7.1) prevent foul air from the drainage system entering the building. As the foul water moves through the system, it can produce a negative pressure which could pull the water from these seals. To prevent this, the system should be well ventilated (⇨ TS 4.2–7). The ventilation will also limit the accumulation of foul gases in the drainage and sewers.

> *Usually the ventilating pipe will be a discharge stack carried up to a suitable height.*

Connect the below-ground drainage directly to a ventilating pipe at or near the head

---

### 4.2–7: Ventilation and foul air

---

of each main drain. Make the same connection to any branch longer than 6m if the drainage is connected to one appliance (and longer than 12m if connected to more than one appliance). The bend at the foot of each pipe should have as large a radius as possible and at least 200mm measured to its centre line.

## Blockages and clearance

The normal method of rodding is with flexible drain rods, which might not always need to be used only in the direction of flow.

> *Provision should be made for clearing blockages but the possibility of these occurring will be reduced if the technical specifications for the layout and construction of the system are followed (⇨ 4.7.1). A gently curved pipe run might reduce the risk of a blockage if it makes a sharp bend unnecessary.*

Mechanical means of clearing drains are also available when the provision for access points in the layout cannot be made.

### Siting access points

Any change of gradient should be combined with an access point but additional access points should be provided only if blockages could not be cleared without them. Slight changes of direction are acceptable if they can be cleared of blockages.

Access points should be provided:
- on long runs (⇨ Table 4.2–4);
- on or near the head of each drain run;
- at a bend or change of gradient;
- at a change of pipe size;
- at a junction of pipes, unless each run can be cleared from an access point.

### Constructing access points

**Table 4.2–4:** *Access points – spacing on long runs (m)*

| From | To | Access Fitting | | Junction | Inspection chamber | Manhole |
|---|---|---|---|---|---|---|
| | | Small | Large | | | |
| Start of external drain | | 12 | 12 | – | 22 | 45 |
| Rodding eye | | 22 | 22 | 22 | 45 | 45 |
| Access fitting<br>small    150 diam<br>           150 x 100<br>large    225 x 100 | | –<br><br>–<br> | –<br><br>–<br> | <br><br>12<br>22 | <br><br>22<br>45 | <br><br>22<br>45 |
| Inspection chamber | | 22 | 45 | 22 | 45 | 45 |
| Manhole | | 22 | 45 | 45 | 45 | 90 |

Under both test conditions and working conditions, access points (⇨ TS 4.2–8) should contain the foul water and also exclude groundwater and rainwater.

## 4.2–8: Constructing access points

Access points (⇨ Diagram 4.2–4) should be one of four types.

**1**    A rodding eye – a capped extension of a drain.

**2**    An access fitting – a small chamber on (or an extension of) a drain but not with an open channel.

**3**    An inspection chamber – a chamber (usually with an open channel) needing working space at drain level.

**4**    A manhole – a large chamber (usually with an open channel) providing working space at drain level.

There are specific dimensions for access points (⇨ Table 4.2–5) and they may be

*Diagram 4.2–4:* **The four types of access points**

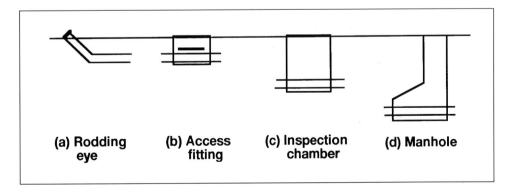

**(a) Rodding eye**    **(b) Access fitting**    **(c) Inspection chamber**    **(d) Manhole**

made of a variety of materials (⇨ Table 4.2–6).

**Table 4.2–5:  *Access points – depths and dimensions***

| Type | Depth to (m) | Internal sizes | | Cover sizes | |
| --- | --- | --- | --- | --- | --- |
| | | Length x width (mm x mm) | Circular (mm) | Length x width (mm x mm) | Circular (mm) |
| Rodding eye | | As drain but min 100 | | | |
| Access fitting | | | | | |
|    small | 0.6 or less | 150 x 100 | 150 | 150 x 100 | 150 |
|    large | | 225 x 100 | – | 225 x 100 | – |
| Inspection chamber | 0.6 or less | – | 190* | – | 190* |
| | 1.0 or less | 450 x 450 | 450 | 450 x 450 | 450† |
| Manhole | 1.5 or less | 1200 x 750 | 1050 | 600 x 600 | 600 |
| | over 1.5 | 1200 x 750 | 1200 | 600 x 600 | 600 |
| | over 2.7 | 1200 x 840 | 1200 | 600 x 600 | 600 |
| Shaft | over 2.7 | 900 x 840 | 900 | 600 x 600 | 600 |

Notes

\*   Drains up to 150mm

†   For clayware or plastics may be reduced to 430mm in order to provide support for cover and frame.

**Table 4.2–6:  *Access-point – materials***

| Material | British Standards |
| --- | --- |
| 1    Inspection chambers and manholes | |
|      Clay | |
|      Bricks and blocks | BS 3921 |
|      vitrified | BS 65 |
|      Concrete | |
|      precast | BS 5911 |
|      *in situ* | BS 8110 |
|      Plastics | BS 7158 |
| 2    Rodding eyes and access fittings (excluding frames and covers) | as pipes<br>See Table 4.2–2<br>BBA Certificates |

Inspection chambers and manholes should have removable non-ventilating covers of durable materials, including cast iron, cast or pressed steel, precast concrete or uPVC, and be of suitable strength. Inspection chambers and manholes in buildings should have mechanically fixed (such as screwed) airtight covers, or the drain itself should have a watertight access cover. Manholes deeper than 1m should have metal step-irons or a fixed ladder.

Where half-round open channels are used in inspection chambers and manholes any branches should discharge over the channel in the direction of flow. Where the angle of the branch is more than 45 degrees, a threequarter section branch-bend (a slipper) should be used.

Channels and branches should be benched up at a slope of 1-in-12, at least to the top of the outgoing pipe and the benching should be rounded to a radius of at least 25mm where it meets the channel.

The depth at which each access point should be used and the dimensions it should have vary (⇨ Table 4.2–5). The dimensions might need to be increased at junctions if they are to allow enough space for branches.

## Special precautions

In some cases, provision may need to be made for one or more situations which arise during construction work. Some of these are discussed below.

### Building settlement

Where a drain runs **under a building**, damage to the drain due to settlement (⇨ TS 4.2–9) of the building must be prevented.

---

#### 4.2–9: Building settlement

---

There are two possibilities to prevent damage to the drain, depending on the position of the crown (the top, including collars).

1    If the crown is **within 300mm** of the underside of a concrete floor slab, the pipe should be encased in concrete integral with the slab (⇨ Diagram 4.2–5(a)).

2    If the crown is **not within 300mm**, the pipe should be surrounded with at least 100mm of granular or flexible material (⇨ Diagram 4.2–5(b)).

Where a drain runs **through a wall or foundation**, there are two alternative approaches.

1    The pipe should have a 50mm clearance all round, with the space blocked with rigid material to prevent the entry of fill and vermin (⇨ Diagram 4.2–6).

2    As short a length of pipe as possible should be built into the wall or foundation (within no more than 150mm of the faces). It should be connected each side to rocker pipes, with a length of, at most, 600mm and flexible joints (⇨ Diagram 4.2–6).

*Diagram 4.2–5:* **Pipe runs under ground-supported floor**

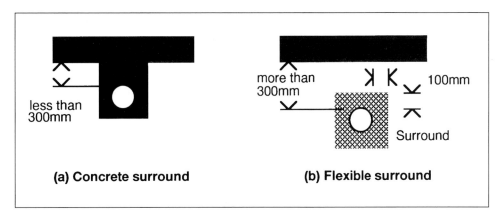

**(a) Concrete surround**                    **(b) Flexible surround**

Where a drain runs **near a building** and the trench has to be excavated to a level lower than its foundations, damage to the building due to settlement of the excavation must be prevented. There are two possibilities depending on the distance between the trench and the foundation.

1    Where the distance is **less than 1m**, the trench should be filled with concrete up to the level of the bottom of the foundation (⇨ Diagram 4.2–7).

2    Where the distance is **at least 1m**, the trench need only be filled with concrete to a level below the bottom of the foundation equal to 150mm less than the distance (⇨ Diagram 4.2–7).

***Diagram 4.2–6*: Pipe runs through walls**

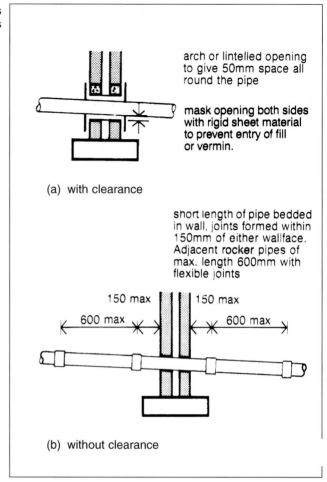

arch or lintelled opening to give 50mm space all round the pipe

mask opening both sides with rigid sheet material to prevent entry of fill or vermin.

(a)  with clearance

short length of pipe bedded in wall, joints formed within 150mm of either wallface. Adjacent rocker pipes of max. length 600mm with flexible joints

150 max      150 max

600 max      600 max

(b)  without clearance

***Diagram 4.2–7*: Pipe runs near buildings**

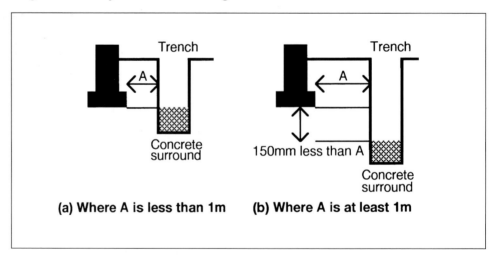

Trench

A

Concrete surround

Trench

A

150mm less than A

Concrete surround

**(a) Where A is less than 1m**     **(b) Where A is at least 1m**

## Surcharging

The local authority should be consulted if there is any suggestion that a drain or sewer might back up, or surcharge, high enough for the contents to flow into the building, not out of it.

## Rodent control

Protection from rodents can be gained from a sealed system. This has access covers to the pipework, instead of open channels, with an intercepting trap (interceptor) between the system and the sewer, although the trap is liable to block unless regularly maintained.

In the worst cases, the provision of access covers and an interceptor, combined with the use of stoneware drainpipes and cast-iron sanitary pipework, might be unavoidable.

> *In some areas, rats are a problem. They might enter a building through the drains and attack both plastic and metal pipes.*

## Ground loads

The protection of pipes is essential (⇨ TS 4.2–10).

### 4.2–10: Ground loads

*Rigid pipes*: if rigid pipes have less than the recommended cover and are liable to damage they should be encased in concrete at least 100mm thick, with movement joints formed from compressible board at the face of each joint (⇨ Diagram 4.2–8).

**Diagram 4.2–8: Protection for rigid pipes (mm)**

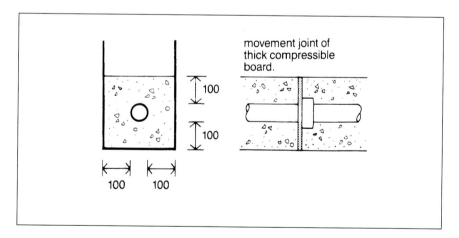

*Flexible pipes*: if flexible pipes are positioned under a road they should, if they have less than 900mm of cover, be protected by reinforced concrete bridging or by a reinforced concrete surround. The bridging should be supported on unexcavated ground. If they are *not* under a road, flexible pipes, if they have less than 600mm of cover, should be protected by concrete paving slabs laid as bridging with at least 75mm of granular material between the top of the pipe and the underside of the slabs. The slabs should be supported on unexcavated ground (⇨ Diagram 4.2–9).

🖳 *Flexible pipes need protection because, although they are unlikely to crack if they are loaded, their capacity will be reduced if they are deformed.*

**Diagram 4.2–9:**
**Protection for**
**flexible pipes (mm)**

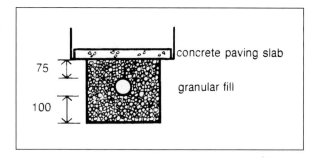

### Alternative approach – foul drainage

The requirements can also be met by following the relevant recommendations of BS 8301: 1985. The relevant clauses are in Sections 1 and 2, also 3 (except Clause 10) and 4 (except Clause 23).

## Final disposal (foul water)

The final disposal (⇨ Appendix F) may be to a foul water, or a combined drain and, sewer, cesspool or a sewage treatment works. Drainage systems need to be ventilated by a pipe connected to the head of the drain and carried up the building to an open outlet. In many cases this ventilating pipe will also be intended to carry foul water – soil ventilating pipe (SVP) – but in some cases it may be intended only for ventilation. Also, older drainage systems were fitted with interceptors (no longer considered necessary or even desirable) installed near the boundary with a length of drain (certainly intended only for ventilation) connecting them to a fresh air inlet (FAI) nearby at or near ground level.

🖳 *Do not connect foul water to a drain connected to a vent pipe or to a drain connected to a FAI without first checking that the drain is suitable. For example, the drain, if it is only for ventilation, may open in the side of a manhole so that any foul water would not discharge into the open channel and be carried away.*

## 4.2.2 Rainwater drainage

> **THE BASICS**
>
> Use 10mm diameter pipes of flexible plasics or rigid stoneware with flexible joints laid at a gradient of 1:40 in suitable bedding (⇨ 4.2.1). The drainage system does not need ventilating.
>
> **Disposal:** connect to a gravity rainwater drainage system if you can (⇨ Appendix F).

&#9744; *The guidance in this section discusses only the requirements for drainage below ground. For surface water systems above ground other arrangements are necessary.*

The Building Regulations do not require a system to be provided, only for the system to be adequate if it is provided. However, where plans are deposited in accordance with the regulations, the Building Act gives the local authority power to reject the plans unless they show that satisfactory provision will be made for the conveyance of surface water.

&#9744; *The means of disposal of surface water must be agreed with the local authority (⇨ Appendix F).*

## Requirements

The rainwater system will be adequate, if:

*   it is **constructed** to carry the flow of rainwater from roofs to a suitable rainwater outfall (a rainwater or combined sewer, a soakaway or an open outlet);
*   it will minimise the risk of **blockages** and be accessible for clearing them.

&#9744; *It is not necessary to ventilate the below-ground surface water drainage system. Special precautions are, however, necessary in some cases. For example, you will have to consider one or more of the following: building settlement, surcharging, rodent control and ground loads.*

### Meeting the requirements

### CHECKLIST
&#9744; Construction
&#9744; Blockages
&#9744; Special precautions
&#9744; Final disposal (rainwater)

## Construction

The layout, depth of pipe cover required, specifications for materials, workmanship and watertightness have been dealt with earlier (⇨ 4.2–1).

### Pipe gradients and sizes
Drains should have enough capacity to carry the flow of water from roofs, pipes (⇨ TS 4.2–11) and the run-off from paved and other hard ground surfaces. This run-off is not covered by the Building Regulations – but the Building Act can require backyards and accesses to houses to be paved.

| 4.2–11: Pipe gradients and sizes |
|---|

The intensity of rainfall which should be assumed for roofs is 75mm an hour and for paved areas 50mm an hour. All drains should be laid to falls (gradients) to the outlet; the capacity depends on size and gradient of the pipes.

Capacities (flow rates) of drains with different diameters and different gradients do vary (⇨ Diagram 4.2–10).

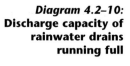

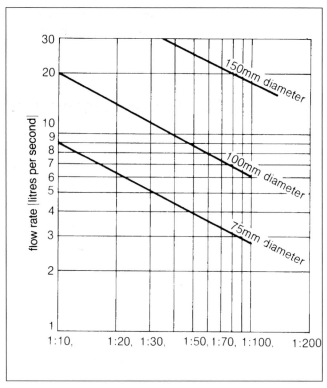

***Diagram 4.2–10:
Discharge capacity of
rainwater drains
running full***

⌷ *Drains should have a diameter of at least 75mm. And 75mm and 100mm drains should have a gradient of at least 1:100. The capacity of a drain is increased according to the gradient. However, if you use a drain with a larger capacity than the expected flow rate requires, simply with the idea of laying it at a lower gradient, it will silt up (⇨ 4.7.1).*

## Blockages

Silt, which is the main cause of blockages in the below-ground rainwater drainage system, should be collected and removed, by providing trapped gullies at the entry points, for example where rainwater downpipes discharge into the system. If access points are provided on long runs, types and dimensions of access fittings and chambers, also materials, will have to be specified (⇨ 4.2.1).

As an alternative to chambers with half-round channels, it might be more convenient to provide a simple brick or concrete box with a sump below the pipe levels where silt can collect and be removed.

⌷ *Do not allow silt to build up. Remove or collect it before blockage occurs.*

## Special precautions

In some cases, provision should be made for at least one of the following: building settlement, surcharging, rodent control and ground loads (⇨ 4.2.1).

### Alternative approach

The regulations can also be met by following the relevant recommendations of BS 6367.

## Final disposal (rainwater)

The final disposal may be to a rainwater drain or sewer, a combined foul and rainwater drain or sewer, a soakaway, a watercourse or some other suitable rainwater outfall, such as a pond (⇨ Appendix F).

# 4.2.3 Groundwater drainage

---
**THE BASICS**

If the water table can rise to within 0.25m of the ground level (dig a trial pit), or you have a basement or cellar, you should consider groundwater drainage if you have access to an open outfall. If you do not, you will have to build with materials which will not be affected by groundwater and will prevent it from entering the building.

---

## CHECKLIST
- ☐ Provision
- ☐ Final disposal (groundwater)

## Requirements

A subsoil drainage system must be provided where it is needed to avoid:
- the passage of moisture to the interior of the building (BR C3a);
- moisture damage to the fabric of the building (BR C3b).

  📖 *Groundwater does not include floodwater.*

---
📖 **Moisture damage** is damage so serious that it would produce deterioration in a material or structure to the point that it would present an imminent danger to health or safety or (if an insulating material) would permanently reduce its performance.

---

### Meeting the requirements

A system will be needed to collect groundwater in the subsoil and dispose of it, unless the construction will effectively prevent groundwater from passing to the interior of the building and **either** the materials which are used will not be adversely affected or they will be protected.

In most cases, the construction materials will be resistant to groundwater. However, if there is a cellar or basement below the level of the water table, or the water table is higher than 0.25m, you should consider a subsoil drainage system to a suitable outfall.

  📖 *The consideration of a subsoil drainage system is necessary because the only alternative – a construction which will prevent groundwater from entering the building – would be expensive. Unfortunately, however, this alternative will be unavoidable if there is no suitable outfall.*

## Provision

Where a subsoil drainage system *is* needed, it will meet the requirements (⇨ 4.2–3) if, **either:**

- an active **system exists** (⇨ Diagram 4.2–11); **or**
- a **system will be provided** if the water table can rise to within 0.25m of the lowest floor of the building, or surface water could adversely affect the building.

## *Existing groundwater drainage*

Where an existing groundwater drainage system or an active subsoil drainage system is in place there is an alternative; **either:**

- any part which will run through the building should be relaid in pipes with sealed joints and a diameter of at least 75mm – or the diameter of the existing pipes, whichever is the greater (⇨ Diagram 4.2–11(a)); **or**
- the system can be re-routed with unsealed joints around the building to rejoin the existing outfall or re-run to another (⇨ Diagram 4.2–11(b)).

**Diagram 4.2–11: Existing subsoil drain cut during excavation**

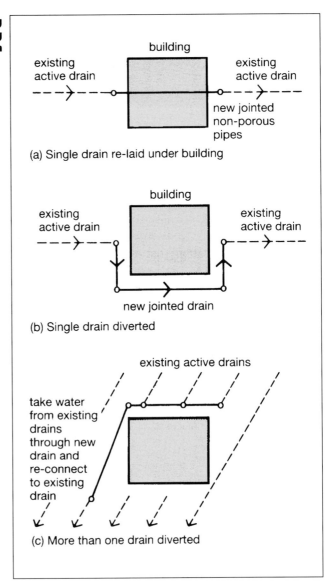

(a) Single drain re-laid under building

(b) Single drain diverted

(c) More than one drain diverted

### *Provision of groundwater drainage*

The groundwater should be collected and drained by gravity to an open outlet. The pipes should have a diameter of at least 75mm. Where they run through the building they should be jointed and non-porous. Refer to BS 1196 and also BS 4962.

## Final disposal (groundwater)

The open outlet should discharge (⇨ Appendix F) to a watercourse or some other suitable open rainwater outfall, such as a pond.

# 4.3
# Walls

## INTRODUCTION

In this section the guidance is for:

| | |
|---|---|
| 4.3.1 | External walls |
| 4.3.2 | Chimneys |
| 4.3.3 | Parapets |
| 4.3.4 | External cladding |
| 4.3.5 | Internal walls |
| 4.3.6 | Internal walls (loadbearing) |
| 4.3.7 | Glazing |

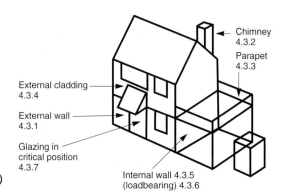

Chimney 4.3.2

Parapet 4.3.3

External cladding 4.3.4

External wall 4.3.1

Glazing in critical position 4.3.7

Internal wall 4.3.5 (loadbearing) 4.3.6

## STRUCTURAL WALLS

The load which a structural wall can support depends on its thickness and on the strength of the materials that are used. But it also depends on the wall itself being stable – not moving under load – and the more stable it is, the more load the wall can carry.

> 📖 A **structural wall** means any external wall and an internal wall if it is load-bearing. It also includes an internal wall which, even if it is non-loadbearing, provides support to an external wall or an internal loadbearing wall.

The stability of a wall depends on its dimensions and on the support which it gets from other parts of the structure (other walls, piers or buttresses, floors and roofs) and the more box-like the building, the more stable it will be.

> 📖 *In this section you can find the thickness that a wall should have – if both your building and your wall meet some conditions, or your design can be changed so that they will (⇨ also Appendices).*

### The conditions

The conditions do assume the worst combinations of conditions likely to occur and for this reason minor departures are possible if they can be justified by, **either:**

- judgement based on experience; **or**
- calculation, when you will only need to calculate the thickness of the wall which is subject of the departure, not the whole building.

> 📖 *Major departures are a strong indication that you should follow the alternative approach, when you will need calculations for the whole building.*

### To find the thickness of a structural wall

Check that your building meets the **conditions for the building** as a whole (⇨ Appendix B1.1 to B.1–3).

Check that the wall meets the **conditions for the wall** (⇨ Appendix B2.1 to B2.8).

If the wall is relied upon to support another wall (that is to say, it is a buttressing wall) remember to check that the thickness of the wall and the limitations on openings in it will satisfy the guidance for a buttressing wall (⇨ Appendix B2.6).

## OPENINGS IN WALLS

You may sometimes have to give special thought to openings in walls not only because there are several requirements which can apply to the **opening** itself but also because it can affect the performance of the **wall** in which it occurs.

### The opening

You may have to think about guarding (where there is a drop), glazing (where it is in critical positions), ventilation (background and rapid), heat loss (the U-value and air infiltration), internal fire spread (fire doors) and means of escape (size and position).

### The wall

You may have to think about the structural support the wall must give (especially if it is loadbearing), support over the opening and its resistance to collapse in the event of fire (and, if the wall is a buttressing wall, its stability), external fire spread (unprotected areas), heat loss (cold bridges, the U-value and the proportion of opening to floor area) and the passage of moisture.

## FIRE SAFETY

The performance of the construction in the event of a fire has two aspects: **resistance** to fire and **reaction** to fire.

### Resistance to fire

**Resistance to fire (collapse)** measures the ability of the construction to maintain its **loadbearing capacity** in the event of its being exposed to fire. The criterion is that **structural frames** (columns and beams) and **loadbearing walls** (and the loadbearing parts of walls) must maintain their loadbearing capacity, or "R", for a given period without collapse. This criterion is expressed in minutes, thus: "R30".

**Resistance to fire (spread)** concerns the ability of the construction to resist the external or internal spread of fire. **External walls, floors,** any parts which are **relied upon to protect a means of escape,** and walls common to two or more buildings must not only meet the R criterion but must also resist:
- the passage of flames and hot gases (the **integrity** or "E" criterion); and
- the transfer of heat from one face to the other (the **insulation** or "I" criterion) for a  given period.

These criteria are also expressed in minutes so full fire resistance is expressed thus: "REI 30/30/30" or "REI 30/15/15".

**Fire doors** must satisfy only the integrity criterion E (measured in minutes but expressed as "FD30" or "FD20").

**Glazed areas** in these walls and doors must satisfy only the insulation criterion "I" (which is expressed in minutes).

## Reaction to fire

The measure of reaction to fire is the extent to which external and internal finishes contribute to the spread and growth of a fire. There are two criteria:
1  Rate of **surface spread of flame**, which measures the speed at which flame travels across the surface of the finish.
2  Rate of **heat release**, which measures the amount of heat which is released by the finish.

## PARTY WALLS

A wall which is shared by two buildings – between semi-detached or terraced houses, for instance – is sometimes called a party wall. The term has been confined to the inner-London area where the rights and duties of neighbours are regulated by a procedure for agreements (Party-wall Awards) under the London Building (Amendments) Act 1936. The Party Wall Act 1996 has now extended the procedure outside London.

> *If you are doing work which may affect a party wall, or exposing the wall of an adjoining building – even if it is a separate wall – you should take professional advice.*

## 4.3.1 External walls

---

**THE BASICS**

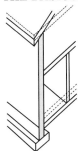

pitched roof 4.5.1
flat roof 4.5.2

upper floor 4.4.2
stairs 4.4.3

external wall 4.3.1
internal wall 4.3.5

ground supported floor 4.1.6
suspended ground floor 4.4.1

site preparation 4.1.4
foundation 4.1.5

**External walls**: can be cavity walls, which rely on the cavity to keep out the rain, or solid walls, which rely on the materials to keep out the rain.

(a) cavity

(b) solid

**Cavity walls**: are usually built with leaves with a 50mm clear space. The outer leaf is usually brickwork. The inner leaf is usually blockwork but it can be timber framing.

(a) both leaves
of masonry

(b) outer leaf of masonry
inner leaf of timber framing

**Solid walls**: can be of masonry without or with external cladding – masonry walls are likely to be thicker than is practical without a weather-resisting external cladding – or of timber framing which will need external cladding.

(a) masonry without
external cladding

(b) masonry with
external cladding

(c) timber framing with
external cladding

**Structural support (masonry walls)**: masonry 190mm thick will generally meet the requirements but needs checking as there are exceptions (⇨ Table 4.3–2). If the height of the wall is more than 3.5m or the length is more than 9m calculate the thickness (⇨ Table 4.3–1). If there are openings in the wall check that the masonry will not be over-loaded (⇨ Appendix B).

Take specialist advice if you want to use a loadbearing timber frame.

Tie the walls to the floors and roof (gable wall) for lateral support.

Provide lintels over openings if there is any load to carry. Lintels come in a variety of materials and designs. Most stockists will, if you tell them the loading conditions and the width of the opening, provide a suitable lintel long enough for each end to bear at least 150mm on a masonry wall.                                                  *continues overleaf*

**THE BASICS** continued from previous page

| (a) brick arch with bearing bar | (b) reinforced concrete | (c) prestressed concrete | (d) pressed metal | (e) timber |

**External fire spread**: the wall – except for any openings – should have a thickness of masonry of 100mm (or 75mm if the wall is non-loadbearing) to meet the requirements for fire resistance. If the thickness will be less ⇨ TS 4.3–4.

If the wall is **less than 1m from a boundary**, openings with an area of less than 0.1m² can be ignored – as long as any such openings are at least 1.5m apart. Openings with an area of less than 1m² can be ignored if they are at least 4m apart (⇨ Diagram 4.3–3), but there should be no other openings.

If the wall is **between 1–6m away from a boundary** (or 12.5m away for small non-residential buildings), larger openings are possible (⇨ Table 4.3–4 and Table 4.3–5).

If the wall is **more than 6m from a boundary**, the size of the openings is unlimited.

**Internal fire spread (finishes)**: plaster or plasterboard will meet the requirement. The use of other materials may be limited, particularly in a circulation area (⇨ 4.6.1).

**Moisture**: tile- and slate-hanging will resist the weather; so also will plastics and timber weatherboarding where you can use a combustible material. If you prefer rendering on a solid masonry wall check the guidance.

Provide damp-proof courses (usually bitumen felt) 150mm above ground level to hold back moisture rising from the ground. They should be continuous with the damp-proof membrane in the floor. Provide damp-proof courses, too, over openings in cavity walls to drain water from the cavity and also at the sides of openings to prevent moisture reaching the inner leaf.

**Heat loss**: unless the building is unheated, heated but non-residential and with a floor area of no more than 30m², or a conservatory extension, you need to limit heat losses.

To limit heat losses through the wall, start by checking the "basic" thicknesses (⇨ Table 4.3–6). These thicknesses depend on the performance of the insulating material you choose (thermal conductivity). You can reduce the basic thickness by making allowances for the construction itself. The thicknesses are called basic because they assume that the average insulating performance (the "U-value") of the openings is no worse than 3.3 W/m²K and their area is no more than 22.5 per cent of the floor area. Find the average U-value of the openings  (⇨ Appendices) and work out their percentage area. Then calculate U-values and the area of openings: trade-offs to vary the average value, the percentage or both to suit your design. Limit the heat losses through gaps in the fabric by sealing any gaps where air could filter through.

*CHECKLIST*
- ☐  Structural support (wall thicknesses)
- ☐  Fire resistance (collapse)
- ☐  External fire spread
- ☐  Internal fire spread, finishes, walls and ceilings
- ☐  Moisture
- ☐  Heat loss

## Requirements

The regulations specify that **external walls** must:
- provide structural support for the combined dead-, imposed- and wind-loads and carry them safely to the foundations (BR A1);
- limit internal fire spread (BR B2[1]);
- maintain their stability in the event of fire for a reasonable period (BR B3[1]);
- limit the external spread of fire (BR B4[1]).

They must also:
- resist the passage of moisture from the ground, as well as rain or snow, to the inside of the building. **Limit on application**: requirement C4 does not apply to windows, doors or similar openings but it does apply to the surrounding construction (BR C4);
- limit heat loss. **Limit on application**: requirement L1 does not apply to buildings other than dwellings, provided the building has an area of no more than 30m² (BR L1).

Even where the requirement applies, it is modified for buildings with low levels of heating (or none) and for extensions to dwellings, provided the extension has an area of no more than 10m².

> 📖 *Remember that some extensions are already exempt (⇨1.2.1).*

## Structural support (wall thicknesses)

> 📖  A conservatory has at least threequarters of the area of its roof and at least one half of the area of its external walls made of translucent material.

The guidance that follows is for external walls. There are different requirements for chimneys (⇨ 4.3.2), parapets (⇨ 4.3.3), and for external cladding (fixings) (⇨ 4.3.4).

For **bay windows**, the minimum thickness requirements for external walls do not apply to any part of the bay window above ground floor sill-level – including the gable, if any.

The guidance which follows gives the thickness of external walls (masonry) required for two types of structure. First, **residential buildings** (up to three storeys) and, second, **annexes** to residential buildings and small buildings (non-residential, single storey).

An alternative approach is also considered, regarding thickness of walls.

### Residential buildings (up to three storeys)

The thickness requirement for the external walls (masonry) of these buildings also applies to walls which separate two or more buildings.

The walls should be supported. There is a minimum thickness requirement (⇨ Table 4.3–1), and thicknesses are subject to some **exceptions**.

---

## 4.3–1: External walls – residential buildings

---

If the wall is relied on to provide vertical or lateral support for another wall, check that the thickness of the wall and the position of any openings in it satisfy the guidance for a buttressing wall (⇨ Appendices).

*The guidance throughout this section is for walls up to 12m long and 12m high. However, if your building is particularly exposed, the conditions relating to the building may limit the maximum height of the building to less than 12m. There are maximum building heights to which the guidance applies (⇨ Appendices).*

**Table 4.3–1:** *External wall thicknesses generally*

| Wall height[1] | Wall length[2] | Wall thickness (minimum) |
|---|---|---|
| not exceeding 3.5m | not exceeding 12m | 190mm for whole of its height |
| exceeding 3.5m but not exceeding 9m | not exceeding 9m | 190mm for whole of its height |
|  | exceeding 9m but not exceeding 12m | 290mm from the base for the height of one storey and 190 mm for the rest of its height |
| exceeding 9m but not exceeding 12m | not exceeding 9m | 290mm from the base for the height of one storey and 190mm for the rest of its height |
|  | exceeding 9m but not exceeding 12m | 290mm from the base for the height of two storeys and 190mm for the rest of its height |

Notes
[1] ⇨ Appendix B, Diagram B-5: The height of a wall and a storey (measurement)
[2] The length is measured between the centre lines and buttressing walls, piers or chimneys.

### Exceptions

As mentioned above, there are exceptions to the general thicknesses required for external walls (⇨ Table 4.3–2).

**Table 4.3-2:** *External wall thicknesses – exceptions*

The thickness of a **solid wall of coursed material** (bricks or blocks) should be at least 1/16th of the storey height if that is more than the thickness given in Table 4.3-1, above.

The thickness of a **solid wall of uncoursed stone** or flint and clunches of burnt or otherwise vitrified materials should be at least one-third more than the thickness given in Table 4.3-1.

The combined thickness of the two leaves of a **cavity wall of coursed material** (bricks or blocks) should be at least 1/16th of the storey height if that is more than the thickness given in Table 4.3-1; ⇨ Table 4.3-3: Spacing of cavity wall ties. The width of the cavity should be between 50 and 100mm.

> ⌕ *If insulating batts are used, the clear width of the cavity should still be at least 50mm to reduce the possibility of moisture passing to the inside of the building. Whatever the width of the cavity it must be kept completely clear of mortar droppings.*

**Table 4.3–3:** *Spacing of cavity wall ties*

| Width of cavity (mm) | Horizontal spacing (mm) | Vertical spacing (mm) | Other comment |
|---|---|---|---|
| 50-75 | 900 | 450 | See notes 1 and 2 |
| 76-100 | 750 | 450 | See notes 1, 2 and 3 |

Notes
1   The horizontal and vertical spacing of wall ties may be varied if necessary to suit the construction provided the number of ties per unit is maintained.
2   Wall ties spaced not more than 300mm apart vertically should be provided within 225mm from the sides of all openings with unbonded jambs.
3   Vertical Twist Type ties, or ties of equivalent performance should be used in cavities wider than 75mm.

### Annexes to residential buildings and small buildings (non-residential, single storey)

In these annexes, external solid walls of coursed bricks or blocks which enclose a floor area of no more than 36m² need be only 90mm thick if they support only wind-loads and the distributed-load of the roof.

> ⌕ *An annex is not defined but it differs from a wing because, in having its height limited to 3m, it has to support only wind-loads and the distributed-load of the roof.*

---

### 4.3–2: External walls – annexes and small buildings

---

If the length or height of the wall is more than 2.5m, it should be bonded at each end (and in between if it is longer than 3m) to buttressing walls or piers. The buttresses and piers are to specified sizes and spacing (⇨ Diagram 4.3–1).

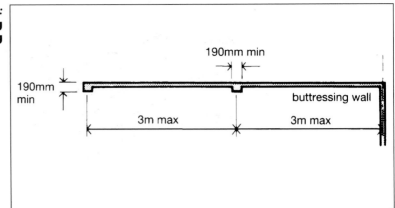

**Diagram 4.3–1:**
**Pier sizing**
**and spacing**

## Alternative approach

The regulations can also be met by following the relevant recommendations of the BS structural design codes.

# Fire resistance (collapse)

⇨ TS 4.3–3.

---

### 4.3–3: Fire resistance (collapse)

External walls should have fire resistance (collapse) of R30 minutes to maintain their loadbearing capacity in the event of a fire. There are qualifications to this figure, however.

Any external wall – whether or not it is loadbearing – which is relied on to support a part of the building is required to have fire resistance. The latter should be at least the same fire resistance as that of the building it is supporting.

---

# External fire spread

The guidance that follows is for **unprotected areas** and the **boundary** of a building (⇨ Diagram 4.3–2).

> *An external wall – whether or not it is loadbearing – might need to resist the spread of fire between buildings. If it does, there will be restrictions on the amount of unprotected area of wall if the distance to the boundary is less than 6m.*

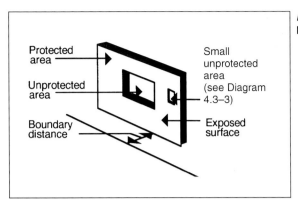

*Diagram 4.3–2:*
**External fire spread – summary**

### Unprotected areas

The definition of an unprotected area is:

*   any part of the wall which has less than the required fire resistance (spread);
*   an opening such as a window or door;
*   an exposed surface which, even if the wall behind it has the fire resistance, is of a combustible material. Some restrictions apply however (⇨ TS 4.3–10).

There is an **exception** to these definitions: small unprotected areas can be disregarded (⇨ Diagram 4.3–3).

> *Remember that a roof which slopes steeper than 70 degrees above the horizontal is treated as though it were a wall. Therefore, it may not be allowed to be an unprotected area or include unprotected areas.*

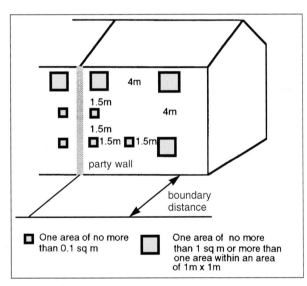

*Diagram 4.3–3:*
**Small unprotected areas**

### The boundary

The boundary will usually be the actual boundary of the curtilage of the property or the centre of a road and, if it makes an angle with the wall of more than 80 degrees, it can be ignored (⇨ Diagram 4.3–4).

> The curtilage is the ground going with a dwelling house and forming one enclosure with it.

*Diagram 4.3–4: Relevant boundary (actual)*

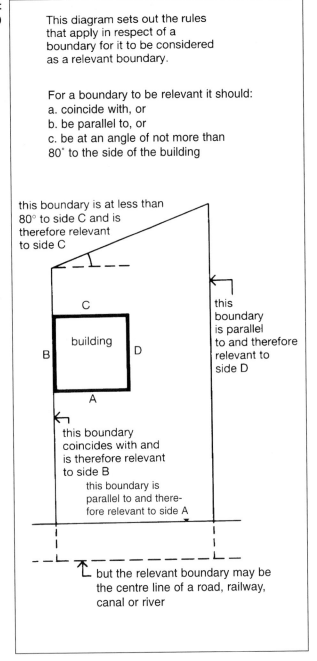

This diagram sets out the rules that apply in respect of a boundary for it to be considered as a relevant boundary.

For a boundary to be relevant it should:
a. coincide with, or
b. be parallel to, or
c. be at an angle of not more than 80° to the side of the building

this boundary is at less than 80° to side C and is therefore relevant to side C

this boundary is parallel to and therefore relevant to side D

C

building

B                D

A

this boundary coincides with and is therefore relevant to side B

this boundary is parallel to and therefore relevant to side A

but the relevant boundary may be the centre line of a road, railway, canal or river

Occasionally, the boundary may not be what it seems. If there is another residential, assembly or recreational building on the site you must assume an imaginary or "**notional**" boundary between them (⇨ Diagram 4.3–5).

> *The limit, if any, on the unprotected area in a wall depends on the distance between the wall and the boundary which it faces. The boundary may be actual or notional and a distance of less than 1m will be particularly important. You can place the notional boundary where you choose but you will then have to work to it.*

**Diagram 4.3-5: Relevant boundary (notional)**

This diagram sets out the rules that apply where there is a building of the residential, or assembly and recreational, purpose groups on the same site as another building, so that a notional boundary needs to be assumed between the buildings.

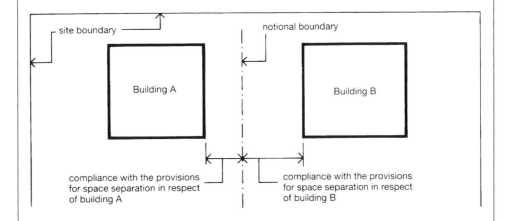

The notional boundary should be set in the area between the two buildings using the following rules:

1. It is only necessary to assume a notional boundary when the buildings are on the same site and either of the buildings, new or existing, is of Residential or Assembly and recreation use.

2. The notional boundary is assumed to exist in the space between the buildings and is positioned so that one of the buildings would comply with the provisions for space separation having regard to the amount of its unprotected area.

In practice, if one of the buildings is existing, the position of the boundary will be set by the space separation factors for that building.

3. The siting of the new building, or the second building if both are new, can then be checked to see that it also complies - using the notional boundary as the relevant boundary for the second building.

## 4.3-4: External fire spread (fire resistance)

30/30/30 minutes REI

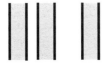

(a) **Masonry (brick or block)**
cavity wall
or
(b) 100mm solid masonry
(75mm if non-loadbearing)
(c) **Masonry/timber frame**
external skin, 100mm brick or block
(75mm if non-loadbearing)
37mm min wide framing at 600mm max spacing
12.5mm plasterboard with 10mm lightweight plaster

30/30/15 minutes REI

(d) **Timber framed**
external skin, any weathering system with
8mm min plywood backing
37mm min wide framing at 600mm max spacing
12.5mm plasterboard with 10mm lightweight plaster

To be sure of your approach to external fire spread, make a checklist.

## CHECKLIST

- ☐ External walls within 1m of the boundary
- ☐ External walls at least 1m from the boundary
- ☐ Canopies
- ☐ Cavity barriers
- ☐ Fire stopping

### External walls within 1m of the boundary

⇨ TS 4.3–5, TS 4.3–6 and TS 4.3–7.

---

#### 4.3–5: Fire resistance

The parts of external walls which are loadbearing must have fire resistance R30 when tested from each side separately to maintain their loadbearing capacity in the event of a fire.

Any non-loadbearing parts can either be given fire resistance REI 30/30/30 when tested from the inside (⇨ 4.3–3) or be treated as unprotected areas.

#### 4.3–6: Unprotected areas

Only certain unprotected areas are acceptable (⇨ Diagram 4.3–3).

#### 4.3–7: Reaction to fire (exposed faces)

The materials used for the exposed face of the wall, even if it has the fire resistance needed for a protected wall, must resist ignition from an external source and the spread of fire across their surfaces. The materials must therefore have a Class 0 classification.

A material is classified as having a Class 0 surface if either it is made of material of limited combustibility or it has a low propagation index (⇨ Table 4.6–1). If the exposed face is of cladding with a drained and ventilated "rain-screen", then the surface facing the cavity should also have a Class 0 surface to prevent a "chimney" effect.

### External walls at least 1m from the boundary

⇨ TS 4.3–8, TS 4.3–9 and TS 4.3–10.

## 4.3–8: Fire resistance

The parts of external walls which are loadbearing must have fire resistance R30 when tested from each side separately to maintain their loadbearing capacity in the event of a fire. Any non-loadbearing parts can either be given fire resistance REI 30/30/15 when tested from the inside or be treated as unprotected areas (⇨ 4.3–3).

## 4.3–9: Unprotected areas

Some **unprotected areas** can be ignored (⇨ Diagram 4.3–3) and more may be acceptable but the amount depends on the distance of the wall from the relevant boundary.

For a **small residential building**, if the building is no more than 24m long and has no more than three storeys (not including a basement) the unprotected area should be no more than a given area (⇨ Diagram 4.3–4).

For a **small non-residential building** the unprotected area should be no more than the given area.

You can, if you wish, calculate percentages for distances between those given (⇨ Table 4.3–5).

*If your wall does not meet the conditions there are two alternative methods for calculating acceptable unprotected areas (⇨ Appendix C).*

**Table 4.3–4:  *Permitted unprotected areas (small residential buildings)***

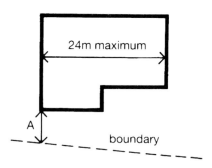

| Minimum distance A (m) between wall and boundary | Maximum total area of unprotected areas (m²) |
| --- | --- |
| 1 | 5.6 |
| 2 | 12 |
| 3 | 18 |
| 4 | 24 |
| 5 | 30 |
| 6 | no limit |

**Table 4.3–5: *Permitted unprotected areas (small non-residential buildings)***

| Minimum distance (m) between wall and boundary | | Maximum total percentage unprotected areas (m²) | Notes |
|---|---|---|---|
| Purpose groups | | | n.a. = not applicable |
| Residential, Office, Assembly and Recreation | Shop & Commercial Industrial storage & other Non-residential | | a. intermediate values may be obtained by interpolation |
| (1) | (2) | (3) | b. For buildings which are fitted throughout with an automatic sprinkler system, meeting the relevant recommendations of BS5306: Part 2. the values in columns (1) & (2) may be halved, subject to a minimum distance of 1m being maintained. |
| n.a. | 1 | 4 | |
| 1 | 2 | 8 | c. In the case of open-sided car parks in purpose group 7(b) the distances set out in column (1) may be used instead of those in column (2). |
| 2.5 | 5 | 20 | |
| 5 | 10 | 40 | |
| 7.5 | 15 | 60 | |
| 10 | 20 | 80 | |
| 12.5 | 25 | 100 | |

## 4.3–10: Reaction to fire (exposed faces)

Materials used for the exposed surface of the wall should, if they are not Class 0, be treated as unprotected areas. However, if the wall has the fire resistance needed for a protected area, and if the thickness of the material is no more than 1mm, you can take the unprotected area as being half its actual area with its position centred on the actual area (⇨ Diagram 4.3–6).

*A material is Class 0 if it is non-combustible or of limited combustibility.*

***Diagram 4.3–6: Combustible surface materials***

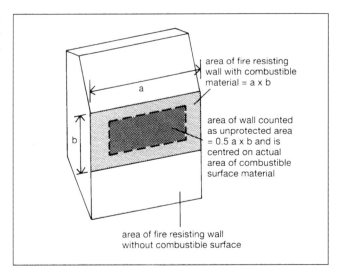

area of fire resisting wall with combustible material = a x b

area of wall counted as unprotected area = 0.5 a x b and is centred on actual area of combustible surface material

area of fire resisting wall without combustible surface

## Canopies

There will be no requirement if the canopy is part of a building which is exempt under Class VI (Small detached buildings) or of an extension which is exempt under Class VII (Extensions) of Schedule 2 of the Building Regulations.

However, even if the building or extension itself is not exempt, any "walls" of the canopy which are at least 1m from the boundary can still be disregarded.

*Because a canopy has no walls, it presents 100 per cent unprotected areas.*

## Cavity barriers

Unless both leaves of an external cavity wall are of masonry and the cavity is closed at the top of any openings, barriers should be provided in the cavity (⇨ TS 4.3–11).

🗒 *Cavity barriers restrict the spread of flame, hot gases and smoke into and within concealed spaces in the construction.*

---

### 4.3–11: Cavity barriers

The thickness of each leaf of the wall should be at least 75mm and the width of the cavity no more than 100mm (⇨ Diagram 4.3–7).

Barriers should be provided in the cavity, at:
- any junction with a wall that separates buildings; and
- the top, unless the cavity is filled with insulation.

A cavity barrier may be made of **either**:
- any material which has 30 minutes integrity and 15 minutes insulation when each side is tested separately to BS 476 (Part 22); **or**
- any construction which, although provided for another purpose, has the same performance.

Each barrier should be fixed firmly to a rigid construction.

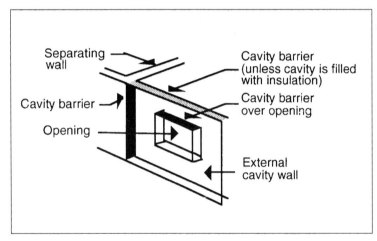

**Diagram 4.3–7: Cavity barriers**

## Fire stopping

Gaps and imperfections of fit should be fire stopped with a suitable material such as cement mortar, gypsum plaster or a proprietary material.

🗒 *Fire stopping restricts the spread of flame, hot gases and smoke from one side of the construction to the other.*

## Internal fire spread, finishes, walls and ceilings

As a reaction to fire the surface finishes on the inside faces of the external walls must have limited rates of surface spread of flame and heat release (⇨ 4.6.1).

## Moisture

The guidance in this section is for external walls and is concerned with moisture from the ground and moisture from outside (⇨ TS 4.3–12 and TS 4.3–13).

---

### 4.3–12: Moisture from the ground

---

Provide a damp-proof course of suitable material, such as bitumen felt, or slates, or engineering bricks laid in cement mortar. The damp-proof course should be continuous with the floor membrane and at least 150mm above the finished ground level unless some part of the building will protect the wall from rain splashes.

🖎 *Requirement C4 does not apply to windows, doors and similar openings.*

---

### 4.3–13: Moisture from outside

---

Provide **either**:
- a solid wall (with a weather-resisting external cladding in conditions of severe exposure); **or**
- a masonry cavity wall; **or**
- any wall (solid or cavity) with a weather-resisting external cladding.

*Solid walls*: if the exposure is *very severe* you should use a weather-resisting external cladding – similar to the covering of a pitched roof (⇨ 4.5.1). If the exposure is *severe* you can use brickwork or blockwork at least 328mm thick, dense concrete aggregate blockwork at least 250mm thick or aerated autoclaved concrete blockwork at least 215mm thick. The exposed face of the blockwork should be rendered in two coats to give a thickness of at least 20mm and given a scraped or textured finish. The rendering mix should be one part cement, one part lime and six parts well-graded sharp sand (nominal mix 1:1:6), unless the blocks are dense concrete aggregate when the nominal mix may be 1:1/2:4.

*Cavity walls*: the outer leaf should be of masonry (bricks, blocks or stone), the cavity at least 50mm wide and the inner leaf of masonry or timber framing. If you intend to insulate the wall with rigid material (batts), you should maintain the width of the cavity. If you intend to insulate with foam or loose insulation filling the cavity further specifications apply (⇨ 4.5.1).

*Openings in walls*: the flow of water down a wall should be carried to the outside face over an opening. The lintel itself may do this but if it will not then use a tray of waterproof material. In either case, openings (weep holes) will be needed to allow the water to escape. In brickwork leave open vertical joints spaced about 450mm apart.

### Alternative approach (moisture)

Where the exposure is less than severe (say, moderate or sheltered) reduced thickness is possible depending on the exposure and the type of brick or block (⇨ BS 5628). For stone walling the specification differs (⇨ BS 5390).

# Heat loss

The guidance in this section is for external walls.

To find the thickness of insulation material, find the thermal conductivity value (the "k" value) of the material you intend to you use. Then find the **base thickness** ($\Rightarrow$ Table 4.3–6) for the insulation.

**Table 4.3–6:** *Insulation thickness: walls*

|  | Thermal conductivity (W/mK) | | | | | | |
|---|---|---|---|---|---|---|---|
|  | 0.02 | 0.025 | 0.03 | 0.035 | 0.04 | 0.045 | 0.05 |
|  | Base thickness of insulation (mm) | | | | | | |
| Exposed walls (U-value 0.45 W/m²K) | 41 | 51 | 61 | 71 | 82 | 92 | 102 |
| Semi-exposed walls (U-value 0.6 W/m²K) | 30 | 37 | 45 | 52 | 59 | 67 | 74 |

*Allowable reductions for masory walls*

The base thickness for **masonry walls** can be reduced as follows (mm):

Thermal conductivity of base insulation (W/mk)

|  | Density | "K" value | 0.02 | 0.025 | 0.03 | 0.035 | 0.04 | 0.045 | 0.05 |
|---|---|---|---|---|---|---|---|---|---|
|  |  |  | Base thickness of insulation (mm) | | | | | | |
| Brickwork (outer leaf) | 1700 | 0.84 | 2 | 3 | 4 | 4 | 5 | 6 | 6 |
| cavity (at least 25mm) |  |  | 4 | 5 | 5 | 6 | 7 | 8 | 9 |
| Concrete block (inner leaf) |  |  |  |  |  |  |  |  |  |
| (medium) | 1400 | 0.51 | 4 | 5 | 6 | 7 | 8 | 9 | 9 |
| (light) | 600 | 0.19 | 9 | 11 | 13 | 15 | 17 | 20 | 22 |
| Concrete block (outer-leaf or single leaf) |  |  |  |  |  |  |  |  |  |
| (heavy) | 2400 | 1.40 | 1 | 1 | 2 | 2 | 2 | 2 | 3 |
| (medium) | 1400 | 0.51 | 3 | 4 | 5 | 6 | 7 | 8 | 9 |
| (light) | 600 | 0.19 | 8 | 10 | 13 | 15 | 17 | 19 | 21 |
| Tile-hanging | 1900 | 0.84 | 0 | 0 | 0 | 1 | 1 | 1 | 1 |
| External render (20mm) | 1300 | 0.50 | 1 | 1 | 1 | 1 | 2 | 2 | 2 |
| Plaster (13mm dense) | 1300 | 0.50 | 1 | 1 | 1 | 1 | 1 | 1 | 1 |
| Plaster (13mm light-weight) | 600 | 0.16 | 2 | 2 | 2 | 3 | 3 | 4 | 4 |
| Plasterboard (13mm) | 950 | 0.16 | 2 | 2 | 2 | 3 | 3 | 4 | 4 |
| air-space (dry lining |  |  | 2 | 3 | 3 | 4 | 4 | 5 | 6 |

*Allowable reductions for **timber-framed walls:***

The base thickness can be reduced as follows (mm):

Thermal conductivity of base insulation (W/mk)

|  | 0.02 | 0.025 | 0.03 | 0.035 | 0.04 | 0.045 | 0.05 |
|---|---|---|---|---|---|---|---|
|  | Base thickness of insulation (mm) for each 100mm of frame[1] | | | | | | |
| Thermal conductivity (k) of insulation within frame[2] |  |  |  |  |  |  |  |
| 0.035 | 42 | 53 | 63 | 74 | 84 | 95 | 105 |
| 0.040 | 38 | 48 | 58 | 67 | 77 | 87 | 96 |

For other reductions see *Masonry wall*, above

Note

[1] The thicknesses assume 48mm framing at 400mm spacing.

[2] The table gives a separate k value for the insulation within the framing so that you can (if you want) use a material which is different from the material you use for the base insulation.

As the construction itself has some insulating value you can then make corresponding deductions from the base thickness.

> *In a masonry wall the insulation can be provided by the masonry used, but the the thickness of material could be considerable and it is more usual to add material chosen for its insulating performance. If the wall is solid the insulation will be fixed to the internal face. If the wall is a cavity wall the insulation may fill the cavity (foam or loose fill) or partly fill the cavity (rigid boards, or batts, fixed to the inner leaf). In a timber-framed wall the insulation (rigid, flexible or loose fill) can probably be contained by the framing and the linings.*

The base thickness assumes that the openings in the walls (windows, doors) have a total area of 22.5 per cent (that is, about one quarter) of the floor area and an average U-value of 3.3W/m²K.

However if, as may well be the case, the actual percentage area of openings is not as stated here and the actual average U-value differs, a limited amount of exchange (trade-off) may be possible.

There are different "k" values for a range of different insulation materials and products.

### CHECKLIST

- ☐ Cavity walls
- ☐ Cold bridges

### Cavity walls

The use of fillings in cavity wall construction is subject to regulation. Foam filling (⇨ TS 4.3–14) should only be used for masonry construction and then only if the exposure conditions and construction of the wall are suitable. These should be assessed using BS 8208.

Alternative materials (⇨ TS 4.3–15) to foam filling include loose mineral fills – suitable for insulating both new and existing walls – and rigid boards (batts) which are only practicable for new walls.

> *If the wall is to be insulated with batts they should be securely fixed to the inner leaf, and the width of the cavity increased to leave a clear space of at least 50mm.*

---

**4.3–14: Foam filling in cavity walls**

---

If the wall is to be insulated with urea formaldehyde (UF) foam cavity fill, you should build the inner leaf with masonry, such as bricks or block. This is to form a continuous barrier that will prevent the UF from penetrating to those parts of the building which will be occupied. Foam filling should only be carried out by a holder of a current BSI Certificate of Registration of Assessed Capability in accordance with BS 5618.

> *On completion of foam filling, rooms should be ventilated for a week or two to disperse any free formaldehyde.*

## 4.3–15: Materials

The materials and workmanship must comply with the relevant British Standards recommendations (⇨ BS 5617 and BS 55618).

### Cold bridges

The insulating value of a cavity wall is reduced if there is an uninsulated pathway – a cold bridge (⇨ Diagram 4.3–8) – along which heat can be lost.

***Diagram 4.3–8: Reducing cold bridging around openings***

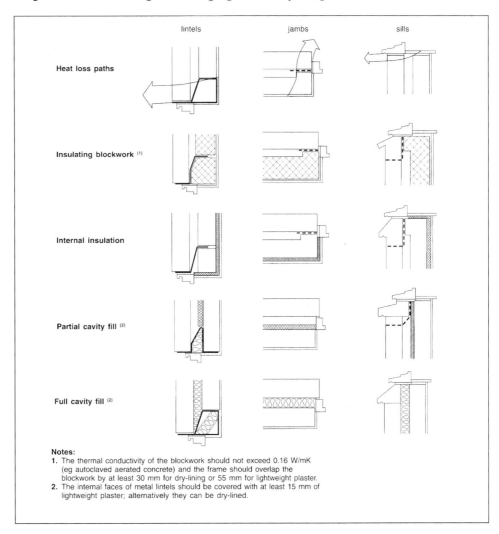

Notes:
1. The thermal conductivity of the blockwork should not exceed 0.16 W/mK (eg autoclaved aerated concrete) and the frame should overlap the blockwork by at least 30 mm for dry-lining or 55 mm for lightweight plaster.
2. The internal faces of metal lintels should be covered with at least 15 mm of lightweight plaster; alternatively they can be dry-lined.

There are a number of ways and means of preventing unnecessary heat loss and local condensation. If one of these is adopted, the losses due to thermal bridging can be ignored.

### Alternative approach (cold bridges)

The Approved Document L gives a detailed method for calculating cold bridges.

# 4.3.2 Chimneys

The guidance in this section is for chimneys above the roof (⇨ 4.9.1).

---

**THE BASICS**

**Stability:** all flue-pipes and chimneys should resist wind-loads. Limit the height of masonry chimneys to no more than 4.5 times their least width.

**Moisture:** seal flue-pipes and chimneys at their junction with the roof.

---

## Requirement

There is only one requirement: chimneys must support the combined dead-, imposed- and wind-loads and carry them safely to the walls below (BR A1).

### *CHECKLIST*
- ☐  Stability (dimensions)
- ☐  Moisture

## Stability

⇨ TS 4.3–16

---

### 4.3–16: Chimneys – stability

---

Chimneys should be self-supporting or adequately stayed by ties or otherwise securely restrained.

In **masonry chimneys** the density of the masonry affects the ability of the chimney to resist high winds (the higher the density the better the resistance) and the height of a chimney of masonry with a density of 1,500 k/m³ should be limited to 4.5 times its least width.

## Moisture

A **flashing** should be provided to close the junction between the flue-pipe or chimney and the roof. A **tray** should be provided to intercept moisture (⇨ Diagram 4.3–9) in a masonry chimney.

*Diagram 4.3–9:*
*Chimneys –*
*moisture*

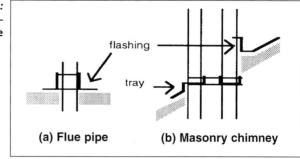

**(a) Flue pipe**          **(b) Masonry chimney**

## 4.3.3  Parapets

---

**THE BASICS**

**Stability:** parapets must resist wind-loads. Limit the height of masonry parapets to the correct height (⇨ Diagram 4.3–10).

**Moisture:** provide a water-resisting coping or a damp-proof course.

---

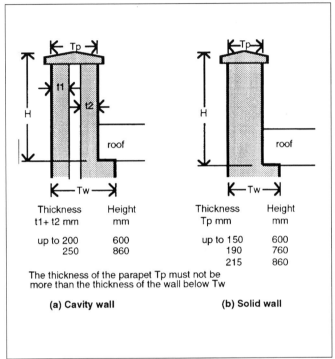

***Diagram 4.3–10: Parapet walls – height***

| Thickness t1+ t2 mm | Height mm |
|---|---|
| up to 200 | 600 |
| 250 | 860 |

| Thickness Tp mm | Height mm |
|---|---|
| up to 150 | 600 |
| 190 | 760 |
| 215 | 860 |

The thickness of the parapet Tp must not be more than the thickness of the wall below Tw

**(a) Cavity wall**                    **(b) Solid wall**

## Requirements

Parapets must support the combined dead-, imposed- and wind-loads and carry them safely to the wall below (BR A1).

### Meeting the requirements

### CHECKLIST
- ☐  Stability
- ☐  Moisture

## Stability

The height of the parapet should be limited by its thickness.

## Moisture

The tops of parapets should be protected by **either:**
- a **coping** which (including the joints) will not let water through; **or**
- any coping with a damp-proof course directly below it.

## 4.3.4  External cladding

**THE BASICS**

**Stability:** fix the cladding securely.

**External fire spread (cladding):** if the wall is **less than 1m from a boundary** you can use only materials of limited combustibility such as tiles and slates.

If the wall is between **1m and 6m from a boundary**, you can use limited amounts of combustible materials such as plastics and timber

If the wall is **more than 6m from a boundary**, you can use unlimited amounts of combustible materials.

*The addition of combustible material to a wall does not, of course, reduce its fire resistance – nor does it increase it – though it does increase the risk of spread of fire across the face of the wall.*

### Requirements

Cladding must safely transfer the dead-, imposed- and wind-loads to the supporting structure (BR A1).

#### Meeting the requirements

Cladding should be securely fixed to the supporting structure so that it will safely carry and transfer the wind-loads and the weight of any fixtures (such as satellite dishes). The anticipated life of the fixings should be at least equal to the anticipated life of the cladding.

## 4.3.5  Internal walls

**THE BASICS**

**Internal walls**: can be masonry (brick or block) or timber framing.

**Internal fire spread (walls)**: these walls protect a route of escape or separate the house from its garage; they should have a thickness of 75mm of masonry (100mm if loadbearing) or, if they are framed, 12.5mm plasterboard both sides.

**Internal fire spread (finishes)**: plaster or plasterboard will meet the requirements. The use of other materials may be limited particularly in a circulation area(⇨ 4.6.1).

**Moisture**: provide a damp-proof course (usually bitumen felt) to hold back moisture from the ground. Position the damp-proof course continuous with the damp-proof membrane in the floor.

**Heat loss**: if the wall separates a heated space from an unheated space you will have to consider heat losses as with an external wall but you can use a U-value of 0.6 instead of 0.45 W/m$^2$K.

## Requirements

Internal walls must:

- limit internal fire spread. **Limit on application:** requirement B3(3) only applies if the wall is relied on to protect a means of escape (BR B2[1] and B3[3]) (⇨ Appendices);
- resist the passage of moisture from the ground to the inside of the building and must not be damaged by that moisture, nor carry it to any part of the building that would be damaged by it (BR C4);
- limit heat loss (BR L1). **Limit on application:** requirement L1 only applies to an internal wall which separates a heated space from an unheated space.

☞ An internal wall separating a dwelling from an enclosed space which is not part of the dwelling may require sound insulation. The space may be another part of the same building (such as another dwelling) or another building. It is outside the scope of *HomeBuilder* but detailed guidance is given in the Approved Document E.

### *Meeting the requirements*

### *CHECKLIST*

☐ Structural support
☐ Internal fire spread
☐ Moisture (ground)
☐ Heat loss, finishes

## Structural support

If an internal wall, even if it is non-loadbearing, is acting as a buttressing wall the number, size and position of any openings in it must not impair the lateral support it gives the supported wall (⇨ Appendices).

## Internal fire spread

The guidance in this section is for internal walls.

> *Internal walls which are loadbearing should have fire resistance (R loadbearing capacity) (⇨ 4.3–6). And walls which, whether they are loadbearing or non-loadbearing, are relied on to protect a means of escape or separate a house from an attached garage should, in addition, have fire resistance (E integrity) and fire resistance (I insulation).*

Doors which are sold as fire resisting (fire doors) should be clearly marked. FD20 and FD30 show that a door will achieve 20 and 30 minutes integrity (I) respectively.

### *Walls protecting a means of escape*

To find which walls are relied on to protect a means of escape:

- for houses with three storeys ⇨ Appendix C2; and
- for houses with a basement storey ⇨ Appendix C3.

⇨ TS 4.3–17 and TS 4.3–18.

### 4.3–17: Fire resistance

*Walls*: should have a fire resistance period of REI 30/30/30 when tested from each side separately.
*Doors*: should be self-closing type FD20.
*Uninsulated glazing*: may only be used in doors and fixed fanlights over doors.

> 📖 **Uninsulated glazing** is glazing which, when tested, fails to achieve the insulation (I) value required for the wall itself.

### Walls separating a house from an attached garage

### 4.3–18: Fire resistance

*Walls*: should have a fire resistance period of REI 30/30/30 when tested from the garage side.
*Doors:* should be self-closing type FD30 and the sill should be at least 100mm above the garage floor.

### Cavity barriers

There is no general requirement for cavity barriers but if the house has three storeys then means of escape regulations will apply (⇨ Appendices).

### Fire stopping

Openings in internal walls which should have fire resistance should be fire stopped to restrict the passage of smoke and fire. Suitable materials include cement mortar and gypsum plaster. There are also proprietary materials.

### Surface finishes

The reaction to fire of surface finishes used on internal walls must have limited rates of surface spread of flame and heat release (⇨ 4.6.1).

## Moisture (ground)

⇨TS 4.3–19.

### 4.3–19: Moisture from the ground

Provide a damp-proof course of suitable material, such as bitumen, felt, or slates, or engineering bricks laid in cement mortar. The damp-proof course should be continuous with the floor membrane.

## Heat loss, finishes

An internal wall which is semi-exposed needs some insulation (though not as much as a wall exposed directly to the outside air).

> 📖 **Semi-exposed** means separating a heated space from an unheated space that has exposed walls which do not meet the recommendations.

To find the thickness of insulating material ⇨ Table 4.3–6. Find the base thickness of material which corresponds with the thermal conductivity ("k") of the material you want to use (you can probably choose another if you want to). This thickness would be sufficient by itself but in practice the construction will also have some insulating value so that you can probably reduce the actual thickness to less than the base thickness (⇨ Table 4.3–6 for the reductions).

# 4.3.6 Internal walls (loadbearing)

> **THE BASICS**
>
> Along with the basic requirement there are additional requirements (⇨ 4.3.5).
>
> **Stability (masonry walls):** a thickness of masonry of half the thickness for an external wall of the same dimensions will meet the requirements unless the wall is relied on to support another wall. If it is it will need at least the same thickness and there are limits on openings in the wall.
>
> ☞  Take specialist advice if you want to use a loadbearing timber frame.
>
> Tie the walls to the floors and roof (gable wall) for lateral support.

## Requirements

An internal loadbearing wall must:
- provide support for the combined dead-, imposed- and wind-loads and carry them safely to the foundations (BR A1);
- maintain its stability in the event of fire for a reasonable period (BR B3[1]).

### Meeting the requirements

### CHECKLIST
- ☐ Structural support (wall thickness)
- ☐ Fire resistance (collapse)

## Structural support

⇨ TS 4.3–20.

---

### 4.3–20: Internal loadbearing walls – thickness

---

The walls should be supported (⇨ Appendices) and, subject to any exceptions, have at least half the thickness for an external wall of the same height and length (⇨ 4.3.1). From this reduced thickness you can then deduct another 5mm.

Exceptions for internal loadbearing walls can be listed as:
**a wall** in the lowest storey of a **three-storey building** which carries a load from both upper storeys and should have a thickness of at least 140mm if that is more than the requisite thickness for a wall of the same height and length (⇨ Table 4.3–1);
**cavity walls** in coursed bricks or blocks, each leaf of which should be at least 90mm thick (⇨ 4.3–3), and tied together with wall ties (⇨ Table 4.3–3). The clear width of the cavity should be not less than 50mm and not more than 100mm.

For the thicknesss of a wall which is relied on to provide **vertical** support for another wall, or a wall which, even if it is not loadbearing, is relied on to provide **lateral** support for another wall ⇨ 4.3–1.

In buttressing walls, if the wall is relied on to support another wall, check that the thickness of the wall and the position of any openings in it satisfy the guidance for a buttressing wall mentioned earlier (⇨ Appendices).

📖 *The number, size and position of openings in the wall must not impair its stability (⇨ Appendices).*

### Alternative approach (stability)

The regulations can also be met by following the relevant recommendations of the British Standard structural design codes.

## Fire resistance (collapse)

For guidance ⇨ TS 4.3.1.

# 4.3.7 Glazing

## Requirements

---

**THE BASICS**

If the glazing is where it would be likely to cause injury to people who come into contact with it (a "critical" position) protect it from impact or use a type of glazing which will either break into small particles on impact or be robust enough to resist impact altogether.

---

Glazing in critical positions in walls must break without causing injury, or resist impact, or be protected from impact (BR N1).

> *The requirement does not apply to replacement glazing although consumer protection legislation may do so. The purpose of the requirement N1 is only to limit injuries from broken glass. Other requirements may also apply. External and internal glazing may also be relied on to act as a barrier to prevent falling accidents and internal glazing may be relied on to provide fire resistance.*

### Meeting the requirements

The guidance which follows is for both external walls and internal walls.

Distinguish between glazing for different purposes:
- glazing where it is most likely to be broken (critical positions) and any sharp piece could cause injuries (BR N1);
- glazing which is intended to act as a barrier to prevent falling accidents (there will be a strength requirement) (BR K3). Not all the types of glazing which meet N1 will meet K3;
- glazing which is intended to protect a means of escape (there may be an insultaion requirement) (BR B1).

### CHECKLIST
- ☐ Critical positions
- ☐ Types of protection

## Critical positions

Critical positions are those where people are most likely to come into contact with glazing. They are at low level in external and internal walls and partitions and in or next to doors (⇨ Diagram 4.3–11).

## Types of protection

Glazing in critical positions should:
- **break safely**;
- be **robust** enough to resist impact without breaking;
- be **permanently protected** or shielded from impact.

### *Diagram 4.3–11: Glazing – critical positions*

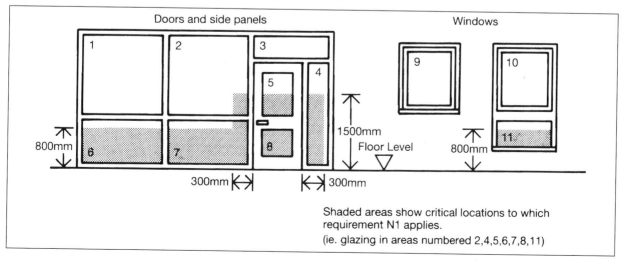

Shaded areas show critical locations to which requirement N1 applies.
(ie. glazing in areas numbered 2,4,5,6,7,8,11)

**Safe breakage**     Breaking should result in **either** a small clear hole with detached pieces of only limited size, **or** complete disintegration into small detached particles, **or** in separate pieces that are neither sharp nor pointed.

**Robustness**       Specially treated or laminated glass will meet the requirement but you can also use ordinary sheet glass (sometimes called annealed glass) provided you choose a suitable thickness (⇨ Diagram 4.3–12).

*Diagram 4.3–12:*
**Glazing – large panes**
**(thickness 8mm or more)**

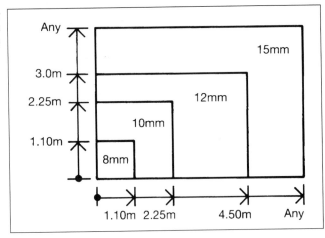

However, you can use glass with a thickness of 6mm in small panes (⇨ Diagram 4.3–13).

*Diagram 4.3–13:*
**Glazing – small**
**panes**
**(thickness 6mm)**

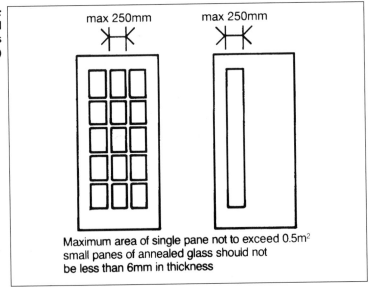

Maximum area of single pane not to exceed 0.5m²
small panes of annealed glass should not
be less than 6mm in thickness

**Permanent protection**      Intended to limit impact, the protection should be at least 800mm high, robust, difficult for children to climb and made so that a 75mm sphere cannot touch the glazing. There are no limits on the size or thickness of glazing which is permanently protected or shielded.

There are no limits on the use of polycarbonates and glass blocks.

   📖 *Glass that behaves in one of these ways is often described as safety glass but do not assume that this means that it is safe in all circumstances – it may not satisfy guarding or fire safety requirements if they apply.*

# 4.4
# Floors and stairs

## INTRODUCTION

In this section the guidance is for:

4.4.1   Suspended ground floors
4.4.2   Upper floors, galleries
         and balconies
4.4.3   Stairways

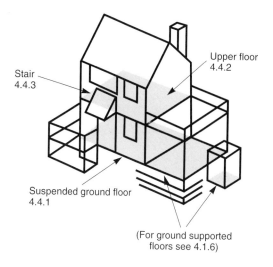

Upper floor
4.4.2

Stair
4.4.3

Suspended ground floor
4.4.1

(For ground supported
floors see 4.1.6)

## 4.4.1  Suspended ground floors

> **THE BASICS**
>
> The following applies to timber floors. If you prefer to use a precast concrete floor, refer to the full text.
>
> **Structural support**: determine joist sizes (⇨ Table 4.4–3). You can reduce the span by building "honeycomb" sleeper walls. Assess if there are any loadbearing internal walls.
>
> **Moisture**: cover the ground below with a 100mm concrete slab on hardcore (⇨ 4.1.6) or, more usually, with a 120mm polythene sheet held down by 50mm of weak concrete or heavy loose material. The ground cover should be laid to falls with outlets to drain any surface water.
>
> **Ventilation**: leave a clear height of at least 75mm between the ground cover and any part of the floor and at least 150mm between the ground cover and the flooring. Provide a 1,500m² run of ventilation openings in the enclosing walls.
>
> ☞   Seek the advice of the local authority if there is any possibility of radon or methane gas (a suspended ground floor may not be advisable).
>
> **Heat loss**: regarding heat loss through the fabric (⇨ Appendix D1) remember that the requirement does not apply to unheated buildings, heated non-residential buildings with a floor area of no more than 30 m², or conservatory extensions.
>
> If you need to insulate, use basic thickness (⇨ Table 4.4.1). The thickness depends on the performance of the insulating material you choose (its "k" value) and the ratio between the perimeter of the floor and its area (the P/A ratio). To limit heat loss through gaps in the floor, seal any gaps where air could filter through (⇨ Appendix D2).

📖 *A suspended ground floor takes its support from the foundations, whereas an upper floor takes its support from the external walls. A suspended timber ground floor is not advisable if the presence of landfill gas or radon gas has been confirmed (⇨ 4.1.4).*

---

📖 The **ground floor** is the lowest floor of a building. If there is a basement, the floor at ground level should be built as an upper floor (⇨ 4.4.2).

---

It is not usual to find ramps in dwellings and there is no requirement to provide them. However, if you do want to install a ramp, other requirements will apply (⇨ BR K1 and Approved Document K).

☞ The structural design of *in situ* concrete suspended floors is outside the scope of *HomeBuilder* and you should take professional advice. However, guidance on the use of concrete suspended floors is given throughout this section.

## Requirements

A suspended ground floor, be it timber or precast concrete must:

- be constructed to support the combined dead- and imposed-loads and carry them safely to the foundations (BR A1);
- avoid risks to health and safety caused by dangerous or offensive substances (BR C2);
- resist the passage of moisture from the ground to the inside of the building, not be damaged by that moisture and not carry it to any part of the building that would be damaged by it (BR C4);
- limit heat loss (BR L1).

📖 *There is no requirement for a suspended ground floor to have fire resistance because it is the lowest floor of the building.*

### Meeting the requirements (timber floors)

Here the requirements are for a timber floor, as in the following checklist. Requirements for a precast concrete floor appear later in this section.

### CHECKLIST

- ☐ Structural support
- ☐ Moisture
- ☐ Ventilation
- ☐ Heat loss

## Structural support

The dimensions of the floor joists can be reduced by providing intermediate support from "honeycomb" brick sleeper walls, or dwarf walls, laid in stretcher bond and spaced between, say, 1.75–2.5m apart (⇨ Diagram 4.4–1).

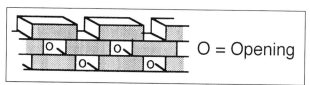

**Diagram 4.4–1: Honeycomb sleeper wall**

O = Opening

If the ground cover is a 100mm concrete slab laid on hardcore, the sleeper walls can be built off the slab, but if the floor supports a loadbearing wall, the thickness of the slab should be increased to 200mm for the width that would be needed for a strip foundation (⇨ 4.1.5) and the sides of the downstand splayed at 45 degrees. If the ground cover is not a slab the sleeper walls should have their own strip foundations. For floor joists, notches and holes, and floorboards (⇨ Diagram 4.4–2).

**Diagram 4.4–2: Suspended timber ground floor – structural support**

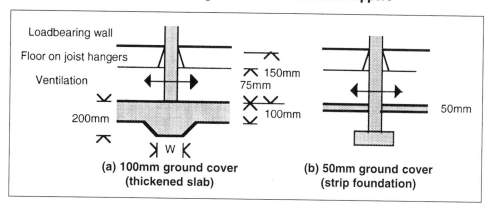

## Moisture

If the floor is to be subject to water pressure or covered with a floor finish which is highly vapour resistant you should follow the alternative approach below.

**Ground cover**     Lay either a hardcore bed and 100mm concrete slab or a polythene sheet covered with either 50mm of concrete or inert fine aggregate. For the hardcore, concrete and polythene sheet there are separate specifications (⇨ 4.1.6). If any part of the ground cover is below the level of the highest ground next to the building it should be set to fall to an opening that is freely draining, to prevent water collecting (⇨ Diagram 4.4–3).

**Damp-proof courses**     Finish all masonry supporting timber joists with a damp-proof course. You should use either two courses of engineering bricks in cement mortar, or a damp-proof course of slates in cement mortar or bituminous or other impervious material.

### Alternative approach
This guidance is for a suspended ground floor.

**Moisture resistant**     You can also meet the requirement to resist the passage of moisture from the ground by following the recommendations in Clause 11 of CP 102:

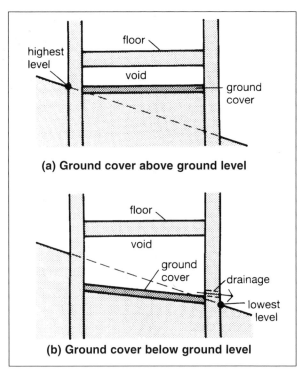

***Diagram 4.4–3:***
**Suspended ground**
**floor – drainage**

**(a) Ground cover above ground level**

**(b) Ground cover below ground level**

1973, or BS 102. The code includes recommendations for floors subject to water pressure.

## Ventilation

There should be a clear space between the ground cover and any part of the suspended floor of at least 75mm. Also a clear space between the ground cover and the underside of the floor itself – and any thermal insulation below it – of at least 150mm.

To promote through ventilation of the air space, openings should be provided in two opposing external walls placed where the air will have a free path between the openings and to all parts. The openings should be large enough to give a free opening of at least 1,500mm² for each 1m run of wall.

The purpose of ventilation provisions is to reduce the passage of moisture from the ground. They may not be sufficient if there is any possibility of the accumulation of radon gas or landfill gas which might lead to an explosion (⇨ 4.1.4).

> *Remember that the free air opening of a typical air brick may be as little as a third of the overall area. If a solid floor lies between the air space and the external wall, you should provide pipes of sufficient area to carry the ventilating air under the floor. Since air moves slowly, each pipe should have a diameter of at least 100mm or an equivalent area.*

## Heat loss

To find the thickness of insulation material (⇨ Table 4.4–1), work out the ratio of floor perimeter (m) to floor area (m²) – the P/A ratio. Then find the thermal conductivity – the "k" value – of the material you intend to use.

**Table 4.4-1:** *Insulation thickness: suspended timber ground floor (U-value 0.35 W/m²K)*

| P/A | Thermal conductivity (k) | | | | | | |
| | 0.02 | 0.025 | 0.03 | 0.035 | 0.04 | 0.045 | 0.05 |
| --- | --- | --- | --- | --- | --- | --- | --- |
| | Insulation thickness (mm) | | | | | | |
| 1.00 | 57 | 67 | 77 | 87 | 96 | 106 | 115 |
| 0.90 | 55 | 66 | 75 | 85 | 94 | 103 | 112 |
| 0.80 | 53 | 63 | 73 | 82 | 91 | 100 | 109 |
| 0.70 | 51 | 60 | 69 | 78 | 87 | 95 | 104 |
| 0.60 | 47 | 56 | 64 | 73 | 81 | 89 | 97 |
| 0.50 | 42 | 50 | 57 | 65 | 72 | 79 | 87 |
| 0.40 | 34 | 41 | 47 | 53 | 60 | 66 | 72 |
| 0.30 | 22 | 26 | 31 | 35 | 39 | 43 | 47 |
| 0.20 | 1 | 1 | 2 | 2 | 2 | 2 | 3 |

Note
The thicknesses assume that the joists are 48mm wide at 400mm spacing

> *The insulation is usually placed below the floorboards when, if it is flexible, it can be draped over the floor joists or, if it is rigid, supported on battens fixed to the sides of the joists. (If you prefer to place it above the floor joists, choose a type which will not be compressed.)*

### Meeting the requirements (precast concrete floors)

You should take professional advice if you are considering precast concrete floors. The guidance and requirements in the checklist which follows are for general use only.

A suspended precast concrete ground floor should be covered with a sealed gas-proof membrane laid under the screed if the presence of landfill gas or radon gas has been confirmed.

### CHECKLIST
- ☐ Structural support
- ☐ Moisture
- ☐ Ventilation
- ☐ Heat loss

## Structural support

The structural design of precast concrete floors is a matter for the manufacturer who should be consulted and who should take into account the guidance given in the Approved Documents A and C.

## Moisture

If the ground below the floor has been excavated below the lowest level of the surrounding ground and will not be effectively drained, the construction should include a damp-proof membrane above or below the air space.

## Ventilation

Where there is a risk of the accumulation of gas which might lead to an explosion (⇨ 4.1.4), the air space should be at least 150mm. It must be ventilated with openings in two opposing external walls placed where air will have a free path between the openings and to all parts. The openings should be large enough to give a free opening of at least 1,500mm² for each 1m run of wall.

> 📖 *If there is any possibility of the accumulation of radon gas these ventilation provisions may not be sufficient.*

## Heat loss

Find the thickness of the insulating material required (⇨ Table 4.4–2).

**Table 4.4–2:** *Insulation thickness: suspended concrete ground floor (U-value 0.35 W/m²K)*

| P/A | Thermal conductivity (k) | | | | | | |
| | 0.02 | 0.025 | 0.03 | 0.035 | 0.04 | 0.045 | 0.05 |
| | Insulation thickness (mm) | | | | | | |
|---|---|---|---|---|---|---|---|
| 1.00 | 37 | 46 | 55 | 64 | 74 | 83 | 92 |
| 0.90 | 36 | 45 | 54 | 63 | 72 | 81 | 90 |
| 0.80 | 35 | 43 | 52 | 61 | 69 | 78 | 87 |
| 0.70 | 33 | 41 | 50 | 58 | 66 | 74 | 83 |
| 0.60 | 31 | 38 | 46 | 54 | 61 | 69 | 77 |
| 0.50 | 27 | 34 | 41 | 48 | 55 | 62 | 69 |
| 0.40 | 22 | 28 | 34 | 39 | 45 | 50 | 56 |
| 0.30 | 14 | 18 | 21 | 25 | 29 | 32 | 36 |
| 0.20 | 0 | 1 | 2 | 2 | 2 | 2 | 3 |

# 4.4.2 Upper floors, galleries and balconies

---

**THE BASICS**

**Structural support**: for joist sizes ⇨ Table 4.4–3 and Table 4.4–4; and for floorboards ⇨ Table 4.4–3.

**Horizontal support for walls**: you might have to strap the joists to the external walls and any internal loadbearing walls at no more than 2m centres (⇨ Appendix B2).

**Internal fire spread**: 15mm tongued and grooved boarding, plywood or chipboard flooring and 12.5mm plasterboard with the joints taped and filled and a 5mm plaster finish will meet the requirements.

**Moisture**: upper floors will not be exposed to moisture from rain or snow or from the ground but if you are using chipboard you should consider a moisture-resisting grade.

**Heat loss**: you need only consider heat loss if the floor will be exposed to the external air or be semi-exposed (⇨ Table 4.4–4).

**Guarding**: where there is a risk of falling more than 600mm – from a landing for example – guard the edge with a wall or a suitable barrier at least 1,100mm high. You can guard a window by carrying the wall below to a height of at least 800mm or providing a rail at that height.

---

## Requirements

Any upper floor, gallery and balcony must:

- provide structural support for the combined dead- and imposed-loads and carry them safely to the supporting walls (BR A1);
- maintain its stability in the event of fire for a reasonable period (BR B3);
- limit the internal spread of fire (this requirement does not apply to a gallery) (BR B2);
- limit heat loss (this requirement does not apply to a gallery or balcony and applies only to a floor if the underside is exposed to external air or to an unheated space [semi-exposed]). **Limit on application:** requirement L1 does not apply to a gallery and it does not apply to a balcony or a floor if the underside is exposed to external air or to an unheated space (BR L1);
- be guarded where there is a risk of people falling. The requirement does not apply to places to which people have access only for the purposes of repair and maintenance. **Limit on application:** requirement K2 does not apply where it would restrict normal use (BR K2).

> 📖 A **gallery** is a floor which projects into an enclosed space and, for the purposes of the regulations, has an area of less than half the area of the space into which it projects.
>
> A **balcony** is a floor which projects from the wall of a building.

### Meeting the requirements

### CHECKLIST

- ☐ Structural support
- ☐ Internal fire spread
- ☐ Moisture
- ☐ Heat loss
- ☐ Guarding

## Structural support

The conditions that apply to the building and its walls (⇨ Appendix B) must be satisfied if the guidance is to be followed.

> 📖 *The guidance assumes that the dead- and imposed-loads to be carried by the floor, whether it is a suspended ground floor or an upper floor, are no more than those given in the notes to the tables.*

### Timber classes

The deeper the section, the less timber you will use for a given span.

Many combinations of species and grade will qualify a timber to be placed in a particular class but fortunately it is sufficient, for strength purposes, to specify by the class.

> The Approved Documents refer to classes SC3 and SC4 which have been
> widely used for general building work and these classes are therefore used in
> HomeBuilder. However, they are being replaced by two new classes: C16
> (nearly equal to SC3) and C24 (nearly equal to SC4). The timber is also being
> marked DRY or KD (kiln dried) and timber marked WET or not marked at all
> can be rejected.

☛ The structural design of concrete upper floors is outside the scope of *HomeBuilder*
and professional advice should be taken; for precast concrete floors, the manufacturer
should be consulted.

### Floor joists
Floor joists dimensions can be found from Table 4.4–3.

**Table 4.4–3: *Floor joists (dimensions)***

| Size of joist (mm) (width x depth) | Span (m) (clear between supports) |
|---|---|
| 50 x 97 | 1.98 |
| 50 x 122 | 2.60 |
| 50 x 147 | 3.13 |
| 50 x 170 | 3.61 |
| 50 x 195 | 4.13 |

Notes
1 These spans assume:
  – Timber of strength-grade **SC3**
  – a dead load of **more than 0.25 but no more than 0.50 kN/m²** excluding the weight of the joists;
  – an imposed load of no more than **1.5kN/m²**
  – a joist-spacing of **400mm;**
  – a minimum bearing at supports of **35mm.**
2 If the joists support the weight of any partitions ⟳ TS 4.4–3.
3 If the joists support a bath double the joists supporting it.

### Alternative approach
The detailed Tables A1 and A2 in the Approved Document give spans for:
* two timber-strength grades (SC3 and SC4);
* three dead-loads (no more than 0.25kN/m², 0.25kN/m² to 0.50kN/m², and 0.5kN/m² to no more than 1.25kN/m²);
* three joist spacings (400mm, 450mm and 600 mm); and
* five joist widths (38mm, 47mm, 50mm, 63mm and 75mm).
  > For a typical floor of 16mm (finished) floorboards and a 12.5mm plasterboard
  > ceiling with a skim coat of plaster and a clear span of 3m, Table 4.4–3 gives a
  > joist size 50x147mm spanning up to 3.13m

Referring to the Tables A 1 and A2 would allow to choose from the following:
* timber grade SC4 instead of SC3, but you would need the same joist size although it would span further – 3.25m, or about 4 per cent;
* a joist width reduced from 50mm to 38mm, but you would need a deeper joist

(38x170mm) and although you would use 12 per cent less timber you might find it difficult to nail two sheets butted together on the same joist;

- a joist spacing increased from 400mm (the most common because it suits standard 1,200x2,400mm plasterboard sheets) to 600mm. This would also suit the sheet sizes but you would need 50x195mm joists and, although you would use fewer joists (and they would span 3.47m), you would still use 20 per cent more timber. You would also need to increase the  thickness of the floorboards from 16mm to 19mm.

## 4.4–1: Notches and holes

**Notches** may be cut either in the top or the bottom of the joist. They should be cut no deeper than 0.125mm of the depth of the joist, no nearer the support than 0.07mm of the span and no further from the support than 0.25mm of the span.

**Holes** should be cut no greater in diameter than 0.25mm of the span; no nearer the support than 0.25mm of the span and no further from the support than 0.4mm of the span. They should be cut only at the mid-point of the depth of the joist and be at least three diameters apart, centre-to-centre.

*Circular holes should always be used. They are not only easier to cut but also lessen the weakening of the joist.*

## 4.4–2: Strutting – if the joist spans more than 2.5m

Floor joists which span more than 2.5m should be **strutted** as:
> **span** between 2.5–4.5m, one row dividing the span into two equal parts;
> **span** of more than 4.5m, two rows dividing the span into three equal parts.

For **solid strutting** the timber should be at least 38mm thick and at least 0.75 the depth of the joists.

For **herringbone strutting** the timber should be at least 38x38mm but should not be used where the distance between the joists is more than three times their depth.

*The strutting will be most effective if the joists are blocked solidly to the walls at the end of each row; it is convenient to use wedges.*

## 4.4–3: Partition loads

Floor joists might need to be increased in size where they carry a partition, or are loadbearing.

The traditional method for calculating partition loads is as follows:
where a partition is lightweight (such as timber framing), non-loadbearing and runs

at right angles to the joists, it is sufficient to take the next higher category of dead-load;

where a partition is lightweight (such as timber framing), non-loadbearing and runs parallel with the joists, it is sufficient to provide **two joists** and spike them together.

If the partition is masonry (such as blockwork) or is loadbearing, a calculation should be made, unless there is a wall nearly below that can provide the necessary support.

*Again, the building control authority may ask for calculations for the joists.*

## 4.4–4: Floorboards – thickness

The span of floorboards is measured between the centres of the joists.

For softwood tongued-and-grooved floorboards, the finished thickness should be:
    **span** between centres of joists up to 500mm, at least 16mm;
    **span** between centres of joists up to 600mm, at least 19mm.

For chipboard tongued-and-grooved boards, the thickness should be:
    **span** between centres of joists up to 400mm, at least 18mm;
    **span** between centres of joists up to 600mm, at least 22mm.

You should use a moisture-resistant flooring grade.

For access purposes, softwood floorboards can easily be lifted. This gives access to services in the floor but if you use chipboard you should provide removable panels.

## 4.4–5: Openings

Floor joists might need to be stopped short (trimmed) for a stairway or other opening. The trimmed joists should then be supported by a trimmer joist and this in turn has to be supported – if it does not bear on a wall – by a trimming joist.

*The building control authority may ask for calculations for the trimmer and trimming joists, but a nineteenth-century rule of thumb for calculating widths runs as follows: "Add 1/8in [3.2mm] to the trimmer and trimming joists for each trimmed joist carried. Alternatively, make them 1in [25mm] thicker, whichever gives the greater width." When more than 25mm is added – that is, more than eight joists have to be carried – it might be cheaper and more convenient to use two joists and spike them together. The rule will be generous where hangers are used in place of traditional tenons because there will be no mortices to weaken the joists.*

### 4.4-6: Fire resistance (collapse)

Upper floors should have fire resistance (collapse) of R30 minutes, when tested from the underside, to maintain their loadbearing capacity in the event of a fire (⇨ Diagram 4.4-4).

*Diagram 4.4-4:* **Internal fire spread – fire resistance**

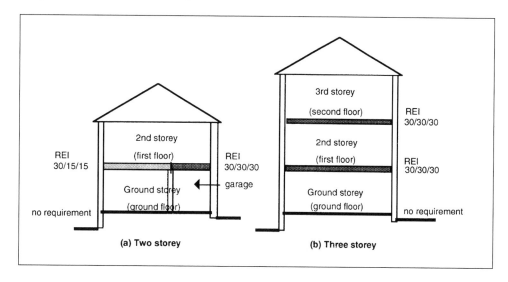

## Internal fire spread

In addition to having 30 minutes fire resistance (collapse) to maintain their loadbearing capacity in the event of a fire, upper floors **except** galleries and balconies, should also have fire resistance (spread) for E and I (integrity and insulation) to resist the internal spread of fire (⇨ TS 4.4-7).

### 4.4-7: Internal fire spread – fire resistance

30/30/30 minutes REI

**(a) 15mm t&g boarding, plywood or chipboard**
37mm min wide joists
12.5mm plasterboard with joints taped and filled with 5mm plaster finish

**(b) 21mm t&g boarding, plywood or chipboard**
37mm min wide joists
12.5mm plasterboard with joints taped and filled

30/15/15 minutes REI

**(c) any flooring**
37mm min wide joists
12.5mm plasterboard with joints taped and filled and backed by timber
or
9.5mm plasterboard with joint taped and filled and 10mm lightweight plaster finish

### Periods of fire resistance

These periods of fire resistance need be only REI 30/15/15 for the upper storey of a two-storey house except for a floor separating the house from its garage, but should be REI 30/30/30 for all other floors including the floor over a garage.

### Reaction to fire

The surface finishes on the underside of a floor (but not its upper side) must have limited rates of surface spread of flame and heat release (⇨ 4.6.1).

### Means of escape (three-storey houses)

The separation of the third storey from the lower storeys could affect the design and construction of the floors (⇨ Appendices).

> 📖 *Means of escape could affect the design and construction of floors.*

### Existing floors

These can be upgraded and the Building Research Establishment (⇨ Useful addresses) has published practical guidance (BRE Digest 208).

### Fire stopping

Imperfections of fit where pipes pass through a floor should be fire stopped.

### Separation between house and garage

A floor separating a house from an integral garage below should have a fire resistance of at least 30 minutes (REI 30/30/30).

## Moisture

If joists are supported on a exposed solid wall you should protect their ends either by treating them with a timber preservative or by wrapping them; even better, you can support them clear of the wall on joist-hangers.

> 📖 *Upper floors will not normally be exposed to moisture but if you are using chipboard flooring, particularly in a kitchen or bathroom, it should be a moisture-resistant flooring grade.*

## Heat loss

If the floor is exposed or semi-exposed you will have to insulate it.

> 📖 **Exposed** means exposed to the outside air.
> **Semi-exposed** means separating a heated space from a space enclosed by elements which do not meet the guidance (such as a garage).

To find the thickness of insulation material, whether the floor is exposed or semi-exposed, first find the thermal conductivity value (the "k" value) of the material you intend to you use. Then find the **base thickness** for the insulation (Table 4.4–4).

You can, if you wish, reduce the base thickness by a given amount (Table 4.4–4).

> 📖 *The insulation in a timber floor may be rigid, flexible or loose fill and may be laid on the ceiling. The insulation on a concrete floor is usually laid above the concrete; choose a rigid type which will not be compressed.*

**Table 4.4–4:** *Insulation thickness – upper floor*

| | Thermal conductivity (k) | | | | | | |
|---|---|---|---|---|---|---|---|
| | 0.02 | 0.025 | 0.03 | 0.035 0.04 | | 0.045 | 0.05 |
| **Timber floor** | **Base thickness** of insulation between joists (mm) | | | | | | |
| Fully exposed (U-value 0.35 W/m²K) | 61 | 76 | 92 | 107 | 122 | 146 | 162 |
| Semi-exposed (U-value 0.6 W/m²K) | 25 | 32 | 38 | 44 | 50 | 57 | 63 |
| The base thickness can be reduced as follow (mm): | | | | | | | |
| 10mm plasterboard | 1 | 2 | 2 | 2 | 3 | 3 | 3 |
| 19mm timber flooring | 3 | 3 | 4 | 5 | 5 | 6 | 7 |

Note
The base thickness assumes that the joists are 48mm wide at 400mm spacing.

| **Concrete floor** | **Base thickness** of insulation between joists (mm) | | | | | | |
|---|---|---|---|---|---|---|---|
| Fully exposed (U-value 0.35 W/m²K) | 52 | 65 | 78 | 91 | 104 | 117 | 130 |
| Semi-exposed (U-value 0.6 W/m²K) | 26 | 33 | 39 | 46 | 52 | 59 | 65 |
| The base thickness can be reduced as follow (mm): | | | | | | | |
| 50mm screed | 2 | 3 | 4 | 4 | 5 | 5 | 6 |

## Guarding

A barrier guarding a landing or balcony will be suitable if it has a height of at least 1,100mm and will resist a horizontal force of at least 0.74kN for each 1m of length applied at that height. Where children under five are likely to use the building, the barrier should be made so that they will not readily be able to climb up it and a 100mm sphere cannot pass through it.

> A suitable barrier should be provided where there is a risk of falling more than 600mm from the edge of any part of a floor (including a window), landing or balcony. Any wall, balustrade or similar may serve as a barrier.

A barrier guarding a window will be suitable if the wall is carried up to, or a rail is provided at, a height of at least 800mm.

Glazing may be used in a barrier but it should either resist impact without breaking or be protected so that impact is limited.

> There is no requirement to guard against the risk of falling from an open window. You might consider fitting suitable bars or window catches unless the window is relied on as a means of escape in case of fire.

## 4.4.3 Stairways

---

**THE BASICS**

The requirements for stairs are too detailed to summarise. The main features are: the rise and going of the steps; the unobstructed space on landings; headroom; the provision of a handrail on at least one side, if the width is no more than 1m; guarding.

There are reduced requirements for loft conversions (⇨ Appendix G4).

---

*CHECKLIST*
- ☐ Construction
- ☐ Dimensions
- ☐ Guarding
- ☐ Special stairs

# Requirements

There is no requirement to make provision for the disabled.

The stairway must be safe for users moving between levels in a building. **Limit on application**: requirement K1 does not apply to stairways providing access only for maintenance. Nor does it apply to steps and ramps on land leading to a building, such as those leading to an entrance, which are not part of the building. To be a part of the building they must be a physical part of it, not simply in contact with it.

A stairway is usually made up of flights and landings. It includes alternating tread stairs and fixed ladders but these can be only used for some loft conversions (⇨ Appendix G).

> 📖 An **alternating tread** stair has alternate steps, left- and right-handed, with part of each tread cut away.
> A **ladder** is a series of rungs or narrow treads which a person using the ladder normally faces, at a typical angle of about 60 degrees.

*Meeting the requirements*

# Construction

There are no specific requirements regarding the construction and fire performance of stairways. Timber construction is widely accepted.

# Dimensions

The requirement for a minimum floor-to-ceiling height for rooms was taken out of the Building Regulations in 1985.

### Width
There is no maximum or minimum width for a stair.

### Length
There is no maximum length for a flight but it should be limited to a maximum of 16 risers.
> 🖺 *A single riser can be a hazard and a minimum of three should be preferred wherever possible.*

### Headroom
For headroom, the clear height on flights and landings should be 2m (⇨ Diagram 4.4–5). Measure the height vertically between a line joining the fronts of the treads and the ceiling under any obstruction, such as a dropped beam.

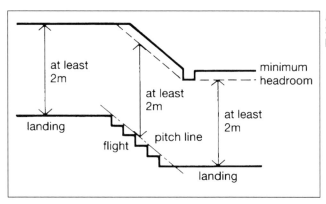

***Diagram 4.4–5:***
**Stairs – measurement of headroom**

## Steps

For steps, any rise between 155–220mm may be used with any going between 245–260mm. Alternatively, any rise between 165–200mm may be used with any going between 223–300mm (⇨ Diagram 4.4–6). Treads should be level.

> *These dimensions are taken from the formula that the sum of two risers, plus one going (2R+G) will be between 550–700mm and the pitch no steeper than 42 degrees.*

> 📖 The **going** is the distance from the front of one tread to the front of the next. The **rise** is the distance from the top of one tread to the top of the next enough to produce deterioration in a material or structure to the point that it would present an imminent danger to health or safety or, if it is an insulating material, would permanently reduce its performance.

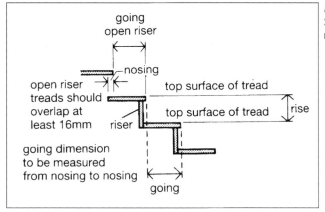

***Diagram 4.4–6:***
**Stairs – measurement of rise and going**

## Landings

Landings should be level **except** where they are formed by the ground – whether paved or not – when they should slope no steeper than 1-in-20.

The space at the top and bottom of every flight should, with two exceptions, be clear of any permanent obstruction for the width of the stair and for a distance equal to at least the width of the stair. A permanent obstruction includes a door.

The two **exceptions** are: first, that a **door to a room** may swing across a landing at the **bottom** of a flight if it will leave a clear space which is the same width of the stair for a distance of at least 400mm; and, second, that a **door to a cupboard** may swing across a landing at the **top** of a flight if it will leave a clear space which is the same width of the stair for a distance of at least 400mm (⇨ Diagram 4.4–7).

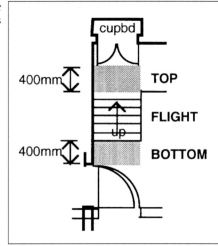

***Diagram 4.4–7:***
**Doors across landings**

### Handrail

Stairs which are less than 1m wide should have a handrail on at least one side; both sides if they are wider. The height of the handrail should be between 900–1,000mm, measured vertically from a line joining the fronts of the treads or from the floor.

## Guarding

Stairs and landings, where they are not against a wall, should be guarded at the sides if the drop is more than 600mm. On stairs which are likely to be used by children under five it should not be possible for children to climb the guarding readily and it should not be possible for a 100mm sphere to pass through it. The height of the guarding should be at least 900mm and it should be able to resist a horizontal force, applied at this height, of 0.36kN for each 1m of length.

> *It is often convenient for the top of the barrier to serve as the handrail.*

If the balustrade is glazed different requirements apply.

## Special stairs

There are a number of special stairs, some of which are discussed below.

### Tapered treads (winders)

The going of the tapered treads should be the same as the going of the straight treads. If the width of the flight is less than 1m, measure the going on the centre line of the flight. If the width is 1m or more, measure the going 270mm in from each side. The going of a tapered tread should be at least 50mm at its narrow end.

> *Winders are better avoided at the top of a flight.*

### Spiral and helical stairs

The geometry of spiral and helical stairs can be complicated and, to meet the requirements, you should read BS 5395.

> 📖 A **helical flight** is a spiral flight rising at a fixed distance from the vertical axis.

### Alternating tread stairs and fixed ladders

Alternating tread stairs and more rarely fixed ladders, are acceptable, but only for loft conversions (⇨ Appendix G).

### Other provisions

Neither sliding and/or folding ladders, nor any other kinds of apparatus that need deploying before they can be used, can be relied on to satisfy the means of escape requirements.

# 4.5
# Roofs

## INTRODUCTION

In this section the guidance is for:

4.5.1    Pitched roofs
4.5.2    Flat roofs
4.5.3    Roof ventilation

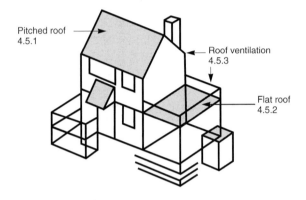

## Requirements

The roof of a building must be capable of resisting a number of threats to its integrity, and ensure the protection and security of the structure itself. It must:

- resist **beetle infestation** in the structural timber (BR 7);
- provide structural **support** for the combined dead-, imposed- and wind-loads and carry them safely to the supporting walls (BR A1);
- maintain its **stability** in the event of fire for a reasonable period. **Limit on application:** requirement B3 does not apply to a pitched roof, nor does it apply to a flat roof except for any part relied on as a means of escape in fire (BR B3);
- limit the **external** spread of fire (BR B4);
- limit the **internal** spread of fire (BR B2);
- resist the penetration of **moisture** from rain and snow to the inside of the building, not be damaged by that moisture and not carry it to any part of the building that would be damaged by it (BR C4);
- limit **heat loss** (BR L1);
- limit **condensation** (BR F2);
- be **guarded** where there is a risk of people falling. **Limit on application:** the requirement K2 does not apply where it would restrict normal use, nor does it apply to a flat roof which is only accessible for maintenance or repair, except any part relied on as a means of escape in fire.

### Meeting the requirements

This section is divided into pitched roofs (⇨ 4.5.1), flat roofs (⇨ 4.5.2) and roof ventilation (⇨ 4.5.3). Pitched roofs are roofs which slope more than 10 degrees.

> 📖 *The Building Regulations leave the choice of a pitched or flat roof to you but the planning authority may not.*

## Beetle infestation

In certain areas (⇨ Table 4.5–1) softwood timber used for roof construction (including any ceiling joists), or fixed in the roof space, should be treated to prevent infestation by the house long-horn beetle.

> *Treatments against beetle infestation are not intended to protect timber against dry-rot, although combined treatments are available. To be fully protected, timber should be treated by the supplier before it is cut to length. If you must cut the timber after treatment, dip the cut ends in a proprietary liquid if you can. Brush them if you cannot.*

**Table 4.5–1:** *Protection against beetle infestation*

| Geographical areas at risk |
| --- |
| Royal boroughs of: |
|     Windsor and Maidenhead, specifically the parishes of Old Windsor, Sunningdale and Sunninghill. |
| The boroughs of: |
|     Bracknell Forest; |
|     Elmbridge; |
|     Guildford (other than the area of the former borough of Guildford); |
|     Spelthorne; |
|     Surrey Heath; |
|     Rushmoor (specifically the area of the former district of Farnborough); |
|     Waverley (other than the parishes of Godalming and Haslemere); |
|     Woking. |
| The districts of: |
|     Hart (other than the area of the former urban district of Fleet); |
|     Runnymede. |

## Wind uplift

Ensure that the roof, whether it is pitched or flat, is strapped vertically to the walls below so that it will withstand uplifting wind forces (⇨ Appendix G5).

If you are replacing the roof covering and the new covering is **heavier** than the existing covering, you should replace any defective timbers and check against the tables of timber dimensions to see if you should strengthen the roof structure with, for example, additional supports. If the new covering is **lighter**, you should check that the necessary fixings to the wall are in place. Otherwise, the wind might lift the roof, particularly if you introduce an underlay to reduce the draughts.

## Snow-loads

Snow-loads are the **imposed-loads** (0.75–1.0 kN/m²) which you should use when you are choosing the sizes of roof timbers. The loads are measured on the plan area of the roof and will depend on the location of your site and its altitude above sea level.

If your site is outside the hatched area (⇨ Diagram 4.5–1) and its height is less than 100m above sea level use 0.75 kN/m². If its height is between 100–200m, use 1 kN/m². If your site is inside the hatched area (⇨ Diagram 4.5–1) and its height above sea level is less than100m, use 1.0 kN/m². To find the snow-load if your site is above these given heights you should refer to BS 6399.

**Diagram 4.5–1: Imposed snow roof loading**

| Site location | Loading | Note: |
|---|---|---|
| Within hatched area at an altitude of less than 100m above ordnance datum | 1.00kN/m² | For sites at greater altitude reference should be made to BS 6399: Part 3 to determine imposed and snow loading. |
| Outside hatched area at an altitude of less than 100m above ordnance datum | 0.75kN/m² | |
| Outside hatched area at an altitude lying between 100m and 200m above ordnance datum | 1.00kN/m² | |

## Roof coverings

Roof coverings have to satisfy two requirements: external fire spread and resistance to weather.

> *Remember that a roof which is pitched steeper than 70 degrees is treated as though it were a wall.*

### External fire spread

The provisions to limit external fire spread do apply to the performance of the roof covering (though not the supporting structure) when exposed to fire on its exposed face. The **performance** which the covering should have depends on its distance from the **boundary**.

**Relevant boundary**      Find the distance to the boundary (⇨ 4.3.1) or the notional boundary (⇨ 4.3.1). You will find that it will usually be the distance to the actual boundary of the curtilage of the property, but if there are other buildings on the site an imaginary "notional" boundary might have to be assumed. On the other hand, the boundary formed by a wall separating a pair of semi-detached houses can be ignored.

Having found the boundary distance ⇨ Table 4.5–2 for the designations which are acceptable. Then, for the notional designations of some common roof coverings, pitched roof coverings and flat roof coverings ⇨ Table 4.5–3.

> 📖 *The performance of a roof covering is given a designation from AA (the best) to DD and this is quite different from the classification given to wall and ceiling finishes (⇨ 4.6).*

### Resistance to weather

The regulations encompass moisture (⇨ 4.5.1) , pitched roofs (⇨ 4.5.2) , and flat roofs (⇨ 4.5.2)

Whichever covering is used, and whatever pitch it is laid at, it should be secured so that it will not be lifted by the wind, particularly at the exposed edges.

> 📖 *Be sure that what you fix the covering to is also secure.*

**Table 4.5–2:** *Limitation on roof coverings*

| Designation of covering of roof or part of roof | Minimum distance from any point on relevant boundary | | | |
|---|---|---|---|---|
| | Less than 6m | At least 6m | At least 12m | At least 20m |
| AA, AB, or AC | ● | ● | ● | ● |
| BA, BB, or BC | ○ | ● | ● | ● |
| CA, CB, or CC | ○ | ● (1) | ● (2) | ● |
| AD, BD, or CD | ○ | ● (1) | ● (2) | ● (2) |
| DA, DB, DC, or DD | ○ | ○ | ○ | ● (1) |
| Thatch or wood shingles, if performance under BS 476: pt 3: 1958 cannot be established | ○ | ● (1) | ● (2) | ● (2) |

Notes
Separation distance considerations do not apply to roofs of a pair of semi-detached houses
● Acceptable
○ Not acceptable
(1) Not acceptable on any of the following buildings:
    a. Houses in terraces of three or more houses.
    b. Industrial, Storage or Other non-residential purpose group buildings of any size.
    c. Any other buildings with a cubic capacity of more than 1,500m³

    And only acceptable on other buildings if the part of the roof is no more than 3m² in area and is at least 1.5m from any similar part, with the roof between the parts covered with a material of limited combustibility
(2) Not acceptable on any of the buildings listed under a, b or c above

**Table 4.5–3:** *Notional designations of roof coverings*

**Part i: Pitched roofs covered with slates or tiles**

| Covering material | Supporting structure | Designation |
|---|---|---|
| 1  Natural slates<br>2  Fibre reinforced cement slates<br>3  Clay tiles<br>4  Concrete tiles | 1. timber rafters with or without underfelt, sarking, boarding, woodwool slabs compressed straw slabs, plywood, wood chipboard, or fibre insulating board | AA |
| 5  Bitumen felt strip slates Type 2E with Type 2B underlayer bitumen felt | 3. timber rafters and boarding, plywood, woodwool slabs, wood chipboard, or fibre insulating board | BB |
| 6  Strip slates of bitumen felt, class 1 or 2 | 2. timber rafters and boarding, plywood, woodwool slabs, compressed straw slabs, wood chipboard, or fibre insulating board | CC |

Note
Any reference in these tables to bitumen felt of a specified type is a reference to bitumen felt as so designated in BS 747: 1977.

**Part ii: Pitched roofs covered with self-supporting sheet**

| Roof covering material | Construction | Supporting structure | Designation |
|---|---|---|---|
| 1. Profiled sheet of galvanised steel, aluminium, fibre reinforce cement, or pre-painted (coil coated) steel or aluminium with a pvc or pvf2 coating | 1. Single skin without underlay or with underlay of plasterboard, fibre insulating board, woodwool slab | Structure of timber, steel or concrete | AA |
| 2. Profiled sheet of galvanised steel, aluminium, fibre reinforce cement, or pre-painted (coil coated) steel or aluminium with a pvc or pvf2 coating | 2. Double skin without interlayer, or with interlayer of resin bonded glass fibre, mineral wool slab, polystyrene, or polyurethane | Structure of timber, steel or concrete | AA |

**Part iii: Flat roofs covered with bitumen felt**

A flat roof comprising bitumen felt should (irrespective of the felt specification) be deemed AA if the felt is laid on a deck constructed of any of the materials prescribed in the Table in part iv, and has a surface finish of:
a.  bitumen-bedded stone chippings covered the whole surface to a depth of at least 12.5mm
b.  bitumen-bedded tiles of a non-combustible material
c.  sand and cement screed, or
d.  macadam

**Part iv: Pitched roofs covered with bitumen felt**

| Number of layers | Type of upper layer | Type of underlayer | Deck of 6mm plywood, 12.5mm wood chipboard, 16mm (finished) T&G or 19mm (finished) plain edged timber boarding | Deck of compressed straw slab | Deck or screeded woodwool slab | Profiled fibre reinforced cement or steel deck (single or double skin) with or without fibre insulating board overlay | Profiled aluminium deck (single or double skin) with or without fibre insulating board overlay | Concrete or clay pot slab (*in situ* precast) |
|---|---|---|---|---|---|---|---|---|
| | Type 1E | Type 1B minimum mass 13kg/10m² | CC | AC | AC | AC | AC | AB |
| 2 or 3 layers built up in accordance with CP 144: Part 3 1970 | Type2E | Type 1B minimum mass 13kg/10m² | BB | AB | AB | AB | AB | AB |
| | Type 2E | Type 2B | AB | AB | AB | AB | AB | AB |
| | Type 3E | Type 3B or 3G | BC | AC | AB | AB | AB | AB |

**Part v: Pitched or flat roofs covered with fully supported material**

| Covering material | Supporting structure | Designation |
|---|---|---|
| 1. Aluminium sheet<br>2. Copper sheet<br>3. Zinc sheet<br>4. Lead sheet<br>5. Mastic asphalt<br>6. Vitreous enamelled steel<br>7. Lead/tin alloy coated steel sheet<br>8. Zinc/aluminium alloy coated steel sheet<br>9. Pre-painted (coil coated) steel sheet including liquid-applied pvc coatings | 1. Timber joists and: tongued and grooved boarding, or plain edged boarding | AA* |
| | 2. Steel or timber joists with deck of: woodwool slabs, compressed straw slab, wool chipboard, fibre insulating board, or 9.5mm plywood | AA |
| | 3. Concrete or clay pot slab (insitu or pre-cast) or non-combustible deck of steel, aluminium, or fibre cement (with or without insulation) | AA |

Note
* Lead sheet supported by timber joists and plain edged boarding may give a BA designation.

## Roof lights

Whether in pitched or flat roofs, roof lights not only have to meet the requirement B4, based on distance to the boundary and a designation, but also requirement B2, based on the use of the space below and a classification.

### Reaction to fire

A roof light of a least 4mm thick **unwired glass** will meet both the designation and classification but a plastic roof light may not.

> *If you wish to use a plastic roof light, you should refer to the Approved Document B which is based on the use of the space below, and Section 14 which is based on the distance to the boundary.*

## Means of escape

There are choices in specifying the means to escape (⇨ Appendix C) and loft conversions (⇨ Appendix G). The choice you make might affect the design and construction of the roof.

## 4.5.1 Pitched roofs

**THE BASICS**

**Structural support**: for the dimensions of the rafters and the purlins supporting them ⇨ Tables 4.5–4 and 4.5–5. In each case two spans are given, one for each of the two different imposed snow-loads. To find the imposed-load to use ⇨ Diagram 4.5–1. Although the imposed-loads given in the diagram are measured "flat" on the plan the dead-loads and the rafter spans given in the table are measured up the slope.

Assess the dimensions of purlins (sheeting or decking) for low-pitched roofs covered with large sheets. Ditto for ceiling joists (⇨ Table 4.5–6) and binders (⇨ Table 4.5–7) supporting ceiling joists. These dimensions do not allow for the weight of water tanks or for trimming around chimneys.

You can use prefabricated roof trusses instead of traditional rafters, although they usually restrict the use of the roof space. Suppliers will provide you with calculations and designs.

**Horizontal support for walls**: you will have to strap the rafters and, in some cases, the ceiling joists, to the gable ends at no more than 2m centres (⇨ Appendix G5).

**Vertical restraint for roofs**: you might have to strap the feet of the rafters down to the external walls at no more than 2m centres to provide restraint against wind uplift (⇨ Appendix G5).

**External fire spread**: roof coverings such as tiles, slates and some types of bitumen felt will meet the requirements. The use of other coverings, such as plastics and thatch, might be possible too (⇨ Tables 4.5–2 and 4.5–3).

**Internal fire spread**: plaster or plasterboard will meet the requirement but the use of other materials may be limited, particularly in a circulation area.

**Moisture**: you have to consider weather resistance and ventilation when planning to limit condensation.

**Weather resistance**: to meet the requirements for weather resistance, materials include tiles, slates, metals and – where the limitations on external fire spread allow – plastics and bitumen felt. Some can be used at pitches as low as 200 degrees.

**Ventilation**: The requirements for roof ventilation are discussed later in this section (⇨ 4.5–3).

**Heat loss**: limit heat loss through fabric (⇨ 4.4–7) and remember that the requirement does not apply to unheated buildings, heated non-residential buildings with a floor area of no more than 30m², or conservatory extensions.

If you need to insulate, start with the basic thickness (⇨ Table 4.5–9). The thickness depends on the performance of the insulating material you choose – its "k" value. From this starting point, you can deduct allowances for the construction itself.

*CHECKLIST*

- ☐ Structural support
- ☐ Fire resistance (collapse)
- ☐ External fire spread
- ☐ Internal fire spread
- ☐ Moisture
- ☐ Heat loss
- ☐ Condensation
- ☐ Guarding
- ☐ Means of escape

## Structural support

The conditions which apply to the building and its walls (⇨ Appendix B) also apply to the following guidance. This assumes that the dead- and imposed-loads to be carried are no more than those given.

> 🕮 *Timber is classified by its strength class and many combinations of species and grade will qualify a timber to be placed in one class or another. However, it is sufficient, for strength purposes, to specify only by class; for example, Class SC3 which is widely used for general building work. More extensive tables are also referred to.*

### Timber dimensions

These are various and apply to the different parts of a timber construction; for example, pitched roof rafters (⇨ Table 4.5–4), purlins supporting pitched roof rafters (⇨ Table 4.5–5), ceiling joists (⇨ Table 4.5–6), binder supporting ceiling joists (⇨ Table 4.5–7), purlins supporting sheeting or decking (⇨ Table 4.5–8).

**Table 4.5–4:** *Pitched roof rafters (dimensions)*

Strength grade SC3
Dead load 0.50–0.75 kN/m² (excluding the rafter)
Imposed load (snow) 0.75 kN/m²

*Imposed load (snow) (1.00 kN/m²)*
Rafter spacing 400mm
Minimum bearing length at supports 35mm
Limited access (for repair or maintenance only)

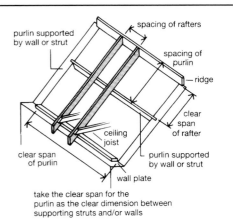

take the clear span for the purlin as the clear dimension between supporting struts and/or walls

**Pitch**

| Size of rafter (mm) (width x depth) | more than 15 no more than 22.5 Span (m) clear between supports (measured along slope) | more than 22.5 no more than 30 | more than 30 no more than 45 |
|---|---|---|---|
| | Table A5 *(A7)* in AD A | Table A9 *(A11)* in AD A | Table A13 *(A15)* in AD A |
| 38 x 100 | 1.93 *(1.93)* | 2.01 *(2.01)* | 2.10 *(2.10)* |
| 38 x 125 | 2.63 *(2.59)* | 2.74 *(2.65)* | 2.87 *(2.75)* |
| 38 x 150 | 3.26 *(3.10)* | 3.34 *(3.18)* | 3.44 *(3.29)* |
| 50 x 100 | 2.35 *(2.28)* | 2.45 *(2.33)* | 2.53 *(2.41)* |
| 50 x 125 | 2.98 *(2.84)* | 3.05 *(2.91)* | 3.15 *(3.00)* |
| 50 x 150 | 3.57 *(3.40)* | 3.65 *(3.48)* | 3.76 *(3.59)* |

Note
For dimensions of purlins supporting rafters ⇨ Table 4.5–5

**Table 4.5–5:** *Purlins supporting pitched roof rafters (dimensions)*

|  | Pitch more than 15 no more than 22.5 | | | |
|---|---|---|---|---|
| **Size of purlin** (mm)<br>(width x depth) | 1500 | 1800 | 2100 | 2400 |
|  | Span between supports (m) | | | |
|  | Table A5 *(A7)* in AD A | | | |

|  | Pitch more than 22.5 no more than 30 | | | |
|---|---|---|---|---|
| **Size of purlin** (mm)<br>(width x depth) | 1500 | 1800 | 2100 | 2400 |
|  | Span between supports (m) | | | |
|  | Table A9 *(A11)* in AD A | | | |

|  | Pitch more than 30 no more than 45 | | | |
|---|---|---|---|---|
| **Size of purlin** (mm)<br>(width x depth) | 1500 | 1800 | 2100 | 2400 |
|  | Span between supports (m) | | | |
|  | Table A13 *(A15)* in AD A | | | |

**Table 4.5–6:** *Ceiling joists (dimensions)*

Strength grade SC3
Dead load 0.25–0.50 kN/m² (excluding the joist)
Imposed load (snow) 0.75 kN/m²
*Imposed load (snow) (1.00 kN/m²)*
Joist spacing 400mm
Minimum bearing length at supports 35mm

**Size of joist** (mm)   Span (m) clear between supports
(width x depth)

| | Table A3 in AD A |
|---|---|
| 50 x 72 | 1.27 |
| 50 x 97 | 1.89 |
| 50 x 122 | 2,53 |

Note
The dimensions do not allow for trimming (for example around flues) or the weight of water tanks

**Table 4.5–7:** *Binders supporting ceiling joists (dimensions)*

Strength grade SC3
Dead load 0.25–0.50 kN/m² (excluding the purlin)

Minimum bearing length at supports 35mm

| | Spacing of binders (m) | | | | |
|---|---|---|---|---|---|
| **Size of binder** (mm) | 1200 | 1500 | 1800 | 2100 | 2400 |
| (width x depth) | Span (m) clear between supports | | | | |
| 50 x 150 | 2.04 | 1.92 | 1.83 | n/a | |
| 50 x 175 | 2.42 | 2.28 | 2.16 | 2.07 | 1.99 |
| 50 x 200 | 2.81 | 2.64 | 2.50 | 2.39 | 2.29 |
| 63 x 125 | 1.82 | n/a | | | |
| 63 x 150 | 2.23 | 2.11 | 2.00 | 1.91 | 1.84 |
| 63 x 175 | 2.65 | 2.49 | 2.37 | 2.26 | 2.17 |
| 63 x 200 | 3.07 | 2.88 | 2.74 | 2.61 | 2.51 |

Note
The dimensions do not allow for weight of water tanks

**Table 4.5–8:** *Purlins supporting sheeting or decking (dimensions)*

Strength grade SC3
Dead load 0.50–0.75 kN/m² (excluding the purlin)
Imposed load (snow) 0.75 kN/m²
*Imposed load (snow) 1.00 kN/m²*
Minimum bearing length at supports 50mm

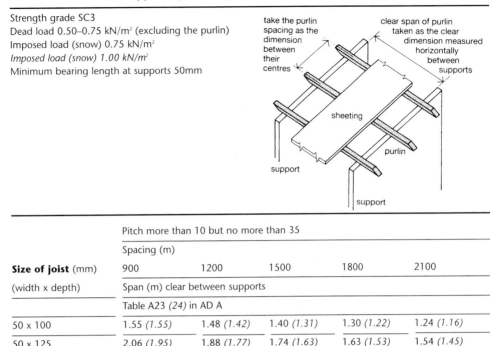

| **Size of joist** (mm) | Pitch more than 10 but no more than 35 | | | | |
| | Spacing (m) | | | | |
| | 900 | 1200 | 1500 | 1800 | 2100 |
| (width x depth) | Span (m) clear between supports | | | | |
| | Table A23 *(24)* in AD A | | | | |
| 50 x 100 | 1.55 *(1.55)* | 1.48 *(1.42)* | 1.40 *(1.31)* | 1.30 *(1.22)* | 1.24 *(1.16)* |
| 50 x 125 | 2.06 *(1.95)* | 1.88 *(1.77)* | 1.74 *(1.63)* | 1.63 *(1.53)* | 1.54 *(1.45)* |
| 50 x 150 | 2.49 *(2.34)* | 2.26 *(2.12)* | 2.09 *(1.96)* | 1.96 *(1.83)* | 1.85 *(1.73)* |
| 50 x 175 | 2.90 *(2.73)* | 2.63 *(2.47)* | 2.43 *(2.28)* | 2.28 *(2.14)* | 2.16 *(2.02)* |
| 50 x 200 | 3.31 *(3.11)* | 3.00 *(2.82)* | 2.78 *(2.60)* | 2.60 *(2.44)* | 2.46 *(2.31)* |

Note
The purlins will support a concentrated load of 0.9 kN instead of the imposed snow load

### *Notches and holes*

Do not cut notches and holes in **rafters**. However, they can be bird-mouthed at the supports to a depth no more than one-third of their depth. You can cut notches and holes in ceiling joists but only in certain places (⇨ TS 4.4–1). You can also cut notches and holes in binders and purlins but only if you have them checked by a competent person.

## Fire resistance (collapse)

There is no requirement for roofs to have fire resistance (collapse).

### *Resistance to fire*

Remember that roofs which slope more steeply than 70 degrees are treated as walls and will need fire resistance.

## External fire spread

The requirements will relate to roof coverings discussed earlier.

### *Reaction to fire*

Remember that a roof which is pitched steeper than 70 degrees is treated as a wall (⇨ 4.3.1).

## Internal fire spread

Requirements for ceilings and internal wall finishes are discussed later (⇨ 4.6.1).

## Moisture

The roof covering should exclude rain and dry and driven snow.

---

### 4.5–1: Roof coverings

Some examples of materials for roof coverings (pitched roofs) are:
  slates and tiles;
  self-supporting rigid sheets: of plastics, metals, mineral fibre-reinforced;
  fully-supported flexible sheets: of plastics, bitumen felt, metal.

**Slates and tiles**: should be laid so that each course overlaps the course next but one below it and the greater the lap, the flatter the pitch can be. However, the pitch of the tile or slate will be flatter than the pitch of the rafters. Therefore, these should be no flatter than 450 degrees (60mm lap) or 40 degrees (75mm lap) for a tiled roof and no flatter than between 450–300 degrees for a slated roof – depending on the size and lap of the slate – under normal exposure. You should use an underlayer of building paper if the exposure is more severe.

**Interlocking tiles**: interlock at the head and sides – but overlap only the course next below and so can be laid flatter, depending on their design.

**Larger sheets**: will be lapped at the heads but interlock at the sides and can be laid even flatter.

**Continuous sheets**: metal or more usually plastics or built-up bitumen felt, need a substructure (decking) to support them but can be laid nearly flat.

## Heat loss

The insulation in a roof may be rigid, flexible or loose-fill where it is laid on the ceiling and rigid or flexible where it is fixed to or between the rafters.

*Remember that a roof which is pitched steeper than 70 degrees is treated as a wall (⇨ 4.3.1).*

To find the thickness of insulation material, whether it is laid over the ceiling or fixed to the rafters, first find the thermal conductivity value (the "k" value) of the material you intend to you use. Then find the **base thickness** (Table 4.5–9) for the insulation. You can, if you wish, reduce the base thickness by specified amounts (Table 4.5–9).

*The thickness applies only to the roofs of extensions. Whether it will apply to the roof of a new dwelling will depend on the energy rating of the dwelling as a whole when calculated using the Standard Assessment Rating (SAP) (⇨ Appendix D1).*

**Table 4.5–9:** *Insulation thickness – roofs (U-values 0.25 and 0.35 W/m²K)*

| | Thermal conductivity (k)[1] | | | | | | |
| --- | --- | --- | --- | --- | --- | --- | --- |
| | 0.02 | 0.025 | 0.03 | 0.035 | 0.04 | 0.045 | 0.050 |
| | **Base thickness** of insulation (mm)[2] | | | | | | |
| Pitched roofs **with** an accessible loft (U-value 0.25 W/m²K) | | | | | | | |
| Between joists or rafters | 114 | 142 | 170 | 199 | 227 | 256 | 284 |
| Between and over joists or rafters | 106 | 120 | 136 | 152 | 169 | 187 | 204 |
| Continuous | 77 | 97 | 116 | 135 | 154 | 174 | 193 |
| Pitched roofs **without** an accessible loft (U-value 0.35 W/m²K) (eg room-in-roof construction) | | | | | | | |
| Between joists or rafters | 69 | 86 | 103 | 120 | 137 | 154 | 172 |
| Between and over joists or rafters | 69 | 86 | 102 | 112 | 124 | 135 | 147 |
| Continuous | 54 | 68 | 82 | 95 | 109 | 122 | 136 |
| The base thicknesses can be reduced as follows (mm): | | | | | | | |
| 10mm plasterboard | 1 | 2 | 2 | 2 | 3 | 3 | 3 |
| 13mm plasterboard | 2 | 2 | 2 | 3 | 3 | 4 | 4 |
| 13mm sarking board | 2 | 2 | 3 | 3 | 4 | 4 | 5 |
| Roof space (pitched) | 4 | 5 | 5 | 6 | 7 | 8 | 9 |
| 19mm roof tiles | 0 | 1 | 1 | 1 | 1 | 1 | 1 |
| 3 layers felt | 1 | 1 | 1 | 1 | 2 | 2 | 2 |
| Roof space (flat) | 3 | 4 | 5 | 6 | 6 | 7 | 8 |

Notes
1 The "k" values of some of the most used insulating materials are given in Appendix D1.
2 The base thicknesses assume that the joists are 48mm wide at 600mm spacing.

## Condensation

Moisture carried up by warm air from the rooms below the roof can do considerable damage if it reaches the cold part of the roof where it can condense. In theory, the problem would be avoided if the moisture could be prevented from passing through the insulation to the cold part above. In practice, this has been found to be virtually impossible. The best course is to ventilate the roof space to remove as much moisture as possible (⇨ 4.5.3).

> *If the ceiling follows the pitch of the roof so that there is no roof space, the ventilation should be as for a flat roof.*

## Guarding

There is no requirement for guarding pitched roofs.

## Means of escape

The bottom of any opening part of a dormer window or rooflight in a pitched roof should be at least 1,100mm above the floor. If the opening is relied on for escape, except from a loft conversion or if the opening is relied on for rescue from a loft conversion, then different requirements will obtain.

# 4.5.2  Flat roofs

---

### THE BASICS

**Structural support**: for joist dimensions ⇨ Table 4.5–10, for roofs, including those where access is limited. In each case, two spans are given: one for each of two different imposed snow-loads. Refer to the map (Diagram 4.5–1) to find the imposed-load for your site.

**Horizontal support for walls**: you will have to strap the joists to the external walls and any internal loadbearing walls at no more than 2m centres (⇨ Appendices).

**Vertical restraint for roofs**: you will have to strap the ends of the joists to the external walls to provide restraint against wind uplift (⇨ Appendices).

**External fire spread**: roof coverings such as metal and some types of bitumen felt will meet the requirements. The use of other coverings may be possible.

**Internal fire spread**: plaster or plasterboard will meet the requirements but the use of other materials may be limited, particularly in a circulation area.

**Moisture**: you have to consider weather resistance and ventilation to limit condensation.

**Weather resistance**: to meet the requirements for weather resistance, materials include metals and – where the limitations on external fire spread allow – plastics and bitumen felt.

**Ventilation**: provide openings to ventilate the air spaces above the insulation ( ⇨ 4.5.3).

**Heat loss**: calculate base insulation thickness and allowable reduction (⇨ 4.5.1) for pitched roofs without an accessible loft.

**Guarding**: where there is a risk of falling more than 600mm and access to the roof is not limited to maintenance, the edges should be guarded with a barrier – it may be a parapet – at least 1,100mm high.

---

### CHECKLIST

- ☐  Structural support
- ☐  Fire resistance (collapse)
- ☐  External fire spread
- ☐  Internal fire spread
- ☐  Moisture
- ☐  Heat loss
- ☐  Condensation
- ☐  Guarding

## Structural support

The conditions which apply to the building and its walls (⇨ Appendices) also apply to the guidance which follows. This assumes that the dead- and imposed-loads to be carried by the roof, whether it is pitched or flat, are no more than those given in the notes to the following for flat roof joists and purlins supporting sheeting. Remember that a flat roof may be for your use, not only for the limited purposes of maintenance or repair.

> 🕮 *Timber is classified by its strength class and many combinations of species and grade will qualify a timber to be placed in one class or another. However, it is sufficient, for strength purposes, to specify only by the class.*

**Table 4.5–10:** *Flat-roof joists – dimensions*

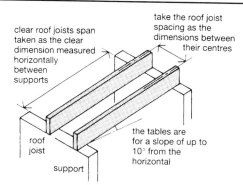

clear roof joists span taken as the clear dimension measured horizontally between supports

take the roof joist spacing as the dimensions between their centres

roof joist

support

the tables are for a slope of up to 10° from the horizontal

**Span (m)** clear between supports

| Size of joist (mm) (width x depth) | Access not limited Dead load 0.25–0.55 kN/m² (excluding the joist) Imposed snow-load | | Dead load 0.5–0.75 kN/m² (excluding the joist) Imposed load |
|---|---|---|---|
| | 0.75 kN/m² | 1.00 kN/m² | 1.50 kN/m² |
| | (A17) in AD A | (A19) in AD A | (A21) in AD A |
| 50 x 97 | 1.89 | 1.89 | |
| 50 x 122 | 2.53 | 2.53 | 2.00 |
| 50 x 147 | 3.19 | 3.19 | 2.59 |
| 50 x 170 | 3.81 | 3.77 | 3.14 |
| 50 x 195 | 4.48 | 4.31 | 3.76 |
| 50 x 220 | 5.09 | 4.85 | 4.38 |

Notes
1 These spans assume:
  – timber-strength grade **SC3**
  – a joist-spacing of **400mm**
  – a mimimum bearing at supports of **35mm**
2 The joists will support a concentrated load of 0.9 kN instead of the imposed snow load

## Notches and holes

Requirements are as discussed earlier (TS 4.4–1).

## Fire resistance (collapse)

There is no requirement for flat roofs to have fire resistance R (loadbearing capacity) if they are only accessible for maintenance or repair. If the roof is to be used as a floor or relied on for escape then different guidance applies.

## External fire spread

### Fire resistance (spread)

Where a door or window which is relied on for a means of escape from a dwelling opens onto a flat roof the part of the roof which is relied on for escape should have fire resistance REI (loadbearing capacity, integrity, insulation) for a period of REI 30/30/30 and the route of escape should also be guarded.

> *It may be impracticable to provide for resistance for a part of a roof without providing fire resistance for the whole roof. However, a ceiling (provided it is of 12.5mm plasterboard or similar with a 5mm plaster finish) together with the*

*deck which will be needed to support the roof covering, provided it is at least
15mm thick and the joints are sealed, will achieve the 30 minute period, which
would seem reasonable.*

### Reaction to fire
For guidance ⇨ **4.6.1**.

> *Remember that a roof which is pitched steeper than 70 degrees is treated as a
> wall (⇨ 4.3.1).*

## Internal fire spread

### Reaction to fire
For ceiling finishes ⇨ **4.6.1**.

### Cavity barriers
There is no requirement for cavity barriers in roof spaces, **except** where a protected
stairway is provided in a house with three storeys (⇨ Appendices).

## Moisture

The roof covering should exclude rain and snow but should also take into consideration
requirements for external fire spread.

> *Continuous sheets should be used and these can be made from a variety of
> materials. Their continued performance depends on compatibility with the
> deck on which they are laid and you would do well to place the responsibility
> for fixing the deck and laying the membrane in the same hands.*

Examples of materials for roof coverings (flat roofs) are:
- self-supporting rigid sheets: of plastics, metals, mineral fibre-reinforced;
- fully-supported flexible sheets: of plastics, bitumen felt, metal.

## Heat loss

There are three possibilities:
1  Insulation between the joists. The thickness of the insulation, which should be laid
   between the roof joists, will be the same as the thickness of the insulation to be laid
   between ceiling joists or roof rafters. This type of roof, which is perhaps the most
   common, is often called a **cold-deck roof**.
2  Insulated deck over the joists. A material which has a suitable insulating performance
   may not provide a suitable base for laying the roof covering.
3  Insulation above the roof finish. Materials are available which are suitable for laying
   over the roof covering – for example, moisture resistant and rigid enough to walk
   on. However, a sufficient weight of material, such as gravel, will have to be placed
   on such coverings to reduce the risk of wind uplift (it will also provide suitable fire
   performance where this is needed).

   > *To find the insulation thickness (⇨ 4.5.1) you should use the basic thickness for
   > a roof without an accessible loft (U-value 0.35 W/m²K) and the same reductions
   > on the basic allowance except the allowance for the roof space.*

### Condensation

For guidance ⇨ 4.5.3.

### Guarding

Unless the roof is accessible only for maintenance and repair it should be guarded where there is a risk of falling more than 600mm from the edge except that, if any part of the roof is relied on for a means of escape, you should consider guarding at least that part (⇨ 4.5.2).

---

#### 4.5–2: Barrier

Any wall, balustrade, or similar, may serve as a barrier. The barrier will be suitable if it has a height of at least 900mm and will resist a horizontal force of at least 0.36kN (about 100kg) for each 1m of length applied at that height.

Glazing may be used in a barrier but with certain restrictions (⇨ 4.4.3).

## 4.5.3  Roof ventilation

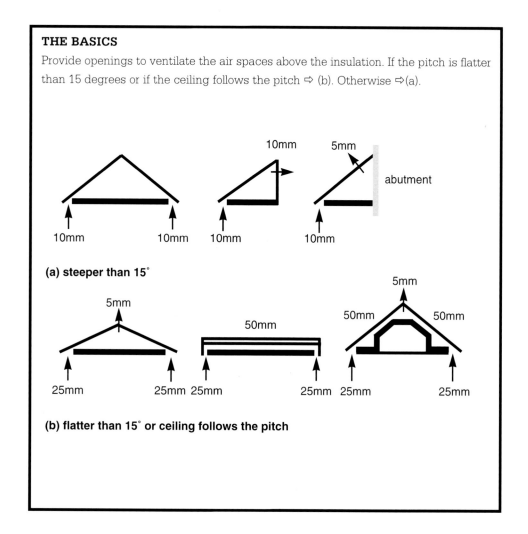

**THE BASICS**

Provide openings to ventilate the air spaces above the insulation. If the pitch is flatter than 15 degrees or if the ceiling follows the pitch ⇨ (b). Otherwise ⇨(a).

**(a) steeper than 15°**

**(b) flatter than 15° or ceiling follows the pitch**

## Requirement

Adequate provision must be made to prevent condensation (⇨ BR F2).

> *It may not be necessary to ventilate a small roof – over a porch, dormer roof or bay window, for example – to ensure reasonable standards of health or safety but you should consider the risk of dry rot before deciding not to do so.*

### Meeting the requirement

Any provision will be adequate if, under normal conditions, the thermal performance of the insulating materials and the structural performance of the roof will not be substantially or permanently reduced.

> *If moisture-laden warm air can rise up into the cold uninsulated part of a roof, the moisture can do considerable damage if it condenses out. In theory, the problem would be avoided if the air could be prevented from getting into the insulation. In practice, this has been found to be virtually impossible.*

### The ventilation strategy

The best course is to use the roof spaces above the insulation to ventilate the cold zone so as to remove as much moisture as possible.

**Pitched roofs**      Where the insulation is between, or on, the ceiling joists it is easy to ventilate the roof space in a normal pitched roof sufficiently to remove much of the moisture. The ventilation will also help to dry out the insulation and the roof structure if there is some condensation. Where the wall and ceiling linings are fixed directly to the rafters, as they may be in a loft space, you will have to take care to leave sufficient air spaces.

**Flat roofs**      You can probably arrange a sufficient air space above the insulation particularly if it is laid between the joists.

### Alternative strategies

If you are using the deck to provide the insulation and to support the roof covering there will be no air space above the insulation and you will have to provide a complete vapour control layer.

> *A vapour control layer will prevent moisture getting into the insulation or through gaps in it (otherwise it will probably condense and accumulate).*

There is another alternative: lay the insulation above the roof covering. You will have to choose the covering carefully because not all materials provide equally effective vapour control (they have to be "gas tight"). You will also have to choose the insulation carefully and fix or weight it down so that it will not blow away.

## Ventilated roofs

If you choose the ventilation strategy, the requisite technical specifications should be met, depending on the pitch of the roof, whether or not the ceiling follows the pitch, and whether the roof finishes against an abutment.

Where quilt or loose-fill insulation is to be used, care should be taken to prevent the insulation from obstructing the flow of ventilating air over the insulation. Purpose-made components, usually of a plastics material, are available.

## 4.5–3: Roofs with an unrestricted roof space

There are roofs with a pitch of 15 degrees or more where the ceiling does not follow the pitch.

A **double-pitched roof** should have ventilation openings at eaves level to promote cross-ventilation. The openings need not be continuous but they should have an area at least equal to a continuous opening 10mm wide (⇨ Diagram 4.5–2).

**Single-pitched roofs not against a wall** should have ventilation openings at eaves level and at high level to promote cross-ventilation. The openings need not be continuous but they should have an area at least equal to a continuous opening 10mm wide (⇨ Diagram 4.5–2).

**Single-pitched roofs against a wall** should have ventilation openings at eaves level and at high level. The openings at eaves level should have an area at least equal to a continuous opening 10mm wide. The openings at high level should be as high as possible, either at the junction of the roof covering and the wall or through the roof covering and should have an area at least equal to a continuous opening 5mm wide (⇨ Diagram 4.5–2).

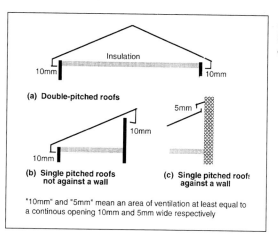

*Diagram 4.5–2:*
**Pitched roofs (15 degrees or more) – ventilation**

## 4.5–4: Roofs with a restricted roof space

These are pitched roofs with an open roof space but with a pitch of **less than 15 degrees,** flat roofs and roofs of any pitch where the ceiling follows pitch.

**Roofs with a ridge** should have ventilation openings at eaves level and at ridge level to promote cross-ventilation. The openings at eaves level should have an area at least equal to a continuous opening 25mm wide. The openings at ridge level should have an area at least equal to a continuous opening 5mm wide. The void should have a free air space between the roof deck and the insulation of at least 50mm (⇨ Diagram 4.5–3).

**Diagram 4.5–3: Roofs (any pitch) where the ceiling follows pitch**

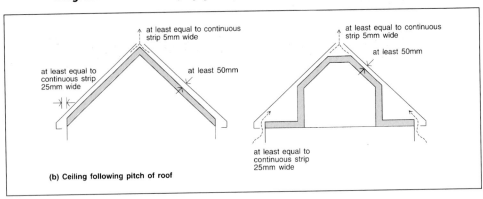

(b) Ceiling following pitch of roof

**Roofs without a ridge** should have ventilation openings at eaves level to promote cross-ventilation. The openings should have an area at least equal to a continuous opening 25mm wide. The void should have a free air space between the roof deck and the insulation of at least 50mm (⇨ Diagram 4.5–4).

**Diagram 4.5–4: Flat roofs**

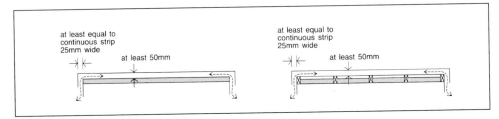

Where the air flow is at right angles to the joists or rafters then **counter-battens** should be used to form a free air space of at least 50mm between the roof deck and the insulation.

For **abutments**, where the edge of the roof abuts a wall or other obstruction so that a free air path cannot be formed to promote cross-ventilation, an alternative form of roof construction should be used.

*Where the distance between the eaves is more than 10m or the plan shape is not a simple rectangle, the openings at eaves level should be increased to give an area at least equal to 0.6 per cent of the roof area.*

## Alternative approach – all roofs

Follow BS 5250 which deals with the control of condensation in buildings. The relevant clauses are 9.1 and 9.3. The code contains additional detailed information about design and construction.

# 4.6
# Finishes – internal (linings)

## INTRODUCTION

In this section the guidance is for:

4.6.1     Walls and ceilings
4.6.2     Roof lights

## Requirements

All finishes must:
- inhibit the spread of flame across their surface (BR B2);
- have a rate of heat release, when ignited, which is reasonable in the circumstances. **Limit on application:** requirement B2 applies only to the internal surfaces of walls and ceilings (the roof, if there is no separate ceiling). It does not apply to the upper surfaces of floors and stairs (BR B2).

> The **surface of a wall** includes the surface of any glazing (except glazing in doors) and any part of a ceiling which slopes more steeply than 70 degrees. It does *not* include: doors and door frames; window frames and frames in which glazing is fitted; narrow items, including architraves, cover moulds, picture rails and skirtings; fireplace surrounds, mantle shelves and fitted furniture.
> The **surface of a ceiling** includes the surface of any glazing (a roof light, for example) and any part of a wall which slopes at 70 degrees or less steeply. It does *not* include the frames of windows, or roof lights, or frames in which glazing is fitted, or narrow items such as architraves, covers, moulds, picture rails and skirtings.

*The surface will usually be the surface of the finish or lining but it will be the surface of the construction itself if it is exposed.*

### Meeting the requirements

### CHECKLIST
- ☐ Reaction to fire

# 4.6.1 Walls and ceilings

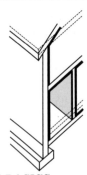

**THE BASICS**

You can use plaster or plasterboard anywhere. In small rooms you can use materials with a Class 3 classification (⇨ Table 4.6–1) and in any other rooms (as long as they are not circulation spaces) you can use a limited amount of Class 3 materials. The amount should be limited to an area of no more than half the floor area of the room and never more than 20m².

Materials with a Class 3 surface include timber and plywood (painted or unpainted) with a density of more than 400kg/m³, particle boards and hardboard (treated or painted) and some plastics.

*Surface-spread of flame and heat-release performance are combined into a single classification: reaction to fire (Class 1 is higher, Class 3 lower). Reaction to fire is not to be confused with fire resistance which, although the finishes might contribute to it, is a separate subject (⇨ 4.3 and 4.4).*

## Reaction to fire

Surfaces of finishes should have at least the following classification:

- small rooms (floor area no more than 4m²), Class 3;
- other rooms, Class 1;
- circulation spaces, Class 1.

However, note that some part of the walls in a room can be Class 3 – but their total area should be no more than half the floor area and never more than 20m².

### Table 4.6–1: *Reaction to fire performances*

**Non-combustible materials (fire propagation)**
A material is non-combustible if, **either**:
- it is classified as non-combustible when tested to BS 476: Part 4: 1970; **or**
- it does not flame or cause a rise in temperature of the specimen and the furnace thermocouples when tested to BS 476: Pt 11: 1982.

**Examples** Materials which are totally inorganic or contain no more than 1 per cent of organic material, such as concrete, concrete blocks, fired clay, bricks and tiles, slate, ceramics, metals, plaster, masonry.

**Materials of limited combustibility (fire propagation)**
A material is of limited combustibility if:
- it is non-combustible (see above);
- it has a non-combustible core, at least 8mm thick with combustible faces no more than 0.5mm thick;
- it has a density of at least 300 kg/m³ and does not flame or cause a rise in temperature of the furnace thermocouple of more than 20 degrees centigrade when tested to BS 476 Pt 11.
  - *Remember that where a flame spread rating is also required the faces must meet the requirements.*

**Classifications for wall and ceiling linings**
Small differences in thickness, substrate (base), colour, form, fixings and adhesives may significantly affect the performance. Test results for the performance of proprietary materials should be obtained from the manufacturers. Some thermoplastics materials cannot be tested to BS 476 (Pt 6) and special tests are needed to measure their performance.

**Class 0 (fire propagation and surface spread)**
The classification 0, combining fire propagation and surface spread, is not directly identified in any British Standard test. A material is classified as Class 0 if, **either**:
- it is composed throughout of non-combustible materials or materials of limited combustibility (see above); **or**
- it is a Class 1 material (see below) which, when tested to BS 476 (Pt 6), has a fire propagation index I of no more than 12 and a subindex $i_1$ of no more than 6. Index I relates to the overall performance. Subindex $i_1$ relates to the performance in the first three minutes of the test.

**Examples** Brickwork, blockwork, concrete and ceramic tiles. Plasterboard (painted or not, or with a PVC facing no more than 0.5mm thick). Woodwool cement slabs. Mineral fibre tiles or sheets with cement or resin bonding.
  - Other materials may achieve Class 0 but their performance should be confirmed by test evidence. They include aluminium-faced fibre insulating board, flame retardant decorative laminates on a calcium silicate base, thick polycarbonate sheet, phenolic sheet and uPVC.

**Class 1 (surface spread)**
A material is classified as Class 1 if, when tested to BS 476 (Pt 7), the flame does not spread further than 165mm after 10 minutes.

**Examples** Any Class 0 material (see above). Any material which has been tested and classified Class 1.
  - *The range of materials, composite materials and possible treatments is very large and you should consult the supplier who should provide test evidence. Some timber products listed under Class 3 (see below) can be brought up to Class 1 with appropriate proprietary treatments.*

  - *Class 2 is not used.*

**Class 3 (surface spread)**
A material is as classified Class 3 if, when tested to BS 476 (Pt 7), the flame does not spread further than 265mm after 1.5 minutes (and 710mm after 10 minutes).

**Examples** Timber or plywood with a density of more than 400 kg/m³ (painted or unpainted). Wood particle board or hardboard (either painted or treated). Standard glass-reinforced polyesters.

  - *Other materials may achieve Class 3 but their performance should be confirmed by test evidence. They include phenolic or melamine laminates on a calcium silicate base and flame retardent decorative laminates on a combustible base.*

## 4.6.2 Roof lights

Roof lights not only have to meet requirement B2 but also requirement B4.

### Reaction to fire

A glass roof light will meet the requirements for both internal and external fire spread if the glass is at least 4mm thick. However, a plastics rooflight may not.

☛ Space does not allow for guidance on plastic roof lights to be given because it takes account of a variety of factors. If you wish to use them you should refer to the detailed guidance in the Approved Document B.

# 4.7
# Piped services

## INTRODUCTION

In this section the guidance is for:

4.7.1    Sanitary pipework
4.7.2    Rainwater collection
         (above ground)
4.7.3    Water services
4.7.4    Gas installation

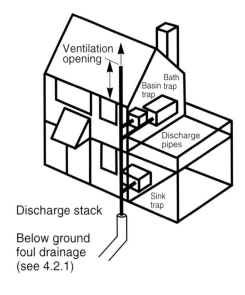

## 4.7.1  Sanitary pipework

The first part of this section gives guidance on foul-water drainage above ground (and sanitary pipework). For guidance on foul-water drainage below ground ⇨ 4.2.1.

### CHECKLIST
- ☐  Traps
- ☐  Discharge pipes (horizontal)
- ☐  Discharge stacks (vertical)
- ☐  Ventilation
- ☐  Blockages
- ☐  Materials and workmanship
- ☐  Testing

### Requirements

The sanitary pipework must be adequate to carry the foul water from the appliances to the drainage system below ground (BR H1).

---

> 📖 **Foul water** is waste from a sanitary convenience – a WC or urinal – or water that has been used for cooking or washing, such as water from a sink, washbasin, bath, shower, or bidet.
> A **sanitary convenience** is a closet (a privy) or urinal.

---

🖛 *The Building Regulations do not require sanitary pipework to be provided; only to be adequate if it is provided. However, where plans are deposited in accordance with the building regulations, Section 21(1) of the Building Act 1984 gives the local authority power to reject the plans unless they show that satisfactory provision will be made for the conveyance and disposal of foul water and this includes sanitary pipework.*

### Meeting the requirements

The sanitary pipework should:

*   be **trapped** to prevent the foul air in it from entering the building;
*   have the **capacity** to carry the flows from the appliances to the drainage system below ground;
*   be **ventilated** where the flow of water through the system can create positive and negative pressures which could draw the water from a trap;
*   **minimise** the risk of blockage or leakage;
*   be **accessible** for clearing blockages and discharges to the foul-drainage system.

🖛 *The system is made up of appliances, appliance traps, horizontal discharge pipes – ventilated where necessary – and vertical discharge stacks (ventilated).*

## Traps

A trap relies on the water seal for its effectiveness – and water moving through the system could "pull" the seal.

🖛 *Ineffective water seals can be avoided by choosing suitable trap sizes and seal depths, suitable discharge pipe sizes, gradients and lengths and ventilation.*

Every appliance discharging to the system should be fitted with a water-sealed trap (⇨ Table 4.7–1) which should retain a seal of at least 25mm under both working conditions and test conditions.

**Table 4.7–1:** *Minimum trap sizes and seal depths*

| Appliance | Diameter of trap (mm) | Depth of seal (mm) |
|---|---|---|
| washbasin bidet | 32 | 75 |
| sink* bath* shower* food waste disposal unit urinal bowl | 40 | 75 |
| wc pan | (siphonic only) 75 | 50 |

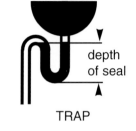

TRAP

* Where these appliances are installed on a ground floor and discharged to a gully, the depth of seal may be reduced to not less than 38mm.

## Discharge pipes (horizontal)

The common minimum and maximum pipe lengths, sizes and slopes (⇨ Table 4.7–1) will usually be sufficient to protect the water seal in the traps, but if they are not then the pipe will need ventilating.

---

### 4.7–1: Discharge pipes

*Layout*: appliances will usually discharge through a discharge pipe into a discharge stack (⇨ Diagram 4.7–1). Discharge pipe connections into a discharge stack should therefore be offset to avoid cross-flow. No discharge pipe should connect into a stack at a height of less than 450mm above the invert of the drain.

*Diagram 4.7–1:* **Branch connections to discharge stacks**

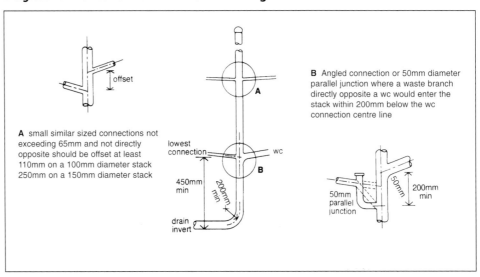

**A** small similar sized connections not exceeding 65mm and not directly opposite should be offset at least 110mm on a 100mm diameter stack 250mm on a 150mm diameter stack

**B** Angled connection or 50mm diameter parallel junction where a waste branch directly opposite a wc would enter the stack within 200mm below the wc connection centre line

*Ground-floor appliances*: Single appliances on the ground floor may discharge directly to the drain, instead of to a discharge stack. If the appliance is a closet, the drop to the drain should be no more than 1.5m (⇨ Diagram 4.7–2).

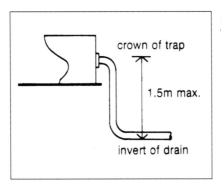

*Diagram 4.7–2:* **Direct connection of a ground floor WC to a drain**

If the appliance carries only waste water, the pipe can discharge to a gully but only between the grating or sealing plate and the top water level of the seal.

*Sizes of discharge pipes:* Unvented pipes serving a single appliance should have maximum diameters, slopes and lengths (⇨ Diagram 4.7–3).

**Diagram 4.7–3: Discharge pipes – unvented single appliances**

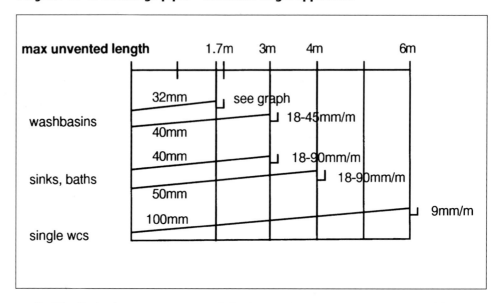

🕮 *The limitations on an unvented discharge pipe sometimes present problems and these will need to be overcome before proceeding further.*

If an unvented pipe serves more than one appliance, **except a WC**, the diameter should be at least 50mm, the slope between 18–45mm per 1m and the maximum length (without bends) 4m. If one of the appliances is a WC, the diameter should be at least 100mm, the slope between 9–90mm per 1m and the maximum length 15m.

*Bends in discharge pipes:* bends should be avoided, otherwise they should have as large a radius as possible. It is recommended that bends in discharge pipes with a diameter up to 65mm should have a radius of at least 75mm (measured on the centre line). Junctions on branch pipes should be made at 45 degrees, or with a sweep of 25mm radius. Connections of branch pipes of 75mm diameter or more to discharge stacks should be made at 45 degrees or with a sweep of 50mm.

## Discharge stacks (vertical)

The "wet" part of a discharge stack – that is, the part below the highest branch pipe connection – should have at least a minimum diameter. It should not reduce in the direction of flow and offsets should be avoided, but where this arrangement is not possible, no discharge pipe connection should be nearer the offset than 750mm.

---

### 4.7–2: Discharge stacks (vertical)

*Diameter:* the diameter of the "dry" part of a discharge stack – the part above the highest branch pipe connection – in a one- or two-storey house may reduce in the direction of the ventilation terminal but should be at least 75mm (⇨ Table 4.7–2)

Discharge stacks should be ventilated and discharge directly to the below-ground drainage with a bend which should have as large a radius as possible – at least 200mm (⇨ 4.1).

**Table 4.7–2: *Minimum diameters for discharge stacks***

| Stack size (mm) | Max capacity (litres/sec) |
|---|---|
| 50* | 1.2 |
| 65* | 2.1 |
| 75† | 3.4 |
| 90 | 5.3 |
| 100 | 7.2 |

Note

*No wcs      †Not more than one siphonic WC with 75mm outlet

## Ventilation

When the length and slope of the discharge pipe are greater than the minimum (⇨ Diagram 4.7–3), the pipe should be ventilated with a branch ventilation pipe to external air or to a discharge stack.

### 4.7–3: Ventilation of discharge pipes and discharge stacks

*Discharge pipes:* branch ventilation pipes to the outside air should finish at least 900mm above any opening into the building nearer than 3m. Branch ventilation pipes to a discharge stack should be connected to the stack above the "spillover" level of the highest appliance served and to the discharge pipe within 300mm of the appliance trap (⇨ Diagram 4.7–4).

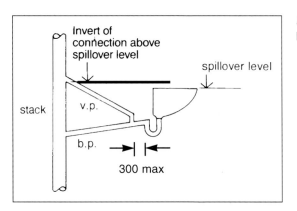

***Diagram 4.7–4: Discharge pipes – ventilation***

Where there are branch ventilation pipes to discharge pipes that serve only one appliance the branch pipes should have a diameter of at least 25mm. Branch ventilation pipes to discharge pipes serving more than one appliance and branch pipes longer than 15m or with more than five bends should have a diameter of at least 32mm.

*Ventilation of discharge stacks*: discharge stacks should be open to the outside air. The diameter above any discharge pipe connection can be reduced to 75mm. The opening should be at least 900mm above any opening into the building nearer than 3m and finished with a cage or other perforated cover which does not restrict the flow of air. The position of the ventilation outlet should be sited with care (⇨ Diagram 4.7–5).

***Diagram 4.7–5*: Termination of ventilation stacks**

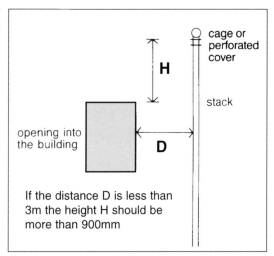

**Blockages**

Although the design and ventilation of pipework reduces the risk of blockages, there is still a necessity to provide for their clearance.

**4.7–4: Traps and clearance of blockages**

Pipework designs should incorporate traps and rodding points in pipework.

*Traps*: if a trap forms a part of an appliance, the appliance (unless it is a WC) should be removable for cleaning. If the trap does *not* form part of the appliance it should be fitted directly after the appliance and be removable or be fitted with a cleaning eye.

*Rodding points*: should be provided to give access to any lengths of pipe which cannot be reached by removing appliances or traps or from any other part of the system. It may be convenient to position these points at bends and junctions so that pipes can be rodded in two directions. All pipes should be reasonably accessible for repair.

## Materials and workmanship

A variety of materials (⇨ Table 4.7–3) are used in sanitary pipework. Different metals should be separated by non-metallic material to prevent electrolytic corrosion.

**Table 4.7–3:** *Materials for sanitary pipework*

| Material | British Standard |
|---|---|
| Pipes | |
| cast iron | BS 416, BS 6087 |
| copper | BS 864, BS 2871 |
| galvanised steel | BS 3868 |
| uPVC | BS 4514 |
| polypropylene | BS 5254 |
| plastics | BS 5255 |
|     ABS | |
|     MUPVC | |
|     polyethylene | |
|     polypropylene | |
| Traps | |
|     copper | BS 1184 |
|     plastics | BS 3943 |

Note
Some of these materials may not be suitable for conveying trade effluent.

> 📖 *Given the wide variety of materials and techniques used in sanitary pipework, you should follow the manufacturer's instructions exactly.*

## Testing

The assembled pipes, fittings and joints should be able to withstand testing for air-tightness. This will be an air- or smoke-test of positive pressure of at least 38mm water gauge for at least three minutes. During this time, every trap should maintain a water seal of at least 25mm. A smoke-test is not recommended for uPVC pipework.

> 📖 *Airtightness is not a good test. It does not take suction into account and it can be difficult to measure the depth of a water seal.*

### Alternative approach

The regulations regarding sanitary pipework can also be met by following the relevant recommendations of BS 5572. Clauses 3, 4 and 7 to 12 are relevant.

## 4.7.2  Rainwater collection (above ground)

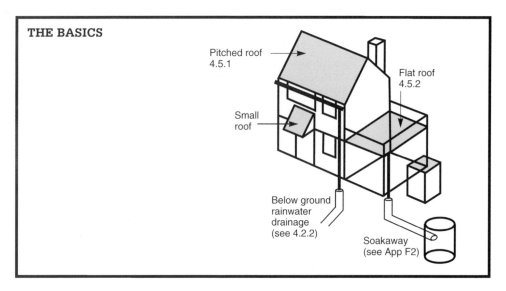

As the above heading states, this section is about rainwater drainage above ground. Drainage and collection of below-ground rainwater was discussed earlier (⇨ 4.2.2). Any rainwater collection system must be adequate to carry rainwater from the roof of a building to the below-ground drainage system.

*CHECKLIST*
- ☐  Gutters and downpipes
- ☐  Discharge to below-ground systems
- ☐  Materials and workmanship
- ☐  Testing

## Requirements

The Building Regulations do not require a rainwater system to be provided, only to be adequate if it is provided. However, where plans are deposited in accordance with the regulations, Section 21(1) of the Building Act 1984 gives the local authority power to reject the plans unless they show that satisfactory provision will be made for the conveyance of rainwater from roofs.

> *The rainfall on areas of 6m² or less – such as small roofs and balconies – need only be collected if they receive a flow from a rainwater pipe or from a paved, or other, hard surface.*

### *Meeting the requirements*
The rainwater collection system should:
- have the **capacity** to carry the **flow** to the drainage-system below ground;
- minimise the risk of **blockage** or **leakage** and be accessible for clearing blockages and discharges to the rainwater drainage system.

**Capacity**   The capacity depends on the sizes of the gutters and pipes.

**Flow**   The flow depends on the area to be drained and the intensity of the rainfall. For example, the rainfall intensity assumed for the design of gutters and rainwater pipes in the UK is 75mm an hour. Gutters should be laid so that any overflow caused by rainfall above the normal, or by obstructions or blockages, will not enter the building.

## Gutters and downpipes

Gutters and downpipes should have a capacity large enough to carry the expected flow at any point. There are maximums and minimum for the largest effective roof area and flow capacities for some common gutter and outlet sizes (⇨ Table 4.7–4).

**Table 4.7–4:** *Effective area of roof*

| Type of surface | | Effective design area (m²) |
|---|---|---|
| 1 | flat roof | plan area of relevant portion |
| 2 | pitched roof at 30° | plan area of portion x 1.15 |
| | pitched roof at 45° | plan area of portion x 1.40 |
| | pitched roof at 60° | plan area of portion x 2.00 |
| 3 | pitched roof over 70° or any wall | elevational area x 0.5 |

### Gutters

The flow into the gutter depends not only on the plan area of the surface being drained but also its pitch. For design purposes, you need to convert some common pitches into an "effective" area (⇨ Table 4.7–5).

**Table 4.7–5:** *Gutter sizes and outlet sizes*

| Max effective roof area (m²) | Gutter size (mm dia) | Outlet size (mm dia) | Flow capacity (litres/sec) |
|---|---|---|---|
| 6.0 | – | – | – |
| 18.0 | 75 | 50 | 0.38 |
| 37.0 | 100 | 63 | 0.78 |
| 53.0 | 115 | 63 | 1.11 |
| 65.0 | 125 | 75 | 1.37 |
| 103.0 | 150 | 89 | 2.16 |

Notes

1 The table assumes that gutter has only one outlet; that it is positioned at one end and that the length of the gutter is not greater than 50 times the water depth. Where the outlet is not at one end, the gutter should be sized for larger of the effective areas draining into it. Where there are two end-outlets, the distance between them may be up to 100 times the water depth.

2 The table assumes that the gutter is laid level and is half-round in section and that the outlet is "square-edged". If a gutter is laid to fall – when the fall should be the outlet – or has a section which gives it a larger capacity than a half-round gutter, or if the outlets are round-edged, the flow capacity will increase. It may be possible, therefore, to increase the effective area which may drained, or to reduce the sizes of the gutter and the downpipe.

### Rainwater pipes (downpipes)

These should have at least the area of the gutter outlet to which they are connected (⇨ Table 4.7–5). A pipe which serves more than one gutter should have at least the combined area of the outlets which it serves.

## Discharge to below-ground systems

The rainwater must eventually discharge into the drainage system or to a soakaway or an open outfall (⇨ Appendix F).

---

### 4.7–5: Connections to below-ground drainage

A rainwater pipe may discharge:

— into **another gutter** or over another drained surface, if it can take the additional flow;

— over a **paved surface**, if it is drained;

— **directly** into the below-ground drainage system.

If the below-ground drainage is connected to a soakway or a rainwater only disposal system, you can discharge the rainwater either directly into it or over a gully (with or without a trap). However, if the drainage is connected to a combined foul water and rainwater disposal system, you must discharge the rainwater over a trapped gully (⇨ 4.2.2).

---

## Materials and workmanship

Materials used should be of adequate strength and gutter joints should stay watertight. Plastics materials are widely used but, because they expand considerably in hot weather and contract in cold weather, you should choose a gutter pattern that can be firmly supported without restricting its thermal movement and has joints that will accommodate the movement.

## Testing

Pour a bucket of water into each gutter to check that the falls, if any, are to the outlet. It is not usual to test the downpipes if they are outside, but if they are inside – in which case they need joints – they should be filled and examined for leaks.

### *Alternative approach*

The regulations can also be met by following the relevant recommendations of BS 6367:1983. The relevant clauses are in Sections 1 and 2, Section 3 (except Clause 9), Section 4, Section 5 (except Clause 18) and appendices. The code contains additional detailed information about design and construction.

# 4.7.3  Water services

Hot-water and cold-water supplies: for heating controls on heating appliances ⇨ 4.9.

### CHECKLIST

☐  Water byelaws
☐  The Building Act
☐  The Building Regulations
☐  Heat loss
☐  Your own needs

## WATER BYELAWS

### Requirements

A tap must be connected to the drinking water supply pipe (BL 96).

> 📖  *This requirement will not stop you from connecting other taps, such as a garden tap, to the supply pipe.*

The supply must also:

•  prevent waste, undue consumption, misuse and contamination of water (BL various);

•  have suitable provision for water expansion if a non-vented water heater is connected to a supply-pipe (BL 91);

•  be protected from frost (BL 30[32;49]).

> 📖  *The Building Regulations have further requirements. Your responsibility for the pipework begins at the stopcock or meter of the statutory water undertaker, usually near the boundary of the site (⇨ Diagram 4.7–6). The water undertaker is responsible for enforcing the byelaws.*

**Diagram 4.7–6: Water services – summary**

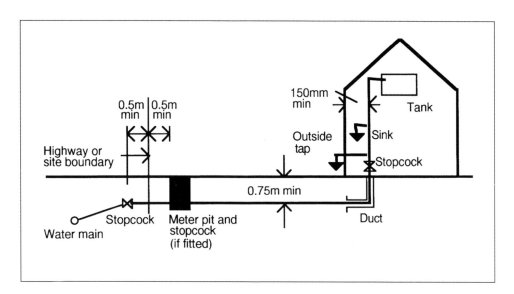

### Meeting the requirements

☞  The Water Supply Byelaws Guide, edited by S F White and G D Mays and published by the Water Research Centre, in association with Ellis Horton Limited, provides detailed guidance for satisfying the byelaws. The UK Water Fittings Byelaws Scheme tests products for compliance.

*⌨ You might have trouble with flushing valves, bidets and extra taps connected to the main.*

**Flushing valves**     These can replace a flushing cistern over a WC. However, they are frowned on by the water authorities but can be accepted by special arrangement.

**Bidets**          If bidets are hand-held or of a spray-type, they will require their own dedicated supplies from the cold-water storage tank and hot-water cylinder, with no water-supplied fittings below the level of the bidet itself. But, dedicated supplies are not necessary if the bidet is fitted with taps with open outlets at least 25mm above the rim.

**Extra taps**     BL 96 does not mean that you are allowed only one tap connected directly to the mains. You can have extra taps, such as a tap used for watering the garden or washing the car, but you will probably have to pay extra for using them. If a tap is fitted with a hose connector it must also be fitted with a double-check valve to prevent backflow (BL 18).

## THE BUILDING ACT

### Requirements

The installation must provide a piped supply of wholesome water sufficient for the domestic purposes of the occupants (BAs. 69).

## THE BUILDING REGULATIONS

### Requirements

The installation must:
*     provide a suitable cold-water supply to any WCs installed as required by the regulations (G1(3), G2);
*     provide suitable hot-water and cold-water supplies to any washbasins, baths, or shower-baths required by the regulations (G1(3), G2);
*     limit the heat loss (L1).

In addition, the hot-water system if it is unvented (that is, not vented to the open air), must:
*     prevent the temperature of the stored water exceeding 100 degrees centigrade;
*     ensure that the hot water discharged from safety devices will be safely taken to where it is visble but will not cause danger;
*     be correctly installed by a competent person. **Limit on application:** the requirement G3 does not apply to a hot-water storage system with a capacity of no more than 15 litres or to a system which only supplies hot water for the purposes of space heating.

*⌨ The building control authority is responsible for enforcing the regulations.*

### *Meeting the requirements*
You can make your own selection of hot-water and cold-water supply systems, pipe

sizes and types of fittings and appliances, but an unvented hot-water system must be installed by a competent person. The requirements will be most conveniently met if that competent person installs a proprietary unit or package. Alternatively, you can choose an individual who is a designated registered operative and is employed by a company included on the list of approved installers published by the British Board of Agrément.

> 📖 A **competent person** means an individual who holds a current registered operative identity card for the installation of unvented hot-water systems issued by one of the following authorities: Construction Industry Training Board (CITB); Institute of Plumbing; or an equivalent body (⇨Useful addresses).

**Unvented hot-water storage systems**     This type of system is directly connected to the water main. It therefore operates under mains pressure which requires that special precautions be taken to prevent excessive pressures when the water is heated. However, with this system you do not need a cold-water storage tank and flow rates of water to all fittings will be considerably increased. This can be of great advantage if headroom for a storage tank is limited, especially in the case of a high-level shower which might otherwise need a pump.

## Heat loss

Hot-water cylinders should be insulated to limit standing heat losses to 1W/litre. For example, a cylinder with a capacity of 120 litres (450mm diameter, 900mm height) should be insulated with at least 35mm of factory-applied polyurethane foam (PU-foam) or its equivalent. The cylinder should comply with BS 5566.

Pipes connected to hot-water storage vessels, including the vent pipe and the primary flow and return, should be insulated with material giving a performance at least equal to material with a thermal conductivity of 0.045 W/mK and a thickness of 15mm. Other hot pipes should also be insulated where they run through an unheated space and use a suitable material which will give a performance at least equal to material with a thermal conductivity of 0.045 W/mK and a thickness equal to the outside diameter of the pipe up to a maximum of 40mm (⇨ Diagram 4.7–7).

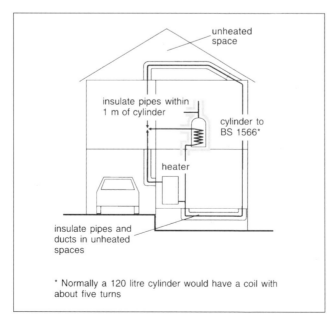

*Diagram 4.7–7:* **Insulation of heating and hot-water pipes and warm-air ducts**

## Your own needs

Compliance with the byelaws and the regulations might not ensure that your chosen installation will meet your needs. For example, storage tanks should be at a height and the pipe sizes large enough to ensure that the rate of supply to appliances will be adequate – particularly showers or bathrooms in a storey directly below the cold-water storage tank. Remember, too, that the insulation requirements in the water byelaws are intended only to protect pipes from being frozen and the insulation requirements in the regulations are only to prevent heat from being wasted. Also remember that no amount of insulation can prevent freezing – it can only delay it. You will find guidance in BS 6700.

☛ If you have any doubts, you should have the work carried out by an experienced contractor, that is a plumber registered by the Institute of Registered Plumbers.

## 4.7.4  Gas installation

For gas burning appliances and heating there are three viewpoints to be considered:
1  Compliance with the Gas Safety Regulations (gas safety).
2  Compliance with the Building Regulations (regarding installation of gas-burning, heat-producing, appliances).
3  Your own needs.

### GAS SAFETY REGULATIONS

### Requirement

The gas installation must be safe in use (GSR).

> 📖 *Your responsibility for the installation begins at the supplier's meter, usually on an outside wall. The supplier is responsible for enforcing the regulations. These cover the pipework and the installation of appliances.*

### Meeting the requirement

☛ *HomeBuilder* cannot give guidance on meeting Gas Safety Regulations. In any event, only a recognised engineer, registered by the Council of Registered Gas Installers (CORGI), may carry out the work.

### THE BUILDING REGULATIONS

### Requirement

Gas burning appliances must be suitably installed.

The building control authority is responsible for enforcing the regulations.

> 📖 *The Building Regulations, unlike the Gas Safety Regulations, only cover the installation of gas appliances.*

*Meeting the requirement*

For guidance on the installation of gas-burning, heat-producing appliances ⇨ 4.9.

## Your own needs

Compliance with the regulations might not ensure that the installation will meet your needs. For example, it is for you to choose whether at all to use gas, which can be from the mains, or bulk or bottled LPG, and what kind of appliances to install.

# 4.8
# Wired services

## INTRODUCTION

In this section the guidance is for:

4.8.1     Electrical installation
4.8.2     Smoke alarms

## 4.8.1  Electrical installation

There are no requirements in the Building Regulations. However, the electrical installation, apart from satisfying your own needs, must comply with the requirements of your regional electricity company (REC), which is responsible for enforcing the Electricity Act. While your responsibility begins on your side of the utility company's main fuse, the latter is concerned that the installation will meet the requirement.

### Requirements

The electrical installation must be safe in operation.

### *Meeting the requirements*

The installation should comply with BS 7671 which has replaced the Institute of Electrical Engineers (⇨ Useful addresses) document known for many years as the IEE Regulations. Although the BS is only a guide to compliance, it usually ensures the acceptance of an electrical contractor's work by an REC under the Electricity Act. Practice among the RECs may vary, but the possibilities include:

*     connection by an accredited electrical contractor or the REC of work carried out by an electrical contractor who has certified compliance with the BS;
*     connection by the REC of any work found satisfactory by an inspector authorised by the REC for a fee;
*     connection by an accredited electrical contractor.


☛ An electrician registered by the National Inspection Council for Electrical Installation Contracting (NICEIC) (⇨ Useful addresses) can give guidance on compliance with the requirements, which is beyond the scope of *HomeBuilder*. However, if you still decide to do the work yourself, at least be sure to have it checked by a registered electrician.

### Your own needs

Compliance with the legislation may not ensure that the installation will meet your needs. For example, you will want to choose the types of appliances and the number and siting of lighting and power points. You should consider using only appliances which carry a recognised safety mark.

## 4.8.2 Smoke alarms

*CHECKLIST*
- ☐ Self-contained alarms
- ☐ Positioning and fixing
- ☐ Large dwelling houses

### Requirements

Smoke alarms must be **self-contained** and suitably **positioned and fixed** (BR B1).

*Meeting the requirements*

### Self-contained alarms

The alarm may be operated at a low voltage via a transformer. The wiring need have no special fire survival properties but the installation should comply with BS 7671.

> 📖 A **self-contained alarm** is one which is permanently wired to a separately fused circuit at the distribution board.

### Positioning and fixing

Alarms, where there are more than one, should be interconnected. This is to ensure that an alarm which picks up smoke in one part of a dwelling will activate alarms which can be heard elsewhere in the dwelling.

### 4.8–1: Smoke alarms – positioning and fixing

Position alarms in circulation areas:
— within 7m (measured horizontally) of doors to kitchens and living rooms;
— within 3m of bedroom doors;
— where they are safely accessible for routine testing and cleaning (not over a stairway or other opening between floors).

Dwellings with more than one storey should have at least one alarm in each storey and a circulation area which is more than 15m long should have more than one alarm.

Do **not** position alarms directly above heaters or air-conditioning outlets, or in bathrooms, showers, cooking areas or any other place where steam, condensation or fumes could give false alarms. Avoid places that get very hot, such as a boiler room, or very cold, such as an unheated porch.

Where possible, **fix** alarms to the ceiling and in a central position. If the alarm cannot be fixed to the ceiling, choose a unit designed for wall mounting and fix it between 150–300mm below the ceiling.

Do **not** fix alarms nearer than 300mm to a ceiling or wall light fitting, or on surfaces which are normally much warmer or colder than the rest of the space.

📖 *Avoid areas where temperature difference might create air currents which move smoke away from the unit.*

## Large dwelling houses

Smoke alarms alone are not considered suitable if the distance from any part of one room to the most distant part of any other room is more than 30m.

A system of detectors and alarms connected to a control and indicating unit should be installed to at least BS 5839 (Pt 1) standard L3.

# 4.9
# Fixtures and fittings

### INTRODUCTION

In this section the guidance is for:

4.9.1     Heat-producing appliances
4.9.2     Cooking appliances
4.9.3     Sanitary appliances
4.9.4     Solid-waste storage (capacity)

## 4.9.1 Heat-producing appliances

### CHECKLIST
- ☐   Solid-fuel burning appliances
- ☐   Gas-burning appliances (including cookers)
- ☐   Oil-burning appliances
- ☐   Heating controls

### Requirements

Heat-producing appliances must:
- have an adequate supply of air for combustion and for the efficient working of the flue-pipe or chimney. **Limit on application:** the requirement J1 applies only to fixed appliances burning solid-fuel, gas or oil (BR J1);
- have adequate provision for the discharge of the products of combustion to the outside air; there is adequate provision for the safe discharge of products of combustion to external air (BR J2);
- be installed, and their flues constructed, so as to reduce to a reasonable level the risk of the building catching fire in consequence of their use (BR J3);
- have controls on the operation of the space heating and hot-water systems. **Limit on application:** the requirement L1 also applies to electrical space heating and water-heating appliances (BR L1).

### Meeting the requirements

Appliances should receive sufficient air for the proper combustion of the fuel and for operation of the flue, be capable of normal operation without the products of combustion being a hazard to health and without causing damage by heat or fire to the fabric of the building.

> *Chimney fires are not considered "normal operation" but the guidance which follows can limit the damage that might result.*

### Existing flues

If you propose to re-use a flue in an existing chimney that is unsatisfactory it may be possible to insert a flexible flue-liner. You should, in any case, consider lining a masonry chimney because the low flue temperatures of some modern appliances can lead to tar-like stains which will be unsightly and difficult to remove and might have an unpleasant smell.

### Chimneys built under former control

The term "former control" refers to the time before the Building Regulations replaced the building byelaws. Chimneys built before 1 February 1966 may not meet requirements J2 and J3. However, they can be accepted if there is no obvious indication that the chimney is unsatisfactory.

### Air supply

The requirements for ventilation to rooms and spaces to promote air quality may already provide a sufficient air supply to heat-producing appliances that draw their air supply from the room or space. However, this should be confirmed and, where the ventilation makes use of an air extract fan, it could actually be counter-productive.

## Types of appliance

An appliance may be open-flued or room-sealed and includes an open fireplace (open fire) (⇨ Diagram 4.9–1).

**Diagram 4.9–1: Types of appliance**

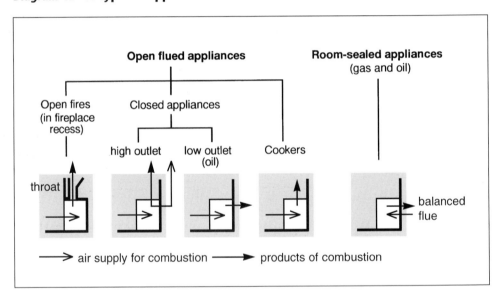

### Open-flued appliance

Open-flued appliances draw most of their air supply from the room or space in which they are installed. They are usually connected to a flue which discharges combustion products to the outside and has its outlets at high level.

An open-flued appliance may be an **open fire** with a chimney (a fireplace recess) or a canopy with a flue-pipe, or a closed stove with doors and a permanent air inlet to maintain the air supply. The air inlet may be fixed or variable.

Some flues might have their flue outlet at a low level – balanced-flue gas-burning and oil-burning appliances and low-level discharge oil-burning appliances – when the outlet will probably need guarding (⇨ Diagram 4.9–2).

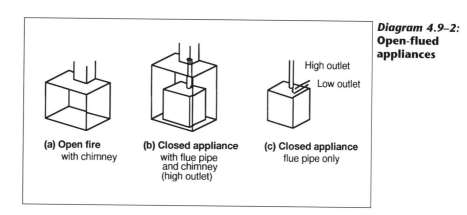

***Diagram 4.9–2:***
***Open-flued***
***appliances***

**(a) Open fire**
with chimney

**(b) Closed appliance**
with flue pipe
and chimney
(high outlet)

**(c) Closed appliance**
flue pipe only

High outlet

Low outlet

Some flues, also, might be fitted with a flue-draught stabiliser, a counter-balanced flap that automatically varies the area of the flue to suit the pull of the flue draught and might even stop it altogether to prevent a down-draught.

### Solid-fuel effect appliances

These are open-flued gas-burning appliances which simulate the burning of coal or wood with a live flame.

### Room-sealed appliances

These balanced-flue appliances draw their air supply from the outside and discharge the combustion products back to the outside at the same level, usually a low level when the inlet and the outlet will probably need guarding. Room-sealed appliances may burn gas or oil but not solid fuel.

## Types of flue

Some of the types of flue (⇨ Diagram 4.9–3) available are discussed in this section.

> 📖 A **flue** is the space enclosed by a flue pipe or a chimney.

***Diagram 4.9–3: Types of flue***

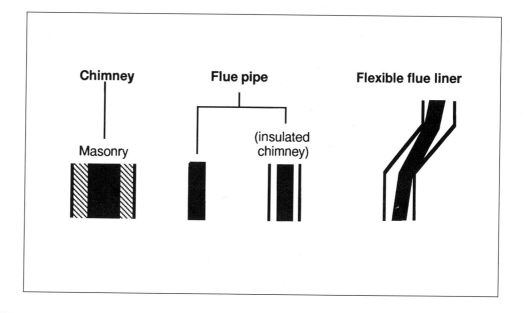

Chimney

Flue pipe

Flexible flue liner

Masonry

(insulated
chimney)

### Masonry chimneys

These may need to be lined, whether they are made of brickwork or blockwork.

### Insulated flue-pipes

These factory-made chimneys should be installed only in accordance with the manu-facturer's instructions.

> *Because this product is accepted as being a chimney it may be carried through a roof space, where the flue-pipe would not be accepted. If you intend to use an insulated chimney with a wood-burning stove you should be sure to tell the supplier.*

### Flexible flue-liners

These circular metal tubes can be dropped down from the top of an existing masonry chimney to line the flue. Liners are needed to protect the flue from the condensation which is likely to occur as a result of the lower temperature of the flue gases from increasingly efficient modern appliances and not simply when the existing flue is in poor condition.

## Summary of provisions

The provisions that will meet the regulations depend mainly on whether the appliance burns solid fuel, gas or oil. For this reason they are described according to the fuel. However, the guidance is very detailed; read the following summary before going into the provisions therefore.

### Supply of air

Appliances must have a supply of air which is sufficient to ensure complete combustion of the fuel and the efficient discharge of the products of combustion. This supply may be taken from any of three sources.

1   From the room or space containing the appliance, if it has a sufficient supply from the open air.
2   From an adjoining room or space, if it has a sufficient and accessible supply from the open air.
3   Directly from the open air (a room-sealed balanced-flue appliance).

If an air extract fan is fitted in a building containing heat-producing appliances – unless they are room-sealed – the supply of air for combustion and the discharge of the products of combustion must be sufficient, whether or not the fan is running. A fan will not affect a balanced-flue appliance because it draws its air supply from the outside.

**Gas-burning appliances**      In a confined space, such as a cupboard, gas-burning appliances also need – in addition to the air for combustion – permanent ventilation. This ventilation is needed to prevent an unacceptable rise in temperature – as described in the Gas Safety (Installation and Use) Regulations.

### Discharge of combustion products

The flue must be of sufficient area, and discharge to external air unless the appliance, such as a cooker, is designed to operate without a flue.

It should be possible to inspect and clean flues so that, **either**:

- the appliance is capable of being removed; **or**
- access openings are provided – which must have rigid, non-combustible and gastight doors or covers.

There must be no other openings in a flue, except to external air. No flue should open into more than one room or space except for the purpose of inspection or access but one flue may serve more than one appliance in the same room.

The **flue-pipes** and **chimneys** should be suitably sited and constructed.

The **flue outlets** should be sited to allow the safe dispersal of combustion products.

### Protection of the building from fire

The flue-pipes and chimneys should be suitably sited and constructed. Ensure that materials for **hearths** and **walls** placed near an appliance, chimney or flue-pipe are non-combustible.

> *This is usually the choice for new work.*

However, appliances, chimneys and flue-pipes can be placed near combustible materials if they are a sufficient distance away and shielded.

> *This is usually the choice for alterations or retro-fitting.*

## Solid-fuel burning appliances

☛ These specifications give guidance only for appliances with a rated output of up to 45kw.

### CHECKLIST
- ☐ Supply of combustion air
- ☐ Discharge of combustion products
- ☐ Protection from fire

---

### 4.9–1: Solid-fuel burning appliances – supply of combustion air

---

*Open-flued appliances*: the space containing the appliance should have at least the following ventilation:

for **open fires** – permanent ventilation with an area that is half that of the throat opening (the throat is the entry to the flue from the combustion space);

for **other appliances** – without a flue-draught stabliser, the requirement is for 550m² of permanent ventilation for each kW of rated output above 5kW.

With a flue-draught stabiliser, the requirement is for 550m² of permanent ventilation for each kW of rated output above 5kW.

### 4.9–2: Solid-fuel burning appliances – discharge of combustion products

Flues in flue-pipes should have an area at least equal to the area of the appliance outlet.

In chimneys the flues should have an area at least equal to the area of the appliance outlet and a given area (⇨ Table 4.9–1) if it is more.

**Table 4.9–1:** *Sizes of flues*

| Installation | Minimum flue-size (mm) | |
| | Round (diameter)[1] | Square (side)[2] |
| --- | --- | --- |
| Fireplace recesses | | |
| – up to 500 x 550mm | 200 | 177 |
| – above 500 x 550mm | 15% of the area of the recess opening | |
| Closed appliances burning bituminous coal | | |
| – up to 20kW rated output | 150 | 133 |
| – burning other fuels, rated output: | | |
| up to 20kW | 125 | 111 |
| 20-20kW | 150 | 133 |
| 30-45kW | 175 | 142 |

Notes
[1] If the flue has an offset: increase the diameter by 25mm.
[2] If the flue has an offset: increase each side of the square by 25mm.

Flues should be vertical, wherever possible. Where an offset is necessary, the flue dimension should be increased by 25mm. Where a bend is necessary, it should make an angle of no more than 30 degrees away from the vertical. Horizontal flues should be avoided, except in the case of a back outlet no longer than 150mm from a closed appliance.

*Flue outlets*: outlets should be above the roof and outside given areas (⇨ Diagram 4.9–3).

*Flue-pipes*: may be used to connect an appliance to a chimney but must not pass through a roof space (use a masonry or factory-made insulated chimney instead).

Flue-pipes may be of cast iron to BS 41: 1973 (1981); mild steel (wall thickness of at least 3mm); stainless steel (wall thickness of at least 1mm) to BS 1449: Part 2: 1983 (Grade 316 S11, S16, S31 or S33); or vitreous enamelled steel to BS 6999: 1989.

Flue-pipes with spigot and socket joints should be fitted with the sockets uppermost.

*Chimneys*: should be able to withstand a temperature of 1,100 degrees centigrade without any structural change which would impair their stability or performance. They may be either masonry (brickwork or blockwork) or factory-made insulated chimneys. Unless the chimney is directly above the appliance a space should be formed for collecting debris and be accessible for emptying.

*Masonry chimneys*: the wall thickness of a masonry chimney, excluding any liner, should be at least 100mm.

*Brickwork chimneys*: should be lined with **either**:
— clay flue-liners to BS 1181: 1971 (1977) with rebated or socketed joints; **or**
— imperforate clay pipes with socketed joints to BS 65: 1981; **or**
— pipes of high-alumina cement and kiln-burnt or pumice aggregate with rebated and socketed joints (or with steel-joint collars).

The linings should be fitted with the sockets or rebates uppermost and jointed with fireproof mortar. Any space between the liners and the brickwork should be filled with weak mortar or insulating concrete.

*Blockwork chimneys*: should be **either**:
— lined (⇨ Brickwork chimneys, above); **or**
— made from refractory material or kiln-burnt or pumice aggregate.

*Factory-made insulated chimneys*: these chimneys should be tested to meet the relevant recommendations in BS 4543: Part 1: 1990, made to meet the recommendations of Part 2 and installed in accordance with **either**:
— the manufacturer's instructions; **or**
— BS 6461: Part 2: 1984.

## 4.9–3: Solid-fuel burning appliances – protection from fire

Protection of the building from fire will involve checking the flues. No combustible material should be nearer to a flue-pipe than a given distance (⇨ Diagram 4.9–4).

*Masonry chimneys*: no combustible material should be nearer to a flue than 200mm and no nearer to the outer surface of a chimney or fireplace recess than 40mm, unless the material is a floorboard, skirting, dado or a picturerail, mantel shelf or architrave. No metal fixing in contact with combustible material should be nearer to a flue than 50mm.

*Hearths*: should be constructed of solid, non-combustible material at least 125mm thick, including the thickness of any solid, non-combustible material below the hearth, and have at least minimum dimensions (⇨ Diagram 4.9–5).

No combustible material should be placed under a hearth unless it is either to support the edges of the hearth or if there is an air space of at least 50mm between the material and the underside of the hearth, or there is a distance of at least 250mm between the material and the top of the hearth (⇨ Diagram 4.9–6). No appliance should be placed on a hearth nearer to the edges than given distances (⇨ Diagram 4.9–7).

*Walls*: using non-combustible material, **fireplace recesses** should be constructed with at least minimum dimensions (⇨ Diagram 4.9–8).

**Diagram 4.9–4: Solid-fuel appliances – separating flue-pipe from combustible material in wall**

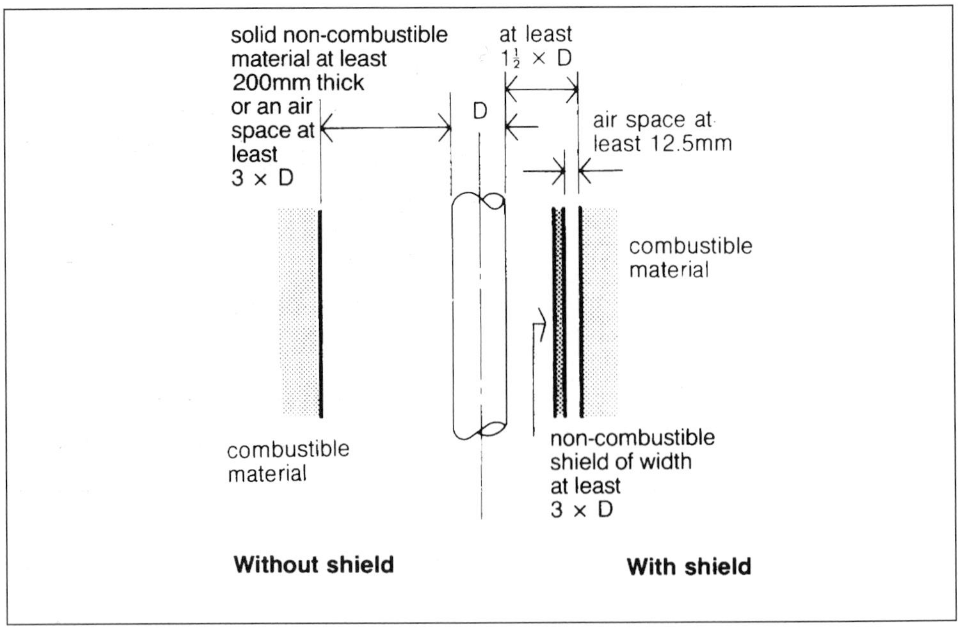

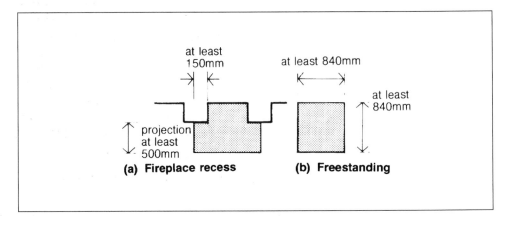

Without shield                                    With shield

**Diagram 4.9–5: Solid-fuel appliances – hearth sizes**

(a) Fireplace recess                  (b) Freestanding

Walls which do not form part of a fireplace recess, but are closer to a **hearth** than 150mm, should be constructed to specification (⇨ Diagram 4.9–9).

Walls near **appliances** should be constructed to specification (⇨ Diagram 4.9–10).

No **factory-made insulated chimney** should be nearer combustible material than a distance $x$ or pass through a cupboard, storage space or roof space, unless it is surrounded by a non-combustible guard farther from the other wall of the chimney than the distance $x$. The distance $x$ is to be found by test in accordance with BS 4543: Part 1: 1976.

*Diagram 4.9–6:* **Solid-fuel appliances – combustible material under hearth**

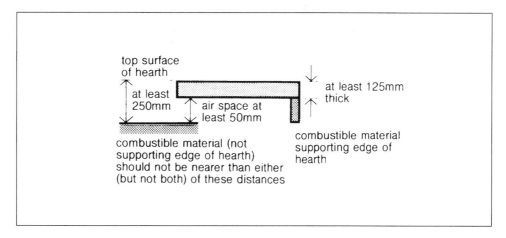

*Diagram 4.9–7:* **Solid-fuel appliances – fireplace recesses**

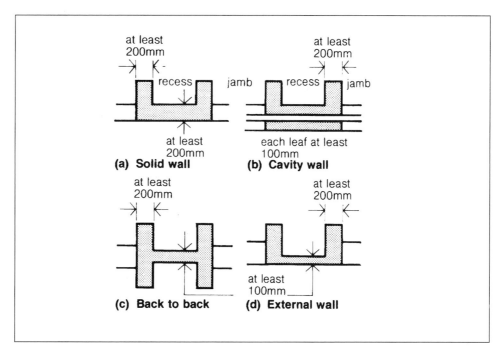

*Diagram 4.9–8:* **Solid-fuel appliances – walls next to hearth**

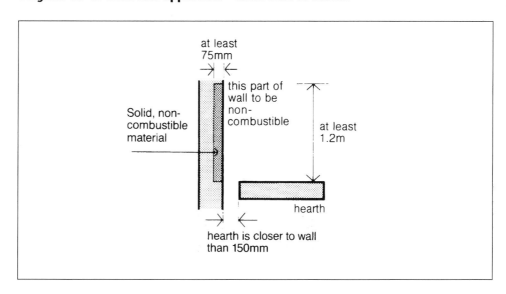

**Diagram 4.9–9: Solid-fuel appliances – placing appliance on constructional hearth**

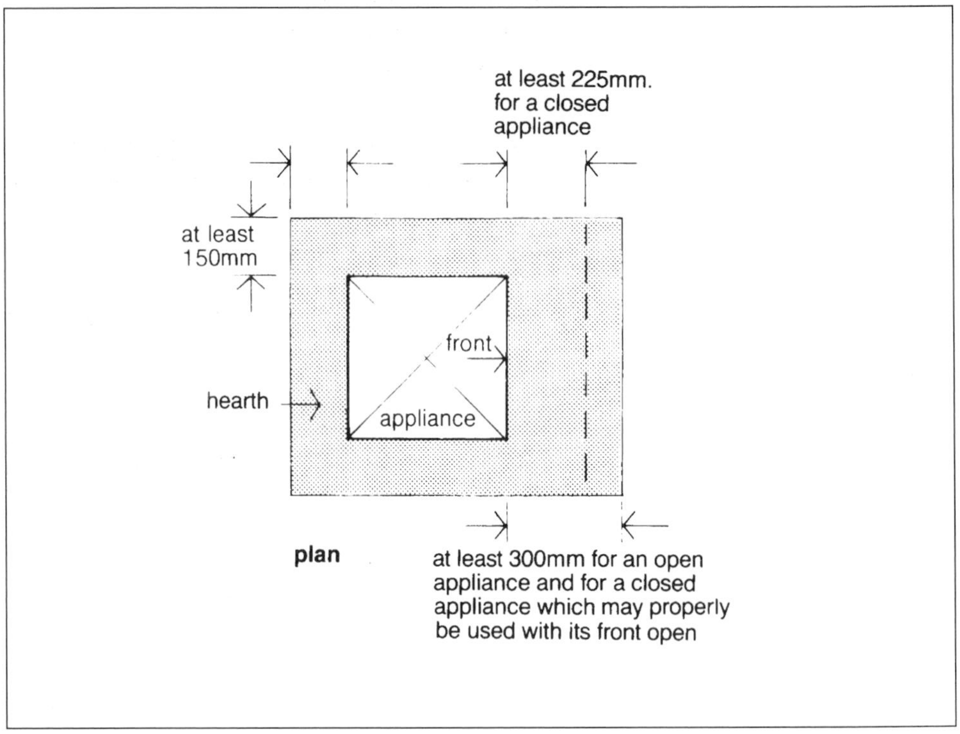

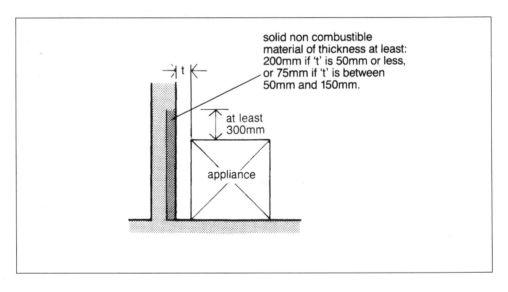

**Diagram 4.9–10: Solid-fuel appliances – separating appliance from combustible material in walls**

### Alternative approach

For solid-fuel appliances the regulations can also be met by following the relevant recommendations of BS 8303: 1986.

## Gas-burning appliances (including cookers)

☛ These specifications apply only to individually flued, non-fan assisted appliances with a rated input of up to 60kW.

A room-sealed appliance needs no air supply from the room or space containing it.

*CHECKLIST*
- ☐  Supply of combustion air
- ☐  Discharge of combustion products
- ☐  Protection from fire

Appliances in baths or shower-rooms and garages must be room-sealed. If the appliance has not been tested, follow the relevant recommendations of BS 5871: Part 1: 1991, Part 2: 1991 or Part 3: 1991.

## 4.9–4: Gas-burning appliances – supply of combustion air

*Open-flued appliances*: the space containing the appliance should have at least the following ventilation:

for **cookers** – either an opening window or some other means of introducing an air supply. If the volume of the space is less than 10cm there should be 5,000mm² of permanent ventilation;

for **bathrooms or shower-rooms and garages** – none; appliances in these spaces must be room-sealed balanced-flue appliances installed as regulated by the Gas Safety (Installation and Use) Regulations;

for **room-sealed appliances** – none; these appliances draw their air supply from outside;

for **other appliances** – these are rated at 450mm² of permanent ventilation, for each kW of appliance input rating above 7kW.

## 4.9–5: Gas-burning appliances – discharge of combustion products

*Flues*: other than for balanced-flue or solid-fuel effect appliances, flues for gas fires should have an area of at least 12,000mm² if the flue is round – and 16,500mm², with a least dimension of 90mm, if the flue is rectangular.

For any other appliance, flues should have an area at least equal to the area of the appliance outlet and should be vertical wherever possible. Where a bend is necessary it should make an angle of no more than 450 degrees away from the vertical. Horizontal flues should be avoided, except in the case of a back outlet from the appliance, and then it should be no longer than 150mm

*Flue outlets*: outlets from **room-sealed gas appliances** (balanced-flue appliances) should be:
- — sited at least 300mm from every opening into the building, partly or wholly above the outlet;
- — fitted with a terminal;

— guarded if they could come into contact with people or be damaged; and

— designed to prevent the entry of material which could obstruct the flue.

Outlets from **all other gas appliances** should be:

— sited at roof level so that air may pass across them at all times;

— at least 600mm from any opening into the building; and

— (except in the case of a gas fire) fitted with a flue terminal if any dimension across the axis of the pipe is less than 175mm.

*Flue-pipes*: may be **either**:

— sheet metal to BS 715: 1986; **or**

— any material listed under solid-fuel appliances.

Flue-pipes with spigot and socket joints should be fitted with the sockets uppermost.

*Masonry chimneys*: the wall thickness of masonry chimneys, excluding any liner, should be at least 25mm.

*Chimneys*: may be **either**:

— masonry (brickwork or blockwork); **or**

— factory-made insulated chimneys.

Unless the chimney is either lined or constructed of flue blocks, a space should be formed for collecting debris and be accessible for emptying. The space should have a volume of at least $0.012m^3$ and a depth of at least 250mm below the connection between the appliance and the chimney.

*Brickwork chimneys*: should be lined with **either**:

— clay flue-liners to BS 1181: 971(1977) with rebated or socketed joints;

— imperforate clay pipes to BS 65: 1981; **or**

— any material described in TS 2.

*Blockwork chimneys*: should be either lined or made of flue blocks to BS 1289: Part 1: 1986 and Part 2: 1989.

*Factory-made insulated chimneys*: these follow the requirements for solid-fuel-burning appliances and discharge of combustion products, except that the chimney should be made to meet the relevant recommendations in BS 4543: Part 3: 1990.

*Although the regulations do not require it, you should also site the flue outlet at least 600mm from the site boundary.*

## Protection from fire

Protecting the building from fire ⇨ TS 4.9–6.

---

### 4.9–6: Gas-burning appliances – protection from fire

*Flue-pipes*: no combustible material should be nearer to a flue-pipe than 25mm and where the flue-pipe passes through a wall, floor or roof it should be separated by a non-combustible pipe sleeve enclosing an air space of at least 25mm. If the pipe is double walled the 25mm may be measured from the outside of the inner pipe.

*Hearths*: other than for a **solid-fuel effect gas appliance**, you must provide a hearth, unless, **either**:
— the flame or incandescent material in the appliance is at least 225mm above the floor; **or**
— the appliance complies with the relevant parts of BS 5258 or BS 5386.

The hearth below a **back boiler** should be of solid non-combustible material at least either 125mm thick or 25mm thick if placed on non-combustible supports at least 25mm thick. The hearth below an appliance which is not a back boiler should be of solid non-combustible material at least 12mm thick.

The size of the hearth should be specified (⇨ Diagram 4.9–11).

For hearths with **solid-fuel effect gas appliances** you must provide a hearth and it must be constructed in the same way as a hearth for a solid-fuel burning appliance.

*Walls*: other than for a solid-fuel effect gas appliance, unless the appliance meets the relevant recommendations of BS 5258 or BS 5386, it should be separated from combustible material by, **either**:
— a shield of non-combustible material thicker than 25mm; **or**
— an air space of at least 75mm (⇨ Diagram 4.9–12).

If a gas appliance is installed in a confined space with a volume of less than 5m$^3$, permanent ventilation should be provided to the space at high and low level. Each ventilator should have an area of at least 900m$^2$ if the ventilation is drawn from a room or space; half that area if it is drawn from outside air. The purpose of this ventilation is to prevent an unacceptable rise in temperature, as regulated by the Gas Safety (Installation and Use) Regulations.

Walls with solid-fuel effect gas appliances should be set in a fireplace recess with the walls constructed in the same way as the recess for a solid-fuel burning appliance.

### Alternative approach

For gas appliances the regulations can also be met by following the relevant recommendations of the following British Standards codes and specifications for gas-fired appliances: BS 5546: 1979 (hot-water supply); BS 5864: 1980 (ducted air heaters); BS 5871: 1980 (1983) (fires, convectors and back-boilers); BS 6172: 1982 (cookers); and BS 6798: 1987 (hot-water boilers).

*Diagram 4.9–11:* **Gas burning appliances – hearth size**

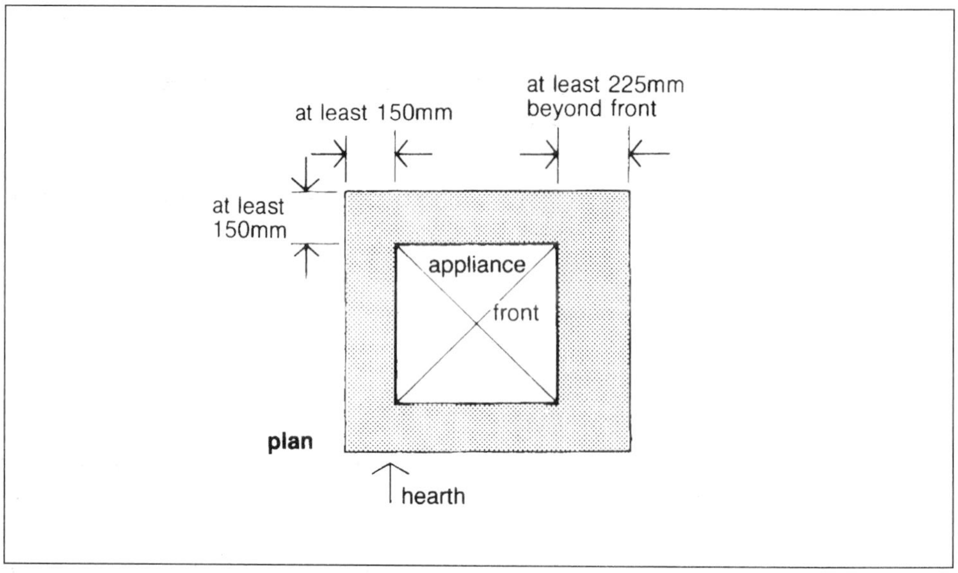

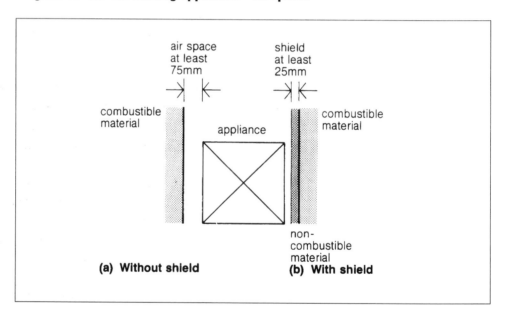

*Diagram 4.9–12:* **Gas burning appliances – air spaces**

## Oil-burning appliances

☞ These specifications give guidance only for appliances with a rated input of up to 45kW.

### CHECKLIST

- ☐ Supply of combustion air
- ☐ Discharge of combustion products
- ☐ Protection from fire

## 4.9-7: Oil-burning appliances – supply of combustion air

*Open-flued appliances*: the space containing the appliance should have at least the following ventilation:

for **room-sealed appliances** – none; these appliances draw their air supply from outside;

for **other appliances** – 550mm$^2$ of permanent ventilation for each kW of appliance input rating above 5kW.

## 4.9-8: Oil-burning appliances – discharge of combustion products

*Flues*: in flue-pipes should have an area at least equal to that of the appliance outlet.

Those flues in chimneys for appliances with a rated output up to 20kW should have an area at least equal to a diameter of 100mm; between 20kW and up to 32kW it should be 125mm, and between 32kW and 45kW, 150mm.

Flues, other than for balanced or low-level flues, should be vertical wherever possible. Where a bend is necessary it should not make an angle of more than 45 degrees from the vertical. Horizontal flues should be avoided, except in the case of the back outlet from an appliance, and then no longer than 150mm.

*Flue outlets*: for **balanced flues** or **low-level flues** should:
— allow the dispersal of the combustion products (and, if a balanced flue, also allow the free intake of air);
— be at least 600mm from any opening into the building;
— be fitted with a terminal guard if people could come into contact with them or if they could be subject to damage;
— designed to prevent the entry of any matter which might obstruct the flue.

Outlets for **pressure-jet appliances** may be anywhere above the roof line.

Outlets for **all other types of appliance** should be above the roof and outside a given area.

*Flue-pipes and chimneys*: if the temperature of the flue gases, under worst operating conditions, is likely to exceed 260 degrees centigrade, the flue-pipes and masonry chimneys should meet the provisions of 4.9–2. If the temperature is unlikely to exceed 260 degrees centigrade, the flue-pipes and masonry chimneys should meet the provisions of 4.9–5.

*Factory-made insulated chimneys*: should meet the provisions for **either** a solid-fuel or gas-burning appliance.

## 4.9–9: Oil-burning appliances – protection from fire

*Hearths*: if the surface of the floor below the appliance is likely to exceed 100 degrees centigrade, a constructional hearth should be provided (⇨ 4.9–2). If the temperature is unlikely to exceed 100 degrees centigrade, no constructional hearth is needed and the appliance may stand on any rigid, imperforate sheet of non-combustible material.

*Walls*: if the surface temperature of the sides and back of an appliance is likely to exceed 100 degrees centigrade, the appliance should be shielded from combustible material by, **either**:
— non-combustible material at least 25mm thick; or
— an air space of at least 75mm (⇨ Diagram 4.9–12).

### *Alternative approach (oil-burning appliances)*
The regulations can also be met by following the relevant recommendations of the British Standard code for oil-fired appliances BS 5410: Part 1: 1977.

## Heating controls

### *CHECKLIST*
☐ Space heating
☐ Hot-water storage

The insulation requirements will be as described for piped services, water, and heat loss (⇨ 4.7–3).

The intention is to control:
• the temperature of the space heating;
• the times when space heating is being used;
• the temperature of the hot-water storage;
• the times when water heating is being used, and to shut down gas-burning and oil-burning boilers when neither is being used.

### *Space heating*
☛ This guidance does not apply to space heating provided by individual solid fuel, gas or electric fires or room heaters that have built-in controls.

The regulations will be met if the following are fitted:
• one or more **zone controls** (thermostats or thermostatic radiator valves), to allow different temperatures to be selected for different parts of a dwelling. In most dwellings, two controls should be fitted but one would be sufficient for a single-storey, open-plan, dwelling;
• a **thermostat** to shut off the supply of space heating when the selected room temperatures are reached;

- a **timing control** (a time clock) to allow one or more different heating periods to be selected;
- a **boiler-control interlock** to ensure that gas-fired and oil-fired boilers will fire only when space heating or hot water is required. If the heating system is controlled only by thermostatic radiator valves it should be fitted with a flow control to stop the boiler from firing, due only to heat losses from the pipework (cycling). **Limit on application:** an interlock is only appropriate for a solid-fuel boiler if it is fan assisted.

### Hot-water storage

The regulations will be met if the **heat exchanger** (the coil) in the storage vessel has sufficient capacity for effective control. Also, the following must be fitted:

- a **thermostat** to shut off the supply of heat to the storage vessel when the storage temperature is reached;
- a **timing control** (a time clock) to allow one or more different water heating periods to be selected.

> *Solid-fuel boilers can simply be switched on and off. The heat exchanger will need sufficient capacity to transfer the heat produced by the boiler when it is idling – the "slumber-load" – to the water in the cylinder to disperse it. The capacity of a coil with five turns should be sufficient. The capacity of the coil in a cylinder which meets the recommendations of BS 5566 will be sufficient.*

If the appliance is a **solid-fuel boiler** and the heat exchanger does not have sufficient capacity for effective control, the regulations will be met if only a **thermostatically controlled valve** is fitted.

> *Programmers are now widely available which allow the heating and hot water supplies to be selected for different times and at different temperatures. The more sophisticated controllers will switch the boiler on and off in advance of the pre-set starting and finishing times, according to the outside temperature, and override the pre-set times to provide background heating in cold weather.*

## 4.9.2  Cooking appliances

The requirements that apply to all fixed heat-producing appliances burning solid fuel, gas or oil also apply to fixed cooking appliances. They concern the supply of air, the discharge of combustion products (unless the appliance is designed to operate without discharging them directly to outside air) and protection of the building from fire.

> *There are requirements for the ventilation of kitchens and other spaces which contain a cooking appliance.*

## 4.9.3  Sanitary appliances

The guidance which follows is for:
  Sanitary conveniences (closets)
  Washbasins
  Bathrooms
  Macerators

*CHECKLIST*
- ☐  Water byelaws
- ☐  Building Regulations

## Water byelaws

The design of a WC must include a flushing cistern which gives a single flush of no more than 7.5 litres. **Limit on application:** the byelaw does not apply to a replacement cistern if the pan is not also replaced (WBL).

## Building Regulations

The following sanitary appliances must be provided:
- adequate sanitary conveniences (water or chemical closets) (BR G1);
- adequate washbasins (BR G1);
- a bathroom with a fixed bath or shower-bath (BR G2).

### Meeting the requirements

**Sanitary conveniences (closets)**     There must be at least one WC in a room provided for the purpose – this includes a bath  or shower-room – separated by a door from any kitchen and any space in which washing-up is done. The closet should have a surface which is smooth, non-absorbent and capable of being easily cleaned.
The WC should discharge through a trap and discharge pipe into a discharge stack or drain (⇨ 4.8). The flushing apparatus should be capable of cleaning the receptacle effectively and no part of the receptacle should be connected to any pipe, other than a flush pipe or discharge pipe.

Where there are water and electrical services, but no suitable connection to a gravity foul-water drainage system, a WC with a macerator may be fitted.

Where there is neither a water supply nor suitable connection to a gravity foul-water drainage system, a chemical or other type of closet may be used.

There are requirements for the ventilation of bathrooms and other spaces which contain a sanitary appliance  (⇨ Appendices).
> *The requirement for a ventilated lobby was taken out of the Building Regulations in 1985.*

The waste should discharge through a trap and discharge pipe into a discharge stack or drain. The flushing apparatus should be capable of cleaning the receptacle effectively and no part of the receptacle should be connected to any pipe, other than a flush pipe or discharge pipe.

**Washbasins**        At least one washbasin should be provided either in the room containing the WC or in a room adjacent to it, with piped hot water and cold water supplies. The hot water supply may be from either a central source or a unit heater. The washbasin should have a surface that is smooth, non-absorbent and capable of being cleaned easily.

The waste should discharge through a grating and trap to a discharge pipe into a discharge stack.

Alternatively, if the washbasin is on the ground floor, it can discharge, **either**:
- into a gully, under the grating but above the water seal; **or**
- direct to a drain.

**Bathrooms**          At least one room in a dwelling should be provided with either a fixed bath or a shower with piped hot-water and cold-water supplies. The hot-water supply may be from either a central source or a unit heater. The bath or shower should discharge through a grating and a trap and may then either discharge as a washbasin or be connected to a macerator.

### Macerators

At installation of the WC, it may be fitted with a macerator and pump. This will be connected by a small-bore discharge pipe to a discharge stack – if there is also access to a WC discharging directly to a gravity system and if the macerator and small-bore drainage system are covered by a current British Board of Agrément Certificate and the conditions of use are in accordance with the certificate.

> *The advantage of a pumped system is that it allows the use of small-bore flexible pipework and this allows appliances to be fitted where a gravity fall to a discharge is neither possible nor practical.*

## 4.9.4  Solid-waste storage (capacity)

For siting the storage, refer to the requirements for site and drainage and solid waste storage (access) described earlier in *HomeBuilder*.

### Requirements

There must be adequate means of storing solid waste (BR H4).

### Meeting the requirements

Each dwelling should have **either** an individual container **or** use of a shared container which is moveable and of sufficient capacity, having regard to the quantity of waste and the frequency of removal.

**Capacity**      An individual waste container (a dustbin) should have a capacity of at least 0.12m³. A shared container should have a capacity of between 0.75m³ and 1m³.

> *These capacities assume a weekly collection and an output of refuse of 0.09m³ (about 90 litres) per dwelling per week. Where the collection is less frequent, larger or more containers will be needed.*

**Design**      Individual and shared containers should have a close-fitting lid. Containers need not be enclosed but, if they are, the enclosure should provide room for filling and emptying a clear space of 150mm between and around the containers and permanent ventilation top and bottom. For shared containers, the height of the enclosure should be at least 2m.

> *In some collection districts, wheeled bins are being introduced. These may need larger enclosures. For example, a container with a capacity (the following*

*dimensions in brackets are for a container with a capacity of 240 litres) of, say, 0.12m³ (120 litres) has a height of 930mm (1,070mm), a width of 480mm (580mm) and a depth of 555mm (740mm). In districts where waste is being collected for recycling, you might wish to consider also increasing the size of the enclosure to include these containers.*

# Appendices

A    **Ground movement and foundations**

B    **Structural stability**

C    **Means of escape**

D    **Energy conservation**

E    **Ventilation**

F    **Drainage disposal**

G    **Loft conversions**

H    **Relevant requirements**

     **Useful addresses**

# Appendix A
# Ground movement and foundations

## INTRODUCTION

In this appendix the guidance is for:

A1 Ground movement
A2 Types of foundations
A3 Designing traditional strip foundations

## A1  Ground movement

### CHECKLIST
- ☐ Swelling and shrinking
- ☐ Frost-heave
- ☐ Other causes

The Building Regulations are concerned only with damage which threatens health and safety and it is rare for damage due to ground movement to be a threat to health – even rarer for it to be an imminent threat to safety – as there are usually warning signs that it may occur. The regulations are not concerned with merely cosmetic damage, although this can have a significant effect on property values.

The main causes of ground movement are **swelling and shrinking** and **frost-heave** and these are discussed below.

☛ While **other causes** are described briefly, it is not possible within the scope of *HomeBuilder* to give detailed guidance. If you are in any doubt, you should consult the building control authority and take professional advice.

### Swelling and shrinking

Swelling and shrinking (volume changes) are the result of changes in the moisture content of the soil. While changes in the moisture content can change the bearing strength of granular soils such as sand (non-cohesive soils), they are unlikely to cause the volume changes which will lead to movement problems. Cohesive soils such as clay can be another matter. Not only will changes in the moisture content change the bearing strength but they will be accompanied by volume changes which can cause movement problems.

A map showing areas where clay subsoils exist – mainly south-east of a line between Exeter, Bristol and Hull – is included in Building Research Establishment Digests 240–242 (three parts): *Low rise buildings on shrinkable clay*.

The moisture content will be less in dry weather, when tree roots take up moisture and the water table is low. The moisture content, naturally, will increase in wet weather, also after tree felling, when the water table is high, and if the house drains are leaking. Seasonal variations usually reach their maximum at depths of between 2–3m, usually below foundation-bearing levels. If there is clay at that depth, the variations will produce movement which will most affect the parts of the building nearest the tree. This can lead to differential settlement, sufficient to cause cosmetic – and even structural – damage.

### Trees

The moisture content below the surface of open ground will not vary greatly, except as a result of flooding and severe drought. However, trees within a distance equal to their height – and some, such as poplar and willow, even farther away – can cause marked seasonal variations in ground moisture content. This also changes the volume of cohesive soils, when the large amounts of water taken up by the roots are not made up by rainfall. Where trees have been felled, the effects will simply be reversed and may still be felt for a decade.

The large volume changes that lead to structural damage are most likely where trees are situated near a building with roots in shrinkable clay. Because these changes will most affect the parts of the building nearest the trees, differential settlement is likely; this can cause not only cosmetic but also structural damage and you should take professional advice. For all but a very low level of risk, the minimum distance between building and tree should be at least half the mature height of the tree, except in the case of high–risk species such as willow, poplar, oak, elm and beech, in that order, when it should be greater than the mature height.

### Concrete strip foundations

The typical depth for concrete strip foundations might be 0.75m but foundations which bear on shrinkable clay in open ground will, if taken to a depth of even 1m, be affected by seasonal clay shrinkage in exceptionally dry summers, with large soil movements possibly leading to structural damage.

## Frost-heave

Frost-heave will occur when the moisture in the ground freezes and expands – the wetter the ground the more it will expand. But while this can affect roads and pavements it is less likely to affect buildings. The depth to which frost can penetrate depends on the severity and duration of the winter period in the area of the site. The depth at which water mains are laid in the area gives a good indication of frost penetration depth: usually between 0.5–0.75m. However, the depth of the foundations will probably be decided by other factors, such as the bearing strength of the ground and, most probably, its susceptibility to swelling and shrinkage movements due to changes in its moisture content.

## Other causes

There are various other causes of ground movement; some are discussed below.

### Landfill sites

These are usually natural or excavated holes in the ground that have been used to take waste material. Sometimes waste is also used to raise low-lying areas. The composition and the amount of waste compaction can make the ground unsuitable for building (⇨ 4.2.1).

### Compressible soils

Soils such as those found in river deposits and peat are compressible soils. Much of their strength is due to the water they contain. This can be squeezed out by the weight of the building which will then settle.

### Landslips

When one layer of ground slides over another, landslips occur. The ground which directly supports the building can slip or slide bodily over ground at some lower level. Slipping is most likely where the layers of ground slope at more than about 30 degrees and are separated by a slip-plane, such as a thin layer of sand or gravel.

### Subsidence

If ground which directly supports the building is no longer supported by ground at a lower level, subsidence occurs. It is likely only where there are underground workings, such as an old coal mine, mineral or salt mine, or some natural weakness such as a swallow hole (a solution cavity much sought after by pot-holers).

## A2  Types of foundations

### CHECKLIST
- ☐ New foundations
- ☐ Raising on existing foundations
- ☐ Extending existing foundations
- ☐ Underpinning existing foundations

The factors which affect the choice of type of foundation include:
- type of construction;
- type of the loading on the ground;
- the bearing strength of the ground; and
- the potential of the ground for swelling, shrinking and frost-heave.

**Diagram A–1: Types of foundations**

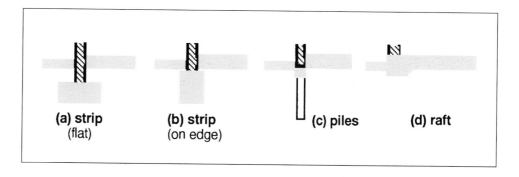

(a) strip (flat)    (b) strip (on edge)    (c) piles    (d) raft

Even when these factors can be foreseen and assessed, the cost of constructing the building so that its stability will never be impaired and cosmetic damage avoided might prove to be unacceptably costly.

Remember that the Building Regulations are concerned only with securing *reasonable* levels of health and safety.

If you cannot adapt your design to accommodate possible movements – perhaps by adopting a flexible form of construction – it is for you to choose whether or not you are prepared to accept some risk of cosmetic damage.

## New foundations

Footings, or **traditional concrete strip foundations** consist of flat strips of concrete, at a suitable depth and of a suitable width, positioned so as to spread loads evenly over ground that is strong enough to bear them and which can be relied upon not to move significantly. The strips support a dwarf wall finishing slightly above ground level to receive a damp-proof course on which the walls can be raised.

For a procedure for designing the traditional foundation ⇨A3.

### Other types of foundations
In some circumstances, other types of foundations have advantages. Some of these are discussed below.

**Vertical strip foundations**     Where the bearing strength of the ground allows you to use a narrow strip it can be laid vertically. This will save brickwork (awkward to lay below ground level) and give a stiffer support (particularly if steel reinforcing bars are dropped in) where there are local weak spots in the ground, or there is a possibility of ground movement.

**Short-bored piles**     This form of foundation is made by drilling a hole in the ground, filling it with concrete poured on-site and capping with a reinforced beam at ground level to replace the normal strip. Short-bored piles are useful where there is a possibility of major ground movement as it greatly reduces the amount of excavation required.

**Reinforced concrete raft**     In this more unusual form of foundation a reinforced concrete raft lays on the surface of the ground. However, this form is expensive and should only be considered where the ground is soft. Never choose it without taking professional advice.

## Raising on existing foundations

Raising the height of a building may not necessarily require an alteration to the foundations as many of them are over-designed. Digging a trial pit will establish the bearing strength of the ground and find the size and depth of the existing foundations, enabling you to calculate the width for the new load. You might find that the existing foundations are adequate.

## Extending existing foundations

Where new foundations are built against old settled foundations – and particularly if the new foundations are also at a different (usually lower) level – the combined effects of settlement and seasonal moisture changes make differential movement likely. Therefore, choose the width of the new foundations to give equal settlement, particularly where a light single storey extension is to be built onto a "heavy" building with two or more storeys. Also, avoid major and abrupt changes of level. You could also consider making a distinct break between the old and new work not only in the foundations but also in any brickwork they support.

## Underpinning existing foundations

Cosmetic damage – such as cracks in masonry not more than 5mm wide – should be made good. Underpinning should not be considered before careful investigation and monitoring has been completed. Even then it should not be partial as this can do more harm than good, by merely reversing the relative movements.

# A3  Designing traditional strip foundations

### CHECKLIST
- ☐  Load
- ☐  Width
- ☐  Projection
- ☐  Thickness
- ☐  Materials

## Supporting the load

When you have chosen a suitable depth for your foundation, next design the concrete strip to support the load. There are four steps involved here.
1  Find the load (L).
2  From the load, find the width (W).
3  From the width, find the projection (P).
4  From the projection, find the thickness (T).

### Step 1: Finding the load—L
Make a trial calculation. Add up the following:
- imposed load of the roof;
- self-weight of the roof;
- imposed-load on floor(s);
- self-weight of floor(s);
- self-weight of the wall itself.

  *For a trial calculation, openings in roofs, floors and walls can be ignored.*

If, for any reason, the foundation width turns out to be critical you can always make a more accurate calculation of the total load.

***Diagram A–2: Strip foundations – summary***

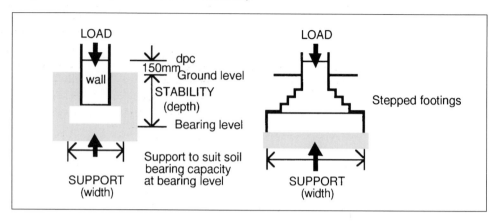

***Diagram A–3: Strip foundations – dimensions***

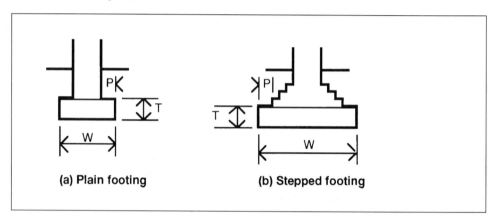

(a) Plain footing          (b) Stepped footing

### *Step 2: Finding the width—W*

Decide which of the types of subsoil exist at the level on which your foundation will bear (⇨ Table A–1). Using the load, L, and the table, find the minimum width of your strip foundation.

> *You might find that the strength of the ground – rock, chalk or firm gravel – will be quite sufficient to bear the load of the wall directly and all that is then needed is a covering of fine concrete to level up the ground for the bricklayer.*

There should be no made ground or wide variation in the type of subsoil in the loaded area. Neither should there be a weaker type of soil at a depth below the bearing level which could impair the stability of the structure. The soil can weaken with depth, particularly where there is a high water table, but the pressure also decreases as the load spreads out. It reduces to about a half at a depth equal to the width of the foundation (and may be only barely appreciable at a depth equal to one-and-a-half times the width).

The more even the pressure on the ground the less the chance of differential settlement so it should be as even as possible. You can arrange this by varying the width of the foundation to suit the load.

> *The more confident you are about the loadbearing strength of the ground, the more you can consider using a more accurate load to calculate a width.*

**Table A-1:** *Minimum width of strip foundations (W)*

| Type of subsoil | Condition of subsoil | Field test applicable | Total load of loadbearing walling not more than (kN/linear metre) | | | | | |
|---|---|---|---|---|---|---|---|---|
| | | | 20 | 30 | 40 | 50 | 60 | 70 |
| | | | **Mimimum width of strip foundation (mm)** | | | | | |
| I<br>Rock | Not inferior to sandstone, limestone or firm chalk | Requires at least a pneumatic or other mechanically-operated pick for excavation | In each case, equal to the width of wall | | | | | |
| II<br>Gravel<br>Sand | Compact<br>Compact | Requires pick for excavation. Wooden peg 50 mm square in cross-section hard to drive beyond 150mm | 250 | 300 | 400 | 500 | 600 | 650 |
| III<br>Clay<br>Sandy Clay | Stiff<br>Stiff | Cannot be moulded with the fingers and requires a pick or pneumatic or other mechanically-operated spade for its removal | 250 | 300 | 400 | 500 | 600 | 650 |
| IV<br>Clay<br>Sandy clay | Firm<br>Firm | Can be moulded by substantial pressure with the fingers and can be excavated with graft or spade | 300 | 350 | 450 | 600 | 750 | 850 |
| V<br>Sand<br>Silty sand<br>Clayey sand | Loose<br>Loose<br>Loose | Can be excavated with a spade. Wooden peg 50mm square in cross-section can be driven easily | 400 | 600 | | | | |
| VI<br>Silt<br>Clay<br>Sandy clay<br>Silty clay | Soft<br>Soft<br>Soft<br>Soft | Fairly easily moulded in the fingers and readily excavated | 450 | 650 | Note<br>In relation to types V, VI, and VII foundation do not fall within the provisions if this section of the total load exceeds 30kN/m | | | |
| VII<br>Silt<br>Clay<br>Sandy clay<br>Silty clay | Very soft<br>Very soft<br>Very soft<br>Very soft | Natural sample in winter conditions exudes between fingers when squeezed in fist | 600 | 850 | | | | |

### Step 3: Finding the projection—P

If the wall is central on the strip the projection P will be half the width W less the thickness of the wall. To avoid the possibility of uplift on one side, the centre line of the load should be kept as near to the centre line of the foundation as possible and always within the middle third (⇨ Diagram A–4) of the width.

**Diagram A–4: Finding the projection – the middle third**

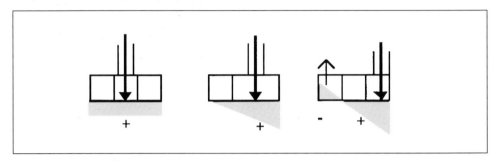

Determine if the foundation is supporting buttresses, piers or chimneys beyond the face of the wall (⇨ Diagram A–5).

**Diagram A–5: Projection of strip foundation**

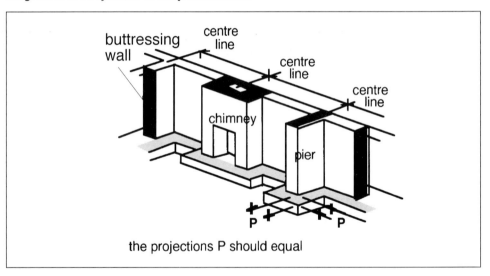

### STEP 4: Finding the thickness—T

Use the projection P to find the minimum thickness T (⇨ Diagram A–5). The thickness should be at least 150mm.

A combination of weak ground and a heavily loaded thin wall can enlarge the projection, and therefore the thickness. You can reduce the projection, and therefore the thickness, by using stepped footings to reduce the projection (⇨ Diagram A–2).

**Stepped foundations**     Stepped foundations should overlap and the height of the step should be no more than the thickness of the strip (⇨ Diagram A–6).

> *It will be convenient to choose the height to suit the masonry courses.*

**Diagram A–6: Stepped strip foundations**

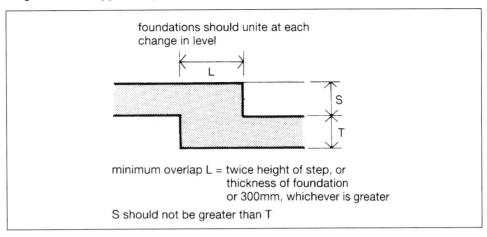

foundations should unite at each
change in level

L

S

T

minimum overlap L = twice height of step, or
thickness of foundation
or 300mm, whichever is greater

S should not be greater than T

## Materials

The concrete mix should be in the proportions of 50kg of cement to not more than 0.1m³ of fine aggregate and 0.2m³ of coarse aggregate or ready-mix concrete Grade ST1 to BS 5328 (Pt 2).

The brickwork should be of frost-resisting bricks or blocks laid in cement/lime mortar 1:1:3 mix.

If the ground is chemically aggressive take the appropriate action (⇨ 4.1.5). If there are significant amounts of sulphates in the ground, use sulphate–resisting cement.

# Appendix B
# Structural stability

### INTRODUCTION

In this appendix the guidance is for:

B1 Conditions: the building
B2 Conditions: the wall

This appendix sets out the conditions which the building and the wall should meet if you want to use the guidance on wall thickness (⇨ 4.3). Minor departures are possible if they can be justified by, **either**:
*      judgment based on experience; **or**
*      calculation, but only for the aspect of the wall which is the reason for the departure and not for the entire wall.
  ▯ *Major departures can only be a strong indication that the Alternative approach should be seriously considered.*

## B1  Conditions: the building

The guidance that follows is for:
    B1.1 Proportions of the building
    B1.2 Floor area enclosed by structural walls (all buildings)
    B1.3 Imposed-loads on the floors, ceilings and roofs (all buildings)

### B1.1 Proportions of the building

The dimensions and proportions of buildings are specified according to their location and other factors which will affect their integrity (⇨ Diagram B–1).

#### Reduced maximum heights

The maximum height H should, in some cases, be reduced depending on the basic wind speed in your part of the country, the location of your proposed building (whether the site slopes and if so how much) and its exposure.
  ▯ *First, use Diagram B–2 to find the basic wind speed for your site. Then, Table B–1 and use the site location and the site exposure to find the height, H.*

### Diagram B–1: Proportions of the building

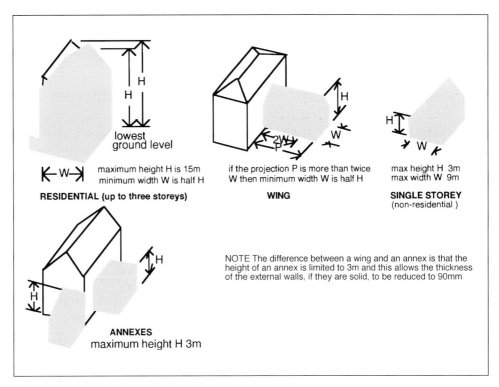

lowest ground level

maximum height H is 15m
minimum width W is half H

**RESIDENTIAL (up to three storeys)**

if the projection P is more than twice W then minimum width W is half H

**WING**

max height H 3m
max width W 9m

**SINGLE STOREY**
(non-residential )

**ANNEXES**
maximum height H 3m

NOTE The difference between a wing and an annex is that the height of an annex is limited to 3m and this allows the thickness of the external walls, if they are solid, to be reduced to 90mm

### Diagram B–2: Basic wind speed

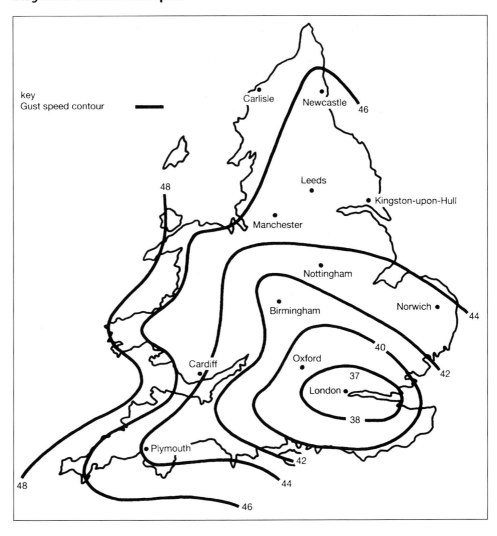

key
Gust speed contour

Carlisle
Newcastle 46
48
Leeds
Kingston-upon-Hull
Manchester
Nottingham
Birmingham
Norwich 44
40
Cardiff
Oxford 37 42
London
38
Plymouth
42
48
44
46

**Table B-1:** *Maximum building heights to which the guidance applies*

Site location: the heights are for a building on a normal or slightly sloping site (use the height in brackets if your building is on a steeply sloping site or hill, cliff and escarpment).

Site exposure:
A  Unprotected sites, open country with no obstructions
B  Open country but with scattered windbreaks
C  Country with many windbreaks, small towns, outskirts of large cities
D  Protected sites, city centres

| Basic wind speed m/s | Maximum height (in metres) Site exposure (and location) | | | |
|---|---|---|---|---|
| | A | B | C | D |
| 36 | 15  (8) | 15  (11) | 15 | 15 |
| 38 | 15  (6) | 15  (9) | 15 | 15 |
| 40 | 15  (4) | 15  (7.5) | 15  (14) | 15 |
| 42 | 15  (3) | 15  (6) | 15  (12) | 15 |
| 44 | 15  (*) | 15  (5) | 15  (10) | 15 |
| 46 | 11  (*) | 15  (4) | 15  (8) | 15 |
| 48 | 9  (*) | 13  (3) | 15  (6.5) | 15  (14) |

Note
(*) shows that the guidance is not applicable

# B1.2 Floor area enclosed by structural walls (all buildings)

The area of a floor enclosed by structural walls (external walls and any internal load-bearing walls) on all four sides should be no more than 70m². The area of a floor enclosed by structural walls on only three sides should be no more than 30m² (⇨ Diagram B–3).

> *These conditions are intended to limit the load placed by a floor on the walls.*

*Diagram B–3:* **Maximum floor area enclosed by structural walls**

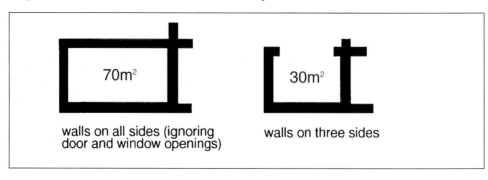

70m²
walls on all sides (ignoring door and window openings)

30m²
walls on three sides

### B1.3 Imposed-loads on floors, ceilings, roofs (all buildings)

The imposed-loads should not be exceeded ($\Rightarrow$ Table B–2).

**Table B-2:** *Imposed-loads*

| Element | Distributed load: |
|---------|-------------------|
| Floors | 2.0 kN/m² for all floor spans |
| Ceilings | 0.25 kN/m² together with a concentrated load of 0.9kN |
| Roof | 1.0 kN/m² imposed loading for roof spans of no more than 12m<br>1.5 kN/m² imposed loading for roof spans of no more than 6m |

# B2  Conditions: the wall

The guidance that follows is for:

| B2.1 | Wall dimensions (height and length) |
|------|--------------------------------------|
| B2.2 | Materials and workmanship |
| B2.3 | Loading on the wall |
| B2.4 | Openings and recesses |
| B2.5 | Overhangs and chases |
| B2.6 | Vertical support for walls |
| B2.7 | Horizontal (lateral) support for walls |
| B2.8 | Vertical restraints for roofs |

### B2.1 Wall dimensions (height and length)

The length of the wall should be no more than 12m between the centre lines of the vertical supports. Determine the length ($\Rightarrow$ Diagram B–4). The height of the wall should be no more than 12m. Determine the height ($\Rightarrow$ Diagram B–5).

*Diagram B–4:* **To determine the length of a wall**

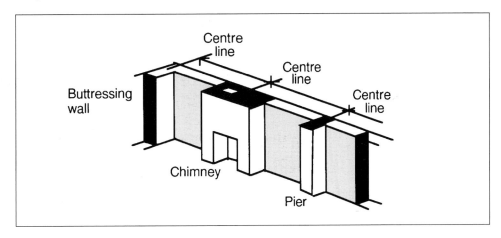

**Diagram B–5: The height of a wall and a storey (measurement)**

Key

**(a) Measuring storey heights**

**A** is the ground storey height if the ground floor is a suspended timber floor or a structurally separate ground floor slab

**A₁** is the ground storey height if the ground floor is a suspended concrete floor bearing on the external wall

**B** is the intermediate storey height

**B₁** is the top storey height for walls which do not include a gable

**C** is the storey height where lateral support is given to the gable at both ceiling level and along the roof slope

**D** is the storey height for walls which include a gable where lateral support is given to the gable along the roof slope

**(b) Measuring wall heights**

**H₁** is the height of a wall that does not include a gable

**H₂** is the height of compartment or separating wall which may extend up to the underside of the roof

**H₃** is the height of a wall (except a compartment or separating wall) which includes a gable

**P** if the parapet height is more than 1.2m the height should be added to H₁

## B2.2 Materials and workmanship

The walls should be properly bonded, solidly put together in suitable mortar and constructed of materials which conform to British Standards (⇨ Table B–3). The bricks and blocks when tested/measured should have compressive strength – at least that shown in Diagram B–6.

## Diagram B–6: Bricks and blocks – strength

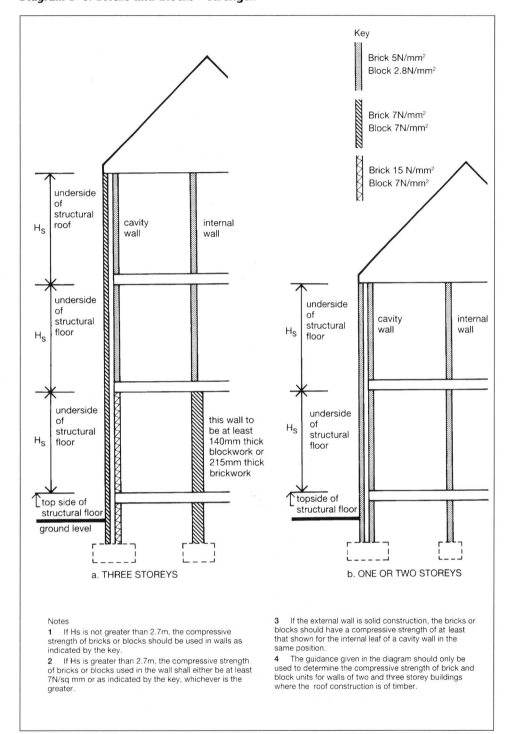

Key

Brick 5N/mm²
Block 2.8N/mm²

Brick 7N/mm²
Block 7N/mm²

Brick 15 N/mm²
Block 7N/mm²

a. THREE STOREYS

b. ONE OR TWO STOREYS

Notes

1    If Hs is not greater than 2.7m, the compressive strength of bricks or blocks should be used in walls as indicated by the key.

2    If Hs is greater than 2.7m, the compressive strength of bricks or blocks used in the wall shall either be at least 7N/sq mm or as indicated by the key, whichever is the greater.

3    If the external wall is solid construction, the bricks or blocks should have a compressive strength of at least that shown for the internal leaf of a cavity wall in the same position.

4    The guidance given in the diagram should only be used to determine the compressive strength of brick and block units for walls of two and three storey buildings where the roof construction is of timber.

**Table B–3:** *Materials*

Bricks and blocks (clay): BS 3921: 1974 or BS 6649: 1985.

Bricks or blocks (concrete): BS 6073: Part 1: 1981

Bricks (calcium silicate): BS 187: 1978 or BS 6649: 1985.

Mortar should be suited to the place where it is to be used and the strength of the masonry units. The proportions will usually be 1 part Portland cement, 1 part lime and 6 parts fine aggregate measured by volume when dry.

*The mortar should be no stronger than necessary. Cement-rich mortars can lead to cracking.*

Wall ties: BS 1243: 1978 or equivalent performance. They should be made of stainless steel or non ferrous material of the wall be severely exposed. For the maximum spacing ⇨ Table 4.3-3

**Table B–4:** *Maximum spacing of cavity wall ties*

| Width of cavity (mm) | Horizontal spacing (mm) | Vertical spacing (mm) | Other comment |
|---|---|---|---|
| 50-75 | 900 | 450 | See notes 1 and 2 |
| 76-100 | 750 | 450 | See notes 1,2 and 3 |

Notes
1. The horizontal and vertical spacing of wall ties may be varied if necessary to suit the construction, provided the number of ties per unit is maintained.
2. Wall ties spaced not more than 300mm apart vertically should be provided within 225mm from the side of all openings with unbonded jambs.
3. Vertical Twist Type ties, or ties of equivalent performance, should be used in cavities wider than 75mm.

## B2.3 Loading on the wall

Some floor and wall loadings and their distribution throughout the building are discussed here.

### Span of the floor

The span should be measured and loads calculated. The span of a floor supported by the wall should be no more than 6m (⇨ Diagram B–7).

> *The loading from the floor may also be limited by the condition restricting the area of floor enclosed by the structural walls (⇨ Diagram B–3).*

*Diagram B–7:* **Floor span (measurement)**

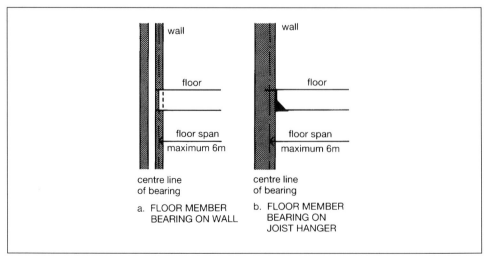

### Vertical loads on the wall

The load should be distributed along the wall. You can assume that the load is distributed if you use a timber floor designed in accordance with the earlier guidance given (⇨ 4.4.2) for suspended floors, a concrete floor cast on-site or a precast concrete floor. The combined dead- and imposed-loads should be no more than 70kN/m at the base of the wall.

For lintel bearings allowance should be made for openings and recesses (support), (⇨ Diagram B–1).

> 📖 *Take into account the guidance given earlier for designing strip foundations to carry loads of no more than 70kN/m and how to calculate the loads (⇨ 4.2.3).*

If the wall carries another wall it should have at least the same thickness.

> 📖 The **thickness** of the wall is measured face-to-face if the wall is a solid wall or a cavity wall with the cavity filled with concrete. If the wall is a cavity wall and the cavity is not filled, the thickness is the sum of the thickness of the two leaves.

### Horizontal (lateral) loads on the wall

There should be no lateral (horizontal/sideways) load on the wall **except** the wind-load and **except** any load due to a difference between the ground level and the ground floor level which is no more than four times the thickness of the wall (⇨ Diagram B–8).

## B2.4 Openings and recesses

The **number and size** of openings and recesses must not impair the stability of the wall (⇨ Diagram B–9).

**Diagram B–8: Differences in ground and floor levels**

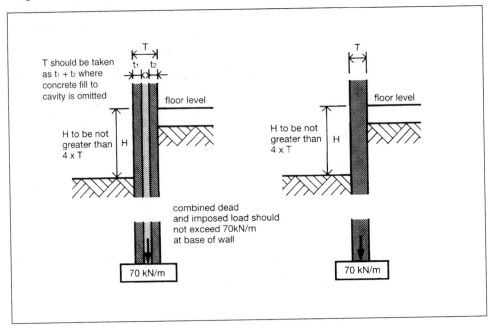

**Diagram B–9: Sizes of openings and recesses**

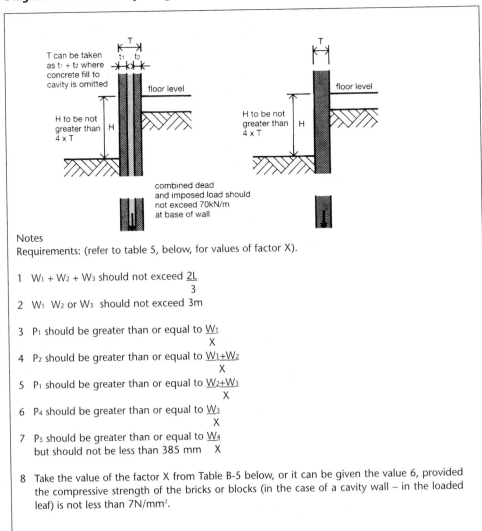

Notes
Requirements: (refer to table 5, below, for values of factor X).

1  $W_1 + W_2 + W_3$ should not exceed $\frac{2L}{3}$

2  $W_1$  $W_2$ or $W_3$  should not exceed 3m

3  $P_1$ should be greater than or equal to $\frac{W_1}{X}$

4  $P_2$ should be greater than or equal to $\frac{W_1+W_2}{X}$

5  $P_1$ should be greater than or equal to $\frac{W_2+W_3}{X}$

6  $P_4$ should be greater than or equal to $\frac{W_3}{X}$

7  $P_5$ should be greater than or equal to $\frac{W_4}{X}$
   but should not be less than 385 mm

8  Take the value of the factor X from Table B-5 below, or it can be given the value 6, provided the compressive strength of the bricks or blocks (in the case of a cavity wall – in the loaded leaf) is not less than 7N/mm².

**Table B–5:** *Values of factor "x"*

| Nature of roof span | Maximum roof span (m) | Minimum thickness of wall inner leaf (m) | Span of floor is parallel to wall | Span of timber floor into wall | | Span of concrete floor into wall | |
|---|---|---|---|---|---|---|---|
| | | | | max 4.5m | max 6.0m | max 4.5m | max 6.0m |
| | | | | | | Value of factor "x" | |
| roof spans parallel to wall | not applicable | 100 | 6 | 6 | 6 | 6 | 6 |
| | | 90 | 6 | 6 | 6 | 6 | 5 |
| timber roof spans into wall | 9 | 100 | 6 | 6 | 5 | 4 | 3 |
| | | 90 | 6 | 4 | 4 | 3 | 3 |

If the load is only the weight of the wall itself a minimum amount of brickwork will be needed and the rest of the wall can be openings, if required. However, if the wall supports a roof and/or floor in addition to its own weight, then the amount of brickwork has to be increased. Calculate, using the factor "x" (⇨ Table B–5).

The construction over openings and recesses should be adequately supported and distributed.

### Support

Lintels vary widely in their design and the materials from which they are made and it is not possible, within the scope of *HomeBuilder*, to give guidance. However, there are many proprietary products which are made to suit a wide range of circumstances.

> *Always refer to the manufacturer's instructions or take professional advice when specifying the use of lintels.*

### Distribution

The bearing load from lintels can be assumed to be distributed where the bearing length is at least 150mm (100mm in the case of lintels with a clear span of no more than 1,200mm).

## B2.5 Overhangs and chases

The stability and thickness of a wall may well affect its design if overhangs and/or chases are envisaged.

### Overhangs

The amount of overhang should not impair the stability of the wall. **Either**:
- the overhanging part of the wall should be adequately supported; **or**
- the upper part should not overbalance on the lower part (if the projection is all on one side it should be no more than one-third of the thickness of the lower part).

### Chases

The dimensions of vertical chases should be no deeper than one-third of the minimum thickness of a solid wall or leaf of a cavity wall. Horizontal chases should not be deeper than one-sixth of the thickness of the wall or leaf.

Deeper chases need a thicker wall.

Chases should not be positioned where they could impair the stability of the wall and, if hollow blocks are used and the chase would take one face away, solid (but easily cut) blocks would be a better choice.

*The support for a wall may be vertical – for example, another wall or a chimney or a pier – or horizontal (usually by a floor or roof), or both (⇨Diagram B–10).*

**Diagram B–10: Vertical and horizontal support**

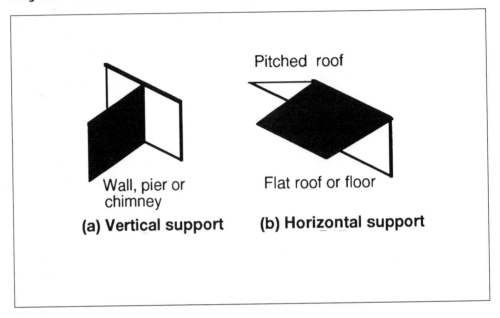

Pitched roof

Wall, pier or chimney

Flat roof or floor

**(a) Vertical support**        **(b) Horizontal support**

## B2.6 Vertical support for walls

The ability of a wall to carry a load depends not only on its dimensions and the strength of the materials used but also on the support it gets from other walls, the floor and the roof (⇨ Diagram B–10). The more box-like the structure is, the stronger it will be and a wall can take a heavier load if it is supported by another part of the structure (⇨ Diagram B–11).

Every external wall and internal loadbearing wall should be bonded at its end or otherwise securely tied from base to top to a buttress which may be another wall, a pier or a chimney. The **exception** to this requirement is a single-leaf wall less than 2.5m in storey height and length in an annex to a residential building or in a small single-storey non-residential building.

*You can divide a wall into shorter lengths by using a buttressing wall, pier of chimney.*

> 📖 A **buttress** is a wall, a chimney, or a pier which is being relied on to give vertical support to a wall. It should be bonded or otherwise securely connected to the wall for its full height and should also meet certain conditions.

## Walls giving vertical support (walls as buttresses)

*A wall is giving horizontal support if it is relied on to keep another wall upright. Assess length, thickness and openings in the wall.*

*Diagram B–11:* **Vertical support**

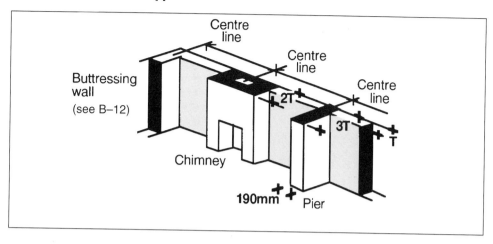

## Length

Measurements of length are made to another buttressing wall, chimney or pier. The length should be at least one-sixth of the height of the supported wall (to measure the height of the supported wall ⇨ Diagram B–5).

## Thickness

If the buttressing wall itself is **restrained** at the other end by a buttressing wall, a pier or a chimney, it should be at least the thickness of the supported wall. And if the wall is **not restrained** it should have at least:

• half the recommended thickness for external wall thickness generally (⇨ Table 4.3–1) and taking into account the **exceptions** (⇨ Table 4.3–2) for a wall of the same height and length (from this reduced thickness you can deduct 5mm);

• 90mm (75mm if the wall forms part of a dwelling house and is no more than 6m high and 10m in length).

## Openings

In a wall relied on to give vertical support to another wall openings are limited (⇨ Diagram B–12).

# Piers giving vertical support (piers as buttresses)

> A pier is giving support if it is relied upon to keep a wall upright.

The pier can be central on the wall or to one side.

## Thickness

The thickness of the pier is the dimension at right angles to the supported wall. It should be at least three times the thickness required for the supported wall.

## Width

The width should be at least 190mm.

# Chimneys giving vertical support (chimneys as buttresses)

> A chimney is giving support if it is relied upon to keep a wall upright. It can be central on the wall or to one side.

**Diagram B–12: Openings in a buttressing wall**

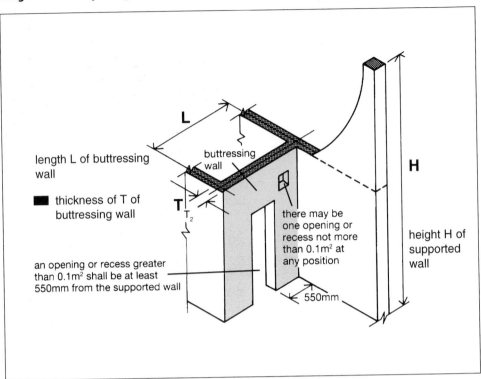

length L of buttressing wall

buttressing wall

L

H

thickness of T of buttressing wall

T

T₂

there may be one opening or recess not more than 0.1m² at any position

an opening or recess greater than 0.1m² shall be at least 550mm from the supported wall

height H of supported wall

550mm

## Thickness

The thickness of the chimney is the dimension at right angles to the supported wall. It should be at least twice the thickness required for the supported wall.

## Area

The plan area of the solid part of a chimney should be at least the area required for a pier.

> Deduct the areas of fireplace openings and flues when measuring the sectional area of a chimney.

## B2.7  Horizontal (lateral) support for walls

Every loadbearing wall in a storey should extend the full height of the storey and have horizontal support (⇨ Diagram B–13) which will prevent it from moving out of the vertical.

Each floor or roof which is being relied on to give the horizontal support should be bonded or otherwise securely connected to the wall and should transfer the forces from the wall to buttressing walls, piers and chimneys.

## Horizontal support from floors

To ensure the stability of the walls each external wall and each internal loadbearing wall should be horizontally strapped to each floor above the ground floor at intervals of no more than 2m.

There are **exceptions** to this requirement and some of these are discussed here.

***Diagram B–13:*** **Horizontal support for gable walls**

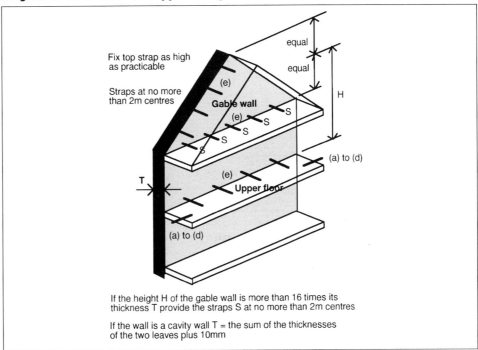

Fix top strap as high as practicable

Straps at no more than 2m centres

equal
equal

H

(e)

**Gable wall**

(e)

S

S

S

S

S

(a) to (d)

T

(e)

**Upper floor**

(a) to (d)

If the height H of the gable wall is more than 16 times its thickness T provide the straps S at no more than 2m centres

If the wall is a cavity wall T = the sum of the thicknesses of the two leaves plus 10mm

## Exceptions

The ends of **timber joists** need not be strapped if the house has no more than two storeys. The joists should have **either**:

- at least 90mm bearing on the supporting wall – or at least 75mm bearing on a timber wallplate – **and** be at no more than 1.2m centres; **or**
- the joists must be carried on the supporting wall by joist hangers of the restraint type **and** be at no more than 2m centres.

A **concrete floor** need not be strapped if it has at least 90mm bearing on the supporting wall.

An **internal loadbearing wall** need not be strapped to floors which are at the same level (or nearly so) on each side of the wall if contact between the wall and floors is either continuous or at intervals of no more than 2m with the points of contact on each side in the same line in plan (or nearly so).

**Straps** should be of galvanised steel or other durable metal, with a cross-section of at least 30x5mm.

  *Remember that the sides of timber floor joists need to be strapped even if the ends do not.*

## Horizontal support from the roof

To ensure the stability of the wall it should be horizontally strapped to the ceiling joists at no more than 2m centres, if the height from the top of the floor next below the ceiling to halfway up the gable is more than 16 times the thickness of the gable wall plus 10mm (⇨ Diagram B–14).

***Diagram B–14:* Horizontal and vertical restraints – details**

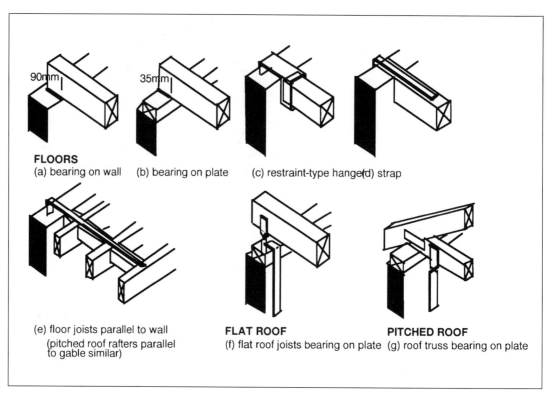

**FLOORS**
(a) bearing on wall    (b) bearing on plate    (c) restraint-type hanger(d) strap

(e) floor joists parallel to wall
(pitched roof rafters parallel
to gable similar)

**FLAT ROOF**
(f) flat roof joists bearing on plate

**PITCHED ROOF**
(g) roof truss bearing on plate

If the roof is a pitched roof each gable wall should be horizontally strapped to the rafters, again at no more than 2m centres.

> *Straps should be of galvanised steel or other durable metal with a cross-section of at least 30x5mm. An example of horizontally strapping a roof to the rafters: if the supported wall is a brick cavity the height will be 344m (two leaves each of 102.5mm = 205mm + 10mm = 215mm x 16).*

## Interruption of horizontal support

An opening in a wall or roof, for example for a stairway, can interrupt the continuity of support, **if**:

*   the length of the opening, measured parallel to the supported wall, is no more than 3m;
*   where the connection is provided by anchors, these are spaced closer than 2m on each side of the opening so that there will be the same number as if there were no interruption;
*   where the connection is not being provided by anchors, whatever form of connection is being provided is continuous on both sides of the opening;
*   there is only one interruption of the support.

## B2.8  Vertical restraints for roofs

To ensure that the roof (whether it is pitched or flat) will withstand uplifting wind forces it should be vertically strapped (⇨ Diagram B–15).

> *Straps should be of metal and at least 1m in length.*

***Diagram B–15:*** **Vertical restraints for roofs**

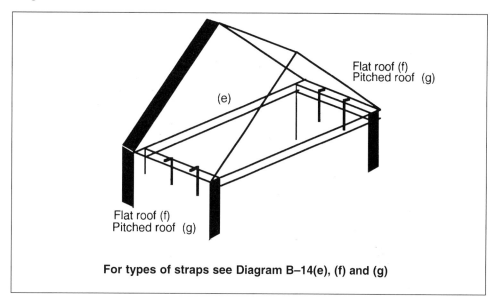

**For types of straps see Diagram B–14(e), (f) and (g)**

The vertical strapping is to the walls below at no more than 2m centres. There are exceptions to this requirement. Some are discussed below.

## Exceptions

The roof need not be strapped if it is:

- pitched at least at 15 degrees;
- tiled or slated;
- of a type which is known by local experience to resist wind gusts; and
- constructed so that the main timbers, such as the roof joists, span onto the walls at no more than 1.2m centres.

# Appendix C
# Means of escape

## INTRODUCTION

In this appendix the guidance is for:

C1 Houses with one or two storeys
C2 Houses with three storeys
C3 Houses with a basement storey

This appendix gives guidance on the provision of means of escape and their protection (BR1). Provisions for the means of escape are supported by requirements for limiting internal fire spread (BR B2 and B3) and external fire spread (BR B4) and for providing access for the fire service (BR B5). Guidance on the provisions which meet these requirements are described with the elements to which they can apply, and the meaning given to basement, ground, first and second storey is demonstrated (⇨ Diagram C–1).

> 🗈 *The purpose of the means of escape makes it possible for people in the house to reach a place of safety unaided and with their backs to a fire, without having to rely on rescue by the fire service.*

## Number of storeys

Count the number of storeys at the position which includes the greatest number, excluding any basement storeys. A basement storey is a storey with a floor which is, at some point, more than 1.2m below the highest level of ground next to the outside walls.

## Requirements

The building must be designed and constructed so that there are means of escape in case of fire from the building to a place of safety whiuch can be used safely and effectively at all material times (BR B1).

*Diagram C–1: Number of storeys*

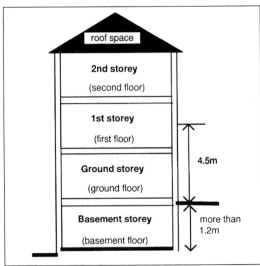

roof space

**2nd storey**
(second floor)

**1st storey**
(first floor)

**Ground storey**
(ground floor)

4.5m

**Basement storey**
(basement floor)

more than
1.2m

*Meeting the requirements*

*CHECKLIST*
- [ ] Smoke alarms
- [ ] Inner rooms
- [ ] Final exit

## Smoke alarms

Houses should be fitted with automatic smoke detectors and alarms (⇨ 4.8.2).

## Inner rooms

If the only escape route from one room is through another room, there is a risk that people in the inner room could be trapped if there is a fire in the outer room. An example of an inner room would be a bedroom in an upper storey which is normally accessible from an open stairway passing through a living room in a lower storey.

With some exceptions, an inner room is acceptable only if it is in a basement, ground storey or first storey and has a **final exit** to a place of safety. No other rooms are acceptable – although there are some exceptions regarding houses with three storeys and there also may be additional requirements if the inner room is in a basement.

## Final exit

The term "final exit" refers to an outside door or opening window through which the occupants of a building can pass to a place of safety.

> 📖 A **place of safety** is a place safe from the effects of fire. It is, ultimately, an unenclosed space in the open air.

If the final exit is into an **enclosed space**, such as a back garden or a yard, from which the only exit is through another building, then the depth of the space should be at least the height of the building (⇨ Diagram C–2).

If the final exit is from a first storey with a floor level which is not more than 4.5m above the ground the intention is that people shall be able to escape unaided by lowering themselves from the sill and dropping to the ground.

If the final exit is from a first storey with a floor level which is more than 4.5m above the ground or from a second storey (which is only acceptable in the case of a loft conversion) it is intended for rescue and not as a means of escape.

There are many other possibilities regarding final exits but these can be judged only on a case-by-case basis.

> 📖 *If the final exit is an opening to a balcony or flat roof, the part of the balcony or roof which is relied on for escape should have fire resistance and be guarded (⇨ 4.5.2).*

**Diagram C–2: Enclosed space**                                  **[B D1]**

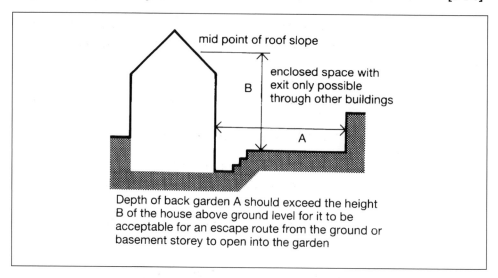

**Openings**    Whether an external door or an opening window, all openings should be unobstructed and at least 850mm high and 500mm wide.

  📖 *The width of a door is the width of the leaf, not the clear width between the door stops.*

**Windows in walls**    The bottom (sill) of the window opening should be between 800–1,100mm above the floor.

**Windows in pitched roofs**    The window may be vertical (a **dormer window**), or sloping (a **roof light**) (⇨ Diagram C–3). The sill of a sloping window may be 600mm above the floor.  In both cases, the distance measured down the slope from the sill of the window to the eaves should be no more than 1.7m.

The final exit from a room in the roof can be in a gable end or in the roof slope, whichever would be more suitable. If the opening is a window, the intention is that people can climb over the sill and drop safely to the ground. If it is in the first storey, it should not be above an obstruction, such as a conservatory.

**Diagram C–3: Windows in a pitched roof**

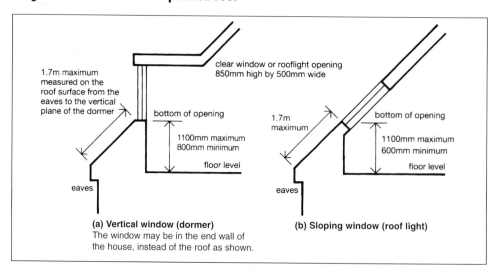

## C1 Houses with one or two storeys

For **smoke alarms** and **inner rooms** and **final exit** ⇨ above.

> *There may be additional requirements if there is a basement storey.*

### CHECKLIST
- ☐ Suitable means of escape

### Suitable means of escape

Each habitable room should, **either**:
- open directly to a hallway or stairway leading to the entrance; **or**
- have a suitable outside door or opening window through which the occupants of the house can reach a place of safety.

## C2 Houses with three storeys

For **smoke alarms** and **inner rooms** and **final exit** ⇨ above.

> *There may be additional requirements if there is a basement storey.*

### CHECKLIST
- ☐ Ground storey and first storey
- ☐ Second storey – protected stairway and alternative means

### Ground storey and first storey

Each habitable room in the ground storey and first storey should, **either**:
- open directly to a hallway or stairway leading to the entrance; **or**
- have a window or door through which escape can be made.

### Second storey

> *If the storey is the result of a loft conversion the provisions may be less demanding (⇨ Appendix G).*

It is possible that, in a few houses, the first floor will be more than 4.5m above some part of the ground next to the building, in which case the provisions described in C2 will apply.

If a fire should start in a lower storey of a house with a floor more than 4.5m above the ground, there is a risk that the people in the top storey could be trapped if the stairway were to become impassable before they had time to use it.

The room heights in a house are likely to be at least 2.8m, so the floor of a second storey will be 4.5m above ground – probably about 6m above ground level (⇨ Diagram C–1).

> *An opening window is not an acceptable means of escape from a second storey.*

You can choose one of two options. The second storey should have, **either**:
- access to a **protected stairway; or**
- its own suitable **alternative means of escape** with fire separation between the first and second storey.

### Protected stairway

A protected stairway is one in a fire-resisting enclosure which provides, **either**:

- **direct access** to a final exit; **or**
- **indirect access**, by separate alternative routes, to each of two final exits.

> *The intention is that a fire in a lower storey will not obstruct the stairway and the occupants of the third storey will be able to use the stairway as a safe means of escape to a place of safety.*

The term "direct access" means that the stairway and the final exit are in the same **protected enclosure** (⇨ Diagram C–4). And "indirect access" means that the stairway itself has no final exit directly from the protected enclosure but opens instead into **two alternative escape routes**, each leading to its own final exit and separated from the other by construction with at least 30 minutes fire resistance (spread) and with self-closing fire doors (FD20) with 20 minutes integrity (⇨ Diagram C–4).

The stairway should be **enclosed by walls** with 30 minutes fire resistance (spread), all openings in the walls should have self-closing fire doors with 20 minutes fire resistance (integrity) (FD20) and any glazing in the walls – but not in the doors – should have fire 30 minutes fire resistance (insulation).

*Diagram C–4: Protected stairway to a final exit*

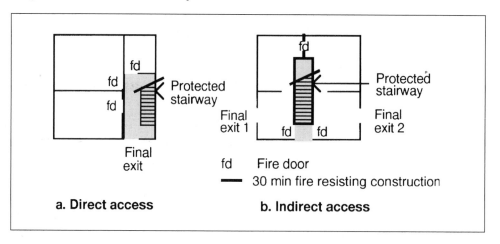

The **stairway** should be separated from the roof space **either** vertically by a cavity barrier **or** horizontally by a fire-resisting ceiling (⇨ Diagram C–5).

**Cavity barrier**     The barrier should have fire resistance of at least 30 minutes for integrity and 15 minutes for insulation when exposed to a fire in the roof space. It must be mechanically fixed and tightly fitted to a rigid part of the construction.

**Fire-resisting ceiling**     The ceiling should have fire resistance of at least 30 minutes for integrity and 30 minutes for insulation when exposed to a fire from the underside and extend over the whole of the roof space above the top storey.

Any **openings** in the ceiling – for example, for access to the roof space – should be fitted with a (trap) door having the same fire resistance.

**Diagram C–5: Protected stairway**

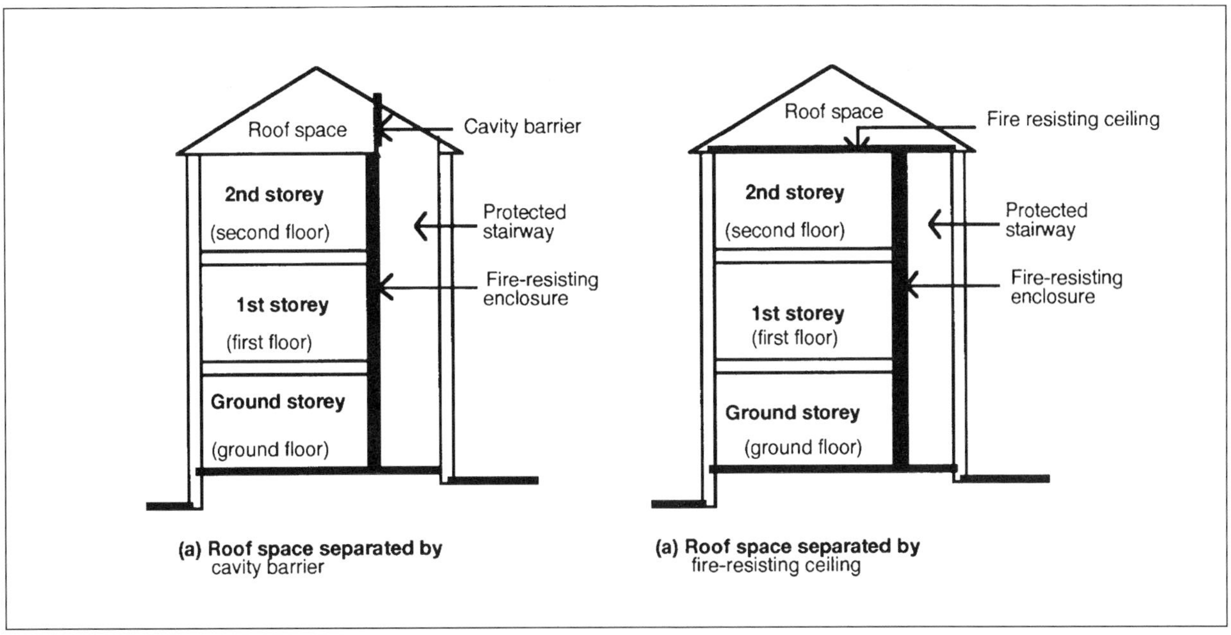

(a) Roof space separated by cavity barrier

(a) Roof space separated by fire-resisting ceiling

**Ducted warm-air heating systems**     Care must be taken to ensure that these ducted systems will not allow smoke or fire to spread into a protected stairway.

## Alternative means of escape

Portable ladders, throw-out ladders and appliances and apparatus of any kind which require handling, such as fold-down ladders, are **not** acceptable as the alternative means of escape from a storey with a floor more than 4.5m above the ground under any circumstance.

> *The intention is that if a fire in the ground or first-floor storey obstructs the stairway the occupants of the second storey will have an alternative means of escape to reach a place of safety.*

The alternative means of escape should be a suitable opening to an outside stair, a fixed ladder or a route across a balcony or flat roof leading to a place of safety. The part of the balcony or roof which is relied on should have fire resistance and be guarded.

> *An opening alone is not suitable as a means of escape from a second storey, but may be accessible (for rescue purposes only) if the storey is the result of a loft conversion (⇨ Appendix G).*

The fire separation between the first and second storeys should be fire resistant and any small openings fire stopped.

> *The regulations do not specify any period of fire resistance but separation will be provided in part by the floor and in part by any walls enclosing the stairway. The floor will have 30 minutes fire resistance. It would seem reasonable for the walls to have the same fire resistance and for doors in them to be self-closing and to have 20 minutes integrity.*

# C3 Houses with a basement storey

There are two possibilities: the fire starts in the basement, or it starts in a floor above the basement.

## CHECKLIST
- ☐ Basement storey
- ☐ Ground storey

## Basement storey

Consider the people in the basement: if the fire starts in the basement they may not be able to escape by the stair up to the ground floor. If the fire starts in a storey above the basement (say, in the ground storey) they will be able to escape up to the ground floor but may not be able to get any further. Either way, they will need an alternative means of escape.

> 📖 A **basement storey** is one with a floor which, at some point, is more than 1.2m below the highest level of the adjacent ground.
> A **habitable room** is one which is used or intended to be used for dwelling purposes. It includes any kitchen but not a bathroom. For ventilation purposes, a habitable room does not include a room which is used solely as a kitchen.

## Storeys above ground

Consider the people in storeys with floors more than 4.5m above ground. If the fire starts in a storey above the basement then the basement is irrelevant but, if the fire starts in the basement, and if the upstairs storey they are on is too high above the ground, the fire may spread into the ground storey before they have time to escape down the stair.

If a house with a basement has a first storey with a floor more than 4.5m above the ground, or has a first and second storey then **either**:
- the ground floor should have 30 minutes fire resistance (spread) to prevent the fire from reaching the ground storey before the people in the upstairs storey have time to escape down the stair; **or**
- the habitable rooms in the ground storey and all the rooms in the upper storeys should be treated as inner rooms (⇨ above) with their own alternative means of escape.

The fire separation should be fire resistant and any small openings fire stopped.
> 📖 *The regulations do not specify any period of fire resistance but separation will be provided in part by the floor which will have 30 minutes fire resistance. It would seem reasonable for any separating walls to have the same fire resistance and for doors in them to be self-closing and to have 20 minutes integrity.*

# Appendix D
# Energy conservation

## INTRODUCTION

In this appendix the guidance is for:

D1 Limiting heat losses through the fabric
D2 Limiting heat losses through gaps in the fabric
D3 Tables (openings)
D4 Technical risks
D5 Alternative methods

## D1  Limiting heat losses through the fabric

### CHECKLIST
- ☐ Extensions
- ☐ Material alterations
- ☐ Material changes of use (conversions)
- ☐ New buildings

If you decide that requirement L1 applies to the work you are planning you then have to consider how you will satisfy it.

> *Remember that the building or the work may be exempt from the application of requirement L1 (⇨ 1.2.1 and 1.2.2) but remember too that conservatories and porches are only exempt if the glazing meets certain requirements (⇨ 4.3.7).*

There are three alternative ways of satisfying requirement L1.

1  The simplest method is the elemental method which limits heat losses through the fabric by setting standard values for the rate of heat loss (the U-values) for the walls, floors and roofs, using familiar types of construction to find a basic thickness of insulation from which allowable reductions can be made. This method is supported by provisions to limit heat losses through gaps in the fabric.
2  The Target U-value method (⇨ D5).
3  The Energy Rating method (⇨ D5).

> 📖 The U-value of a wall, roof, etc. (U), shows how much heat (W) passes through one square metre ($m^2$) of area when the temperature of the two faces differs by 1 degree (K). Thus: $U = W/m^2K$. The higher the number the worse the insulating performance.

# Extensions

The floors, walls and roofs, except in the case of **small extensions**, should achieve the standard U-values (⇨ Diagram D–1).

To ensure the standards are met use **basic insulation thicknesses** and take advantage of the **allowable reductions** (⇨ 4.1.6).

*Diagram D–1:* **Standard U-values**

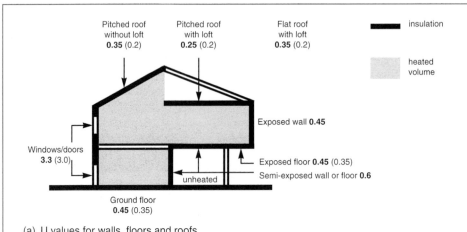

(a) U values for walls, floors and roofs
The values in bold type apply to new dwellings with a SAP rating over 60 and to all extensions
The values in brackets (light type) apply to new dwellings with a SAP rating of 60 or less
(they do not apply to extensions)

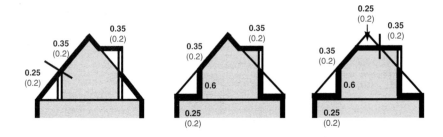

(b) U values (room-in-the-roof construction)
The values in bold type apply to new dwellings with a SAP rating over 60 and to all extensions
The values in brackets (light type) apply to new dwellings with a SAP rating of 60 or less
(they do not apply to extensions)

Notes
1  *SAP energy rating*  the lower the energy rating the better the overall energy efficiency of the dwelling
2  The U values assume that the combined area of the doors and windows is 22.5% of the floor area
3  If any part of the roof has a pitch of 70 or steeper it should have the same U value as a wall
4  A loft means a roofspace which is not intended to be habitable (but may be used for storage)

## *Insulation materials*

There is a variety of insulation materials with different thermal conductivity values ("k" values) (⇨ Table D–1). Wherever possible, use the manufacturers' values.

**Table D-1:** *Insulating materials – U-values*

| Material | Density (kg/m²) | k value (W/mK) |
|---|---|---|
| Expanded polystyrene (EPS) slab | 25 | 0.035 |
| Mineral wool quilt | 12 | 0.040 |
| Mineral wool slab | 25 | 0.035 |
| Phenolic foam board | 30 | 0.020 |
| Polyurethane board | 30 | 0.025 |

## Openings

The basic thickness measurements assume that the **area of the openings** expressed as a percentage of the **floor area** is no more than 22.5 per cent of the floor area. They also assume that the average rate of heat loss through the windows, doors and roof lights – their **average U-value** – is no worse than 3.3W/m²K. However, there is some allowance for trade-off between the actual percentage area and the actual average U-value. Calculate the average U-value (⇨ Tables D–2 and D–3).

> 📖 To calculate the **floor area**: measure between the finished internal faces of the external walls, including any projecting bays. Include non-usable spaces such as ducts and stairwells.

**Table D–2:** *Indicative U-values of openings (windows, doors and roof lights)*

| Item | Type of frame | | | | | | | |
|---|---|---|---|---|---|---|---|---|
| | Wood | | Metal | | Thermal break | | PVC-u | |
| Air gap in sealed unit (mm) | 6 | 12 | 6 | 12 | 6 | 12 | 6 | 12 |
| Window, double-glazed | 3.3 | 3.0 | 4.2 | 3.8 | 3.6 | 3.3 | 3.3 | 3.0 |
| Window, double-glazed low-E | 2.9 | 2.4 | 3.7 | 3.2 | 3.1 | 2.6 | 2.9 | 2.4 |
| Window, double-glazed, Argon fill | 3.1 | 2.9 | 4.0 | 3.7 | 3.4 | 3.2 | 3.1 | 2.9 |
| Window, double-glazed, low-E, Argon fill | 2.6 | 2.2 | 3.4 | 2.9 | 2.8 | 2.4 | 2.6 | 2.2 |
| Window, triple-glazed | 2.6 | 2.4 | 3.4 | 3.2 | 2.9 | 2.6 | 2.6 | 2.4 |
| Door, half double-glazed | 3.1 | 3.0 | 3.6 | 3.4 | 3.3 | 3.2 | 3.1 | 3.0 |
| Door, fully double-glazed | 3.3 | 3.0 | 4.2 | 3.8 | 3.6 | 3.3 | 3.3 | 3.0 |
| Rooflights, double-glazed at less than 70° from horizontal | 3.6 | 3.4 | 4.6 | 4.4 | 4.0 | 3.8 | 3.6 | 3.4 |
| Windows and doors, single-glazed | 4.7 | | 5.8 | | 5.3 | | 4.7 | |
| Door, solid timber panel or similar | 3.0 | | – | | – | | – | |
| Door, half single-glazed, half timber or similar | 3.7 | | – | | – | | – | |

Notes
1 Single glazed panels in doors are acceptable provided they do not increase the average U-value of the doors, windows and roof lights beyond the limit for the total area of the openings after applying Table D–3.
2 Single glazed windows and doors protected by unheated, enclosed, draughtproof porches or conservatories can be assumed to have a U-value of 3.3 W/m²K.

**Table D–3:** *U-values and areas of opening – trade-offs*

| Average U-value (W/m²K) | Maximum permitted area of windows and doors as a percentage of floor area for SAP Energy Ratings of: | |
|---|---|---|
| | 60 or less | over 60 |
| 2.0 | 37.0% | 41.5% |
| 2.1 | 35.0% | 39.0% |
| 2.2 | 33.0% | 36.5% |
| 2.3 | 31.0% | 34.5% |
| 2.4 | 29.5% | 33.0% |
| 2.5 | 28.0% | 31.5% |
| 2.6 | 26.5% | 30.0% |
| 2.7 | 25.5% | 28.5% |
| 2.8 | 24.5% | 27.5% |
| 2.9 | 23.5% | 26.0% |
| **3.0** | **22.5%** | 25.0% |
| 3.1 | 21.5% | 24.0% |
| 3.2 | 21.0% | 23.5% |
| **3.3** | 20.0% | **22.5%** |
| 3.4 | 19.5% | 21.5% |
| 3.5 | 19.0% | 21.0% |
| 3.6 | 18.0% | 20.5% |
| 3.7 | 17.5% | 19.5% |
| 3.8 | 17.0% | 19.0% |
| 3.9 | 16.5% | 18.5% |
| 4.0 | 16.0% | 18.0% |
| 4.1 | 15.5% | 17.5% |
| 4.2 | 15.5% | 17.0% |

Note
The data in this table is derived assuming a constant heat loss through the elevations amounting to the loss when the basic allowance for openings of 22.5% of floor area is provided and the standard U-values given in Table D–2 apply. It is also assumed for the purpose of this table that there are no roof lights.

### Small extensions

If the floor area is no more than 10m² the requirements will be met if the construction is "no less effective" for the conservation of fuel and power than is the existing construction.

The term "no less effective" might mean **either** using a similar construction and proportion of openings, **or** achieving an average rate of heat loss which would be similar. However the extension is constructed the potential for energy saving seems to be rather small (even if it is to be heated) given that the heat loss through what is at present an outside wall will be reduced.

## Material alterations

An alteration is material if, as a result of the work and at any stage, the building will not comply or will comply to a lesser extent with a relevant requirement in Part A or Part B (except B2) of the Building Regulations.

The requirement may be satisfied by the provisions summarised here but the extent of the provisions will depend on the circumstances in each case.

### Ground floors

Where substantially replacing the structure of a ground floor provide insulation in heated rooms to the standard for new work (⇨ 4.1.6).

### Walls

If you are substantially replacing a complete exposed wall provide a "reasonable" thickness of insulation and limit the heat loss through gaps in the wall.

> 📖 *The term "reasonable" used here is not defined but the intention seems to be that you should take advantage of opportunities to reduce heat losses where you can, without significant alteration to the design or additional expense.*

### Roofs

Where you are substantially replacing a roof structure, provide insulation to the standard for new work (⇨ 4.1.5).

> 📖 *The term "substantially replacing" is not defined but, because a reference to a building includes a reference to a part of a building (TBR 2) it could mean the replacement of, say, a complete ground floor (perhaps not just the floor in one room), a complete wall, or a complete roof (perhaps not just one slope) but probably not only a section of a floor, wall or roof (in short, a part of a part).*

### Space-heating and water-heating installations

When you are carrying out building work on a space-heating or water-heating installation provide controls and insulation to the standard for new work (⇨ 4.7.1 and 4.9.1).

## Material changes of use (conversions)

A change of use is material if the building will be used as a dwelling where previously it was not. The requirement may be satisfied by the provisions summarised here but the extent of the provisions will depend on the circumstances in each case.

### Ground floors

Where substantially replacing the structure of a ground floor, provide insulation in heated rooms to the standard for new work (⇨ 4.1.6).

### Walls

Where substantially replacing a complete exposed wall, provide a "reasonable" thickness of insulation and limit the heat loss through gaps in the wall. Where renovating a substantial area of the internal surfaces, upgrade the insulation of exposed and semi-exposed walls – for example, by providing a reasonable thickness of insulated dry lining and sealing the gaps and junctions.

### Windows

Where replacing windows provide draught-stripped windows with an average U-value no worse than $3.3W/m^2K$ (⇨ Table D–1), except in conservation work and other situations where the existing window design needs to be kept.

### Space-heating and hot-water systems

Where you are carrying out building work on a space-heating or water-heating installation, provide controls and insulation to the standard for new work (⇨ 4.7.1 and 4.9.1).

### Accessible lofts

Where the U-value of the existing insulation is worse than 0.45W/m²K, upgrade the insulation to a U-value no worse than 0.35W/m²K (⇨ 4.5.1).

## New buildings

Except in the case of **conservatories** and **buildings with low levels of heating**, the floors, walls and roofs should achieve the requisite U-values (⇨ Diagram D–1). You can if you wish achieve these values if you use the basic insulation thicknesses and make the allowable reductions.

### Conservatories

When a conservatory is attached to, and built as part of, a new dwelling:

• where it is **not separated** from the dwelling, it should be treated as part of the dwelling; and

• where it is **separated** from the dwelling, there will be energy savings unless the conservatory is heated (if it will be heated by a fixed installation this should have its own separate temperature and on/off controls).

Here, "separated" means having the separating walls, and the floor cover if any, insulated as a semi-exposed wall and floor (0.6 W/m²K) and any separating doors and windows having the same U-value and draught-stripping as the exposed windows and doors.

> 📖 A **conservatory** has at least threequarters of the area of its roof and at least one half the area of its external walls made of translucent material.

> 🔖 *Translucent material is material through which light can pass. It may be clear or opaque and of glass or other material, usually a plastic material. However, this defintion depends on how the conservatory is built and not on how you might use it.*

### Buildings with low levels of heating

The insulation of buildings with low levels of heating (and with no heating) will be unnecessary. A **low level** is where the output of the space-heating system is no more than 50 W/m² of floor area if the building is for industrial or storage use or no more than 25 W/m² for any other building which is not a dwelling.

## Standard Assessment Procedure (SAP)

This is the procedure used to calculate the energy rating for a dwelling. The calculation is for information only, does not affect the levels of insulation, and can be made at any time (even after the work has been completed).

# D2  Limiting heat losses through gaps in the fabric

Some ventilation is needed to ensure air quality, to limit condensation, and to provide the air supply to fuel-burning appliances, which is essential if they are to function safely and efficiently. Too much air (⇨ Diagram D–2) can, however, cause problems.

> 🗏 *If too much air enters the building unintentionally it might not only be unwel-*
> *come: it will increase the need for space heating.*

**Diagram D–2: Limiting unintentional air movement**

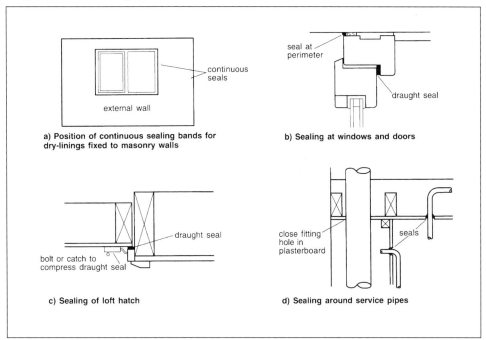

a) Position of continuous sealing bands for dry-linings fixed to masonry walls

b) Sealing at windows and doors

c) Sealing of loft hatch

d) Sealing around service pipes

## Air infiltration

To limit unintentional air infiltration as far as practicable:

*   **fit** draught-stripping in the frames of opening parts of windows, doors and rooflights;
*   **seal** gaps between dry lining and masonry walls at the edges of openings and at the junctions with walls, floors and ceilings;
*   **seal** vapour-control membranes in timber-framed constructions;
*   **seal** around loft hatches;
*   **seal** boxing for concealed services at both floor and ceiling levels; and
*   **seal** piped services where they penetrate or project into hollow constructions and voids.

# D3  Tables (openings)

When you calculate the actual **area of the openings** as a percentage of the floor area, you can choose, **either**:

*   the area of openings in the extension as a percentage of the floor area of the extension; **or**
*   the combined area of the openings in the extension **and** the existing dwelling as a percentage of the combined floor areas of the extension and the dwelling.

> 🗏 *You will probably find that the latter choice will allow you to have a larger area*
> *of glass in your extension.*

If you find that the average U-value of the openings is more than the value assumed for the basic allowance (3.3 W/m²K), then you can choose either to reduce the average value or to reduce the area of the openings. If of course the U-value is less you can increase the area.

If you find that the area of the openings is more than the percentage assumed for the basic allowance (22.5 per cent), then you can choose either to reduce the area or to increase the average value. If of course the area is less you can reduce the U-value.

# D4 Technical risks

The application of some energy conservation measures can give rise to technical risks, such as rain penetration, condensation, reduced ventilation rates, etc. You should check existing provisions for compliance with the technical guidance elsewhere in *HomeBuilder*, particularly the guidance on ventilation.

> *Where there is any history of existing problems you are strongly advised to refer to the Report 262 Thermal insulation: avoiding risks published by the Building Research Establishment and to Thermal insulation and ventilation: Good Practice Guide published by the National House-Building Council ( ⇨ Useful addresses).*

# D5 Alternative methods

A number of alternative methods of energy conservation are discussed below.

### Standard Assessment Procedure (SAP)
The procedure used to calculate an energy rating – the SAP rating – for a dwelling, is based on the energy cost for space heating and water heating. It is expressed as a number between 1 and 100, the higher the number the better the rating.

### Target U-value method
This method relies on calculating the average U-value for the design, then calculating a target average based on the SAP rating and comparing the two. The method allows you limited flexibility in the form of trade-offs between parts with levels of insulation which are better than the standard against parts with levels which are worse (usually glazed openings). It also allows you to take account of solar gains (which depend on which way the dwelling faces) and the efficiency of your central gas-fired or oil-fired hot-water and space-heating system.

### Energy rating method
Using this method gives you the flexibility to use any valid energy conservation measures including not only levels of insulation, solar gains and the efficiency of the hot-water and space-heating systems but also internal heat gains, ventilation rates, the exposure of the building and even fuel costs. Your design will comply with the requirements if its SAP rating is no less than the appropriate rating in Table 4 of the Approved Document L which also has a worksheet with guidance which you can use to find the rating.

# Appendix E
# Ventilation

## INTRODUCTION

In this appendix the guidance is for:

E1  Space ventilation and air quality
E2  Air supply to fuel-burning appliances

Some requirements combine to advantage, such as room ventilation designed to improve air quality, which reduces potentially troublesome moisture at source because it reduces the need for roof ventilation. It can also contribute to the air supply to fuel-burning appliances, which is vital for them to function safely and efficiently. Similarly, the appliances themselves – particularly open fires – can contribute to room ventilation.

Remember, however, that if the ventilation opening that supplies air to a room or space can be closed – and if there is a heat-producing appliance in the room or space which needs an air supply – it must be separate if the appliance is not to be starved of air when the opening is closed.

Some requirements conflict. For example, an extractor fan – for a quick fix on a muggy day – can pull carbon monoxide from boiler flues when the building is fitted with draught-stripping designed to reduce air infiltration, vital to improving energy economy.

*Ventilation probably faces the regulators with their most taxing problem.*

Balancing these requirements makes the presentation of the provisions designed to meet them particularly difficult. Steps should be taken to resolve any apparent conflict. This appendix gives guidance on three ventilation strategies, designed to:
1  **Promote** air quality.
2  **Provide** the air supply to heat-producing appliances.
3  **Limit** condensation.

Each of these three strategies makes use of a least one of the following provisions:
*       rapid natural ventilation, mainly opening windows, doors and louvres;
*       background natural ventilation, adjustable openings which will not prejudice security;
*       mechanical extract ventilation, controlled manually or automatically.

## Air infiltration

While it is necessary to promote ventilation to ensure air quality and a supply of air to any heat-producing appliance, it is also necessary to limit excess ventilation – air infiltration – which, if it enters the building unintentionally through gaps in the fabric, might not only be unwelcome but will also increase heat loss and the need for space heating (⇨ D2).

# E1  Space ventilation and air quality

## CHECKLIST
☐  E1.1 Space ventilation
☐  E1.2 Open-flued appliances

## Requirements

The means of ventilation will meet the requirements for air quality if they provide adequate means of ventilation for people in the building (BR F1). **Limit on application:** the requirements do not apply to a building or space in a building:

- into which people do not normally go; or
- is used solely for storage; or
- is a garage used solely in connection with a single dwelling.

The spaces which need some means of ventilation are:

- habitable rooms;
- kitchens;
- utility rooms if they are accessible from inside the building;
- bathrooms and shower-rooms, with or without a WC;
- sanitary accommodation separate from a bathroom.

### Meeting the requirements

The ventilation will be adequate if, under normal conditions, it is capable of:

- extracting moisture and pollutants which are a hazard to health before they become widespread;
- diluting pollutants rapidly where necessary;
- providing a minimum supply of fresh air for the occupants.

The provisions make use of three strategies:

1  **Background ventilation.** One or more small openings to external air, such as trickle, or "hit-and- miss", ventilators, typically fixed about 1.75m above the floor level to avoid draughts, reasonably secure, adjustable, and rain-screened (⇨ Diagram E–1).

2  **Rapid ventilation.** One or more larger openings to external air, such as opening windows and doors, with some part of the opening at high level, typically 1.75m above the floor level.

3  **Extract ventilation.** This type of ventilation can take two forms:

- mechanical ventilation using fans with suitable extract rates and controls;
- passive-stack ventilation (PSV), a system of ducts rising from the ceiling level to terminals at roof level. The ducts operate by a combination of the natural stack effect – that is, the movement of air due to the difference between indoor and outdoor temperatures and the flow of air passing over the roof.

  *Detailed design guidance can be found in  Information paper 13/94 published by the Building Research Establishment, and product information obtained from the British Board of Agrément.*

### *Diagram E–1:* **Background ventilation**

The following are examples of provisions for background ventilation. In each case, the ventilation opening should be located (typically 1.75m above floor level) so as to avoid discomfort due to cold draughts.

**1. Trickle ventilators**

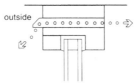

**a) In window frames**

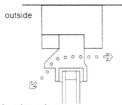

**b) In glazed openings**

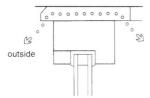

**c) Above window frames**

**2. Airbrick with "hit and miss" ventilator**

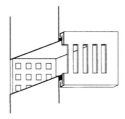

Notes to examples 1 and 2:

To minimise resistance to air flow, the main air passages (not insect screens or baffles, etc.) of an installed ventilation opening (when fully open) should have a smallest dimension of at least 5mm for slots or 8mm for square or circular holes.

**3. Vertical sliding sash windows with adjustable fixed locking positions**

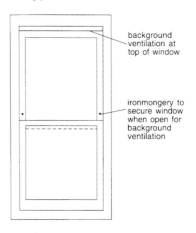

For background ventilation, the opening of the window should be adjustable to provide the required area and lockable so it is secure when open for background ventilation.

**Note:** Provisions in B1 for certain windows to be usable for means of escape.

**4. High-level top-hung window with adjustable locking positions** (because of the risk to security, this should generally be restricted to use above ground floor level)

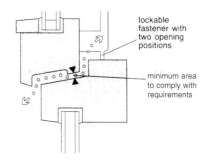

For background ventilation, the opening of the window should be adjustable to provide the required area and be lockable with a removable key or similar device so it is secure in at least two opening positions for background ventilation.

## E1.1 Space ventilation

### *CHECKLIST*

- ☐ Habitable rooms
- ☐ Kitchens
- ☐ Utility rooms
- ☐ Bathrooms and shower-rooms
- ☐ Sanitary accommodation

Where rooms serve a combined function, such as a kitchen-diner, the individual ventilation provisions need not be duplicated if you provide for the more demanding function.

## Habitable rooms

There are three possibilities:

1 Ventilating a single habitable room.
2 Ventilating two habitable rooms with a permanent opening between them as one habitable room.
3 Ventilating a habitable room through an adjoining space, such as a conservatory or similar space, with a closable opening between them.

> 📖 A **habitable room** is a room used or intended to be used for dwelling purposes which is not a kitchen. Remember, however, that for means of escape purposes. a habitable room **includes** a kitchen.

### E.1: Habitable rooms

Ventilating a single room requires provision of:

**background ventilation** –  one or more openings with a total area of 8,000mm²; and

**rapid ventilation** – one or more openings with a total area of at least one-twentieth of the floor area.

Ventilating two rooms as one (a permanent opening to another habitable room) ⇨ Diagram E–2.

Ventilating through an adjoining space (a closeable opening to a conservatory or similar space) ⇨ Diagram E–3.

### E.2: Kitchens

> 📖 *These provisions only apply to a room used solely as a kitchen. However, if the room serves a combined function the provisions need not be duplicated but they should meet the more onerous standard. For example, a dining kitchen (serving as a kitchen and as a habitable room) should have background ventilation (8,000mm²) plus rapid ventilation (one-twentieth floor area), plus extract ventilation with a fan rate of 60 litres/second (or 30 litres/second if near the hob).*

With an opening to external air provide:

**background ventilation** – **either** one or more openings with a total area of 4,000mm²; **or**

**mechanical ventilation** by increasing the performance of the extract ventilation so as to be capable of operating continuously for one hour and extracting the volume of the kitchen in that time; and

**rapid ventilation** – an opening such as a window or door of any size and

**Diagram E–2:** **Ventilating two rooms as one**

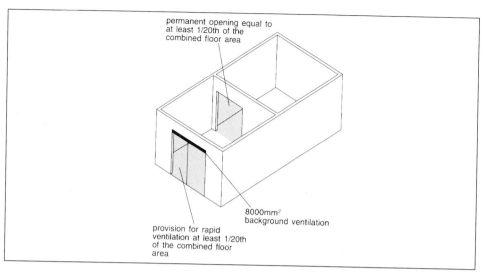

**Diagram E–3:** **Ventilating through an adjoining space**

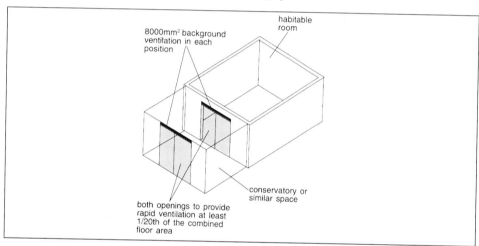

**extract ventilation** – by **either** a fan, or passive-stack ventilation, or a suitable open-flued appliance. There should be a 10mm gap under the door

If you choose the fan option it must be capable of operating intermittently and of extracting at least 60 litres/second (or at least 30 litres/second if it is near the hob). Near the hob means within a cooker hood or, when sited near the ceiling, not mote than 300mm from the centre line of the hob space and under the control of a humidistat.

Without an opening to external air (allowing an internal kitchen) provide:
**extract ventilation** – as above except that, if you choose the fan option, the fan should have a 15 minute overrun unless there is also an open-flued heating appliance in the kitchen.

*In rooms without natural light it is convenient to connect the fan to the light switch.*

## E.3: Utility rooms

A **utility room** is any space, except a kitchen, which is directly accessible from a building and which might reasonably be expected to produce significant quantities of water vapour from clothes washing and the like.

With an opening to external air provide:

**background ventilation** – one or more openings with a total area of 4,000mm²; and

**rapid ventilation** – an opening such as a window or door of any size; and

**extract ventilation** – as E.2 except that, if you choose the fan option, it need only be capable of extracting at least 30 litres a second.

Without an opening to external air (allowing an internal utility room) provide:

**extract ventilation** – as above **except** that, if you choose the fan option, the fan should have a 15 minute overrun **unless** there is also an open-flued heating appliance in the kitchen.

## E.4: Bathrooms and shower-rooms

A bathroom or shower-room is any space containing a bath or shower with or without a WC.

With an opening to external air provide:

**background ventilation** – one or more openings with a total area of 4,000mm²; and

**rapid ventilation** – an opening such as a window or door of any size; and

**extract ventilation** – as E.2 **except** that, if you choose the fan option, it need only be capable of extracting at least 15 litres per second.

Without an opening to external air (allowing an internal bathroom) provide:

**extract ventilation** – as above except that the fan should have a 15 minute overrun **unless** there is also an open-flued heating appliance in the room.

## E.5: Sanitary accommodation

Sanitary accommodation is any space with a WC or urinal which is separate from a bathroom.

With an opening to external air provide:

**background ventilation** – one or more openings with a total area of 4,000mm²; and either

**rapid ventilation** – one or more openings with a total area of at least one-twentieth of the floor area; or

**extract ventilation** – a fan capable of extracting at least 6 litres/second.

Without an opening to external air (allowing internal sanitary accommodation) provide:

**extract ventilation** – as above **except** that, the fan should have a 15 minute overrun **unless** there is also an open-flued heating appliance in the space.

## Alternative approach

For background ventilation, you could provide an average of 6,000mm$^2$ for each of the rooms with at least 4,000mm$^2$ in each. However, this is the minimum area anyway except for habitable rooms (8,000mm$^2$) so they are the only ones which could be different.

## E1.2 Open-flued appliances

To be effective, an open-flued appliance should be **either**:

- an open fire; **or**
- a solid fuel primary source of heating, cooking or water heating; **or**
- an appliance with a flue equal in area to a 125mm diameter duct with the combustion air and dilution air inlets permanently open.

The open-flued appliance could be, say, a closed stove which might be thought unlikely to make a significant contribution to room ventilation, unless it has doors and they are open. A draught diverter will maintain the flow of air.

> *An open fire can clearly contribute significantly to room ventilation but an open-flued appliance is one which "draws its combustion air from the room or space in which it is installed" (BS 5440).*

### Extract fans

If an open-flued appliance and an extract fan are fitted in the same dwelling, the fan can pull the flue gases from the appliance – "spillage" – whether it is in the same room or another.

Precautions are essential. For example:

- a solid-fuel open-flued appliance and an extract fan should not be in the same room;
- if a gas-fired open-flued appliance and a fan are both in a kitchen, the fan extract rate should be reduced to no more than 20 litres/second (even if the two appliances are in different rooms, the fan rate may need to be reduced);
- an oil-fired open-flued appliance should be installed only in compliance with Technical Information Note T1/112 issued by the Oil Firing Technical Association for the Petroleum Industry (OFTEC) (⇨ Useful addresses).

> *Flue gases contain carbon monoxide which can cause drowsiness, sickness and even death, if it mixes with the air in a room. Usually the cause is a blocked flue but, more rarely, it can be due to spillage. The growing tendency to weather-strip doors and windows to limit draughts only makes the situation worse.*

Given the dangers inherent in flue gases, all appliances should be regularly maintained and tested. You can easily find out for yourself whether spillage is occurring, particularly where the open-flued appliance and the fan are in the same room and the room is a small one.

To carry out the test, two steps are necessary:

1  Open any doors between the appliance and the fan. Close all other doors and windows in the house/flat. Switch the fan on.
2  Hold the flame from a lighted taper just below the lower edge of the draught-diverter. There is spillage if the flame is drawn away from the draught-diverter.

The ventilation provision will be suitable if it includes:

- habitable rooms (direct ventilation from outside air);
- habitable rooms (indirect ventilation from an adjoining space);
- kitchens;
- utility rooms;
- bathrooms and shower-rooms with or without a WC;
- sanitary accommodation, if separate from a bathroom or shower-room.

  *Remember that internal kitchens, utility rooms, bathrooms and sanitary accommodation are possible if you have mechanical extract ventilation.*

# E2  Air supply to fuel-burning appliances

## Requirements

Air supply must be adequate for combustion and for the efficient working of any flue-pipe or chimney. **Limit on application:** the requirement applies only to fixed heat-producing appliances designed to burn solid fuel, gas or oil and to incinerators (BR J/1/2/3).

### Meeting the requirements

The air supply will be adequate if the room or space containing an appliance which is not room-sealed has a suitable ventilation opening to outside air, or to an adjoining room or space with a ventilation opening to outside air and of the same size. No ventilation opening should be in an internal wall needing fire resistance (⇨ 4.3).

Most heat-producing appliances draw their air supply from the room in which they are installed but some appliances may be room-sealed; gas appliances in bathrooms or shower-rooms and private WCs must be room-sealed. With one exception, this section does not apply to them because they draw their air supply directly from the outside air (and discharge the products of combustion direct to outside air).

The **exception** is a room-sealed gas appliance in a cupboard or similar small space which, to prevent an unacceptable rise in temperature, needs ventilation either from an adjoining room or space or from outside air (⇨ 4.9).

  *Ventilation might be needed for air quality but this may not be enough to provide the air supply which the appliance needs: you should check whether it is enough and increase it if it is not.*

---

The above section gives the provisions for the following:

**Solid-fuel burning appliances:** an appliance with a rated output no more than 45kW. Solid fuel includes wood. These appliances include open fires and other appliances, either with or without a flue-draught stabiliser.

**Gas-burning appliances:** an individually flued non-fan assisted appliance with a rated input no more than 60kW. These appliances include cookers, solid-fuel effect and other appliances.

**Oil-burning appliances:** an appliance with a rated output of no more than 45kW. These appliances include all appliances with a rated output above 5kW.

---

# Appendix F
# Drainage disposal

## INTRODUCTION

In this appendix the guidance is for:

F1 Foul-water disposal
F2 Rainwater disposal
F3 Groundwater disposal

This section sets out the methods for the final disposal of foul water, rainwater and groundwater from drainage systems. The design and construction of the drainage systems carrying the flow to the final disposal was discussed earlier (⇨ 4.1.2).

## F1 Foul-water disposal

Foul water means waste water which consists of, or includes, waste from a sanitary appliance or other soil appliance or water which has been used for cooking and washing.

### CHECKLIST
- ☐ Connection to a sewer or drain
- ☐ Sewage treatment works
- ☐ Cesspools

### Requirements

The Building Act requires that:
- satisfactory provision must be made for the disposal of foul water from the building (BA 21).

The Building Regulations require that:
- any septic tank, settlement tank or cesspool shall be of adequate capacity and impermeable to liquids, adequately ventilated, and so sited and constructed that it is not prejudicial to the health of any person, will not contaminate any underground water or water supply, and have adequate means of access or emptying (BR H2).

### Meeting the requirements

There are three ways to dispose of foul water. In order of preference, they are:
- discharge it untreated into a sewer;
- treat it in a sewage treatment works and discharge it as clean water;
- store it untreated for collection from a cesspool.

   *Whichever of these three methods for the disposal of foul water is chosen, it must be agreed with the local authority.*

> 📖 A **sewer** means any sewer or drain used for the drainage of buildings and paved areas except a drain used for the drainage of one building or the buildings in one **curtilage**.

Discharge to a **public gravity sewer** is the best option, but you will need to have access to it – preferably not across other properties – and it will be important to know the distance, depth and the method of connection. This latter information is important because the connection in this case could be only a simple "saddle" on a shallow sewer close by, or it could mean the necessity of building a new manhole on a deep sewer down the road.

> 📖 *There will be an annual charge for discharging foul water into a sewer. This will usually be payable to the water undertaking, separate from but paid with the charge for the water supply.*

Where a gravity discharge to a drain or sewer is not possible or practicable, foul water can be treated in a **septic tank**. However, it will still be necessary to treat the effluent and dispose of it satisfactorily. This requires either space to disperse treated effluent over suitable ground or an outfall discharging to a suitable watercourse.

In the last resort, foul water can be stored, untreated in a **cesspool** for collection but the frequency and cost of collection might be high. Although Environmental Agency consent is not needed, local authority agreement is unlikely to be given unless all the other possibilities have been exhausted.

### Combined systems

Some sewers take both foul water and rainwater. However, this is a matter to be agreed with the local authority.

> 📖 *Although a combined system has to be designed and built to foul-water standards it will be cheaper than building separate foul-water and rainwater drainage systems.*

### Gravity systems

The great majority of sewers and drains depend on gravity for ensuring a flow to the outfall. Gravity systems need inspection and maintenance – and occasional repair – but they are not liable to mechanical breakdown and you should try to connect to one wherever the local authority judges that the capacity and condition of the system is suitable.

### Pumped systems

Where the ground levels make a gravity discharge impossible or impractical a pumped discharge may be considered, but only as a last resort.

> 📖 *A pumped system can be expensive to build and maintain and is liable to breakdown, especially over the Christmas period, so it should not be even considered without first consulting the drainage authority. The authority might be prepared to adopt, operate and maintain the pump and discharge pipe, but only if it agrees to the siting, design and construction.*

### Public and private sewers

A public sewer is owned and maintained by the water undertaking although it may run through private property. A private sewer is owned and maintained by the owner through whose land it passes but others may have the right to use it.

### Building over sewers

If you intend to build or extend over a sewer or drain that is shown on the authority's sewer map the local authority must reject your plans, unless it is satisfied that it can agree unconditionally or subject to conditions.

This is to ensure that the drain or sewer will not be damaged in the course of the work or later by subsidence and that access for maintenance and repair will still be possible.

> *Where a conflict arises as to the siting of the new sewer, the authority may accept a combination of bridging and additional access points.*

## F1.1 Connection to a sewer or drain

The connection may be made into a manhole or onto a length of pipe between manholes. For a connection into a manhole, the drain should discharge over the channel and in the direction of flow (⇨ 4.4.2).

### Clearance of blockages and construction of access points

Where the level of the incoming drain is substantially above the level of the sewer there are implications for drainage.

### Pipe gradients and sizes

A connection onto a pipe will usually be made with a saddle. This is a short length of drainpipe projecting through a flange. The projection enters a hole cut in the sewer and the flange, which is curved to suit the size of the sewer, is bedded against the outside. The connection should be no lower than the centre line of the sewer.

> *A connection to a sewer should be no lower than the centre line of the sewer itself.*

## F1.2 Sewage treatment works

A sewage treatment plant, as its name implies, will treat foul water continuously and therefore has an inlet and an outlet. It consists of:

*   a **settlement tank** to collect solids;
*   a **septic tank** to break down organic matter;
*   a **filtration system** to produce a flow of clean water that will not contaminate any water supply source. Efficient proprietary equipment is now available which can be hidden below ground level but will still discharge the effluent above ground level for eventual dispersal or disposal. Such equipment will, of course, require an electricity supply.

The consent of the Environmental Agency might be required for dispersal of untreated effluent over the ground and certainly will be required even for the discharge of treated effluent to a watercourse, lake or pond. Consent is not given automatically and will not normally be given where discharge to a public foul sewer is reasonably practicable.

Septic tanks can be expensive to build and maintain. You will have to pay the Environmental Agency initial and annual charges for its consent. You also will have to pay a contractor for regular de-sludging and cleaning. Despite the expense, it might be unwise to share a septic tank with a neighbour if it can be avoided.

You should be sparing with detergents during the first six months use of a new septic tank. This will give the very necessary bacteria time to establish themselves.

A sewage treatment works will comply with the Building Regulations if it is:
- **designed** to have sufficient capacity to enable the breakdown and settlement of solid matter in foul water from the building and constructed so as to prevent leakage of the contents and entry of subsoil water;
- **ventilated** – if it is covered;
- **sited** so as not to prejudice health or contaminate water supplies; and is
- accessible for de-sludging and cleaning.
  - *The purpose of the settlement tank is to allow solids to be deposited for removal, while the septic tank holds the foul water long enough for bacteria, in the absence of air (anaerobic action), to break down the matter which it contains before it passes to the filtration (aerobic) system.*

### Maintaining sewage treatment works and cesspools
The local authority is responsible for the provision of a de-sludging and cleaning service for sewage-disposal works and an emptying and cleaning service for cesspools. It may sublet these services and you may go to a private service if one is available.
  - *It is advisable to find out what services are available in your area because they might be expensive. For example, the media in a filter bed will need lifting, drying out and returning from time to time.*

## Settlement tanks and septic tanks

The capacity below the inlet should be at least 2,700 litres (2.7m³) for both settlement and septic tanks.
  - *The figure given here is a minimum size and the local authority should be consulted before a new system is built, or the use of an existing system is increased.*

### Design
The inlet and outlet of both a settlement tank and septic tank should be provided with access for inspection.

The inlet and outlet of a septic tank should also be designed to prevent disturbance to the surface scum or settled sludge. Unless the width of the tank is at least 1,200mm, the inlet should be via a dip-pipe. To limit turbulence, provision should be made to limit the flow rate of the incoming foul water. For steeply-laid drains with a diameter of up to 150mm the velocity may be limited by laying the last 12m of the incoming drain at a gradient of 1-in-50, or flatter.

Settlement tanks and septic tanks should be **fenced or covered**.

### Construction
Settlement tanks and septic tanks may be constructed of masonry, concrete or glass-reinforced concrete. The two tanks will usually be combined in one construction with a

T-shaped dip-pipe through the dividing wall. The brickwork should be at least 220mm thickness of engineering bricks laid in mortar (1:3 cement:sand). The *in situ* concrete should be at least 150mm thick (C/25/P mix).

A tank, if covered, should be ventilated and its cover should be durable, non-ventilating and of suitable strength – such as heavy concrete slabs – and be provided with an access for de-sludging and cleaning. The access should have no dimension less than 600mm and be fitted with a lockable cover of durable quality, having regard to the corrosive nature of the contents. Where the depth is more than 1m, metal step-irons or a fixed ladder should be provided.

> *It is important that, for safety reasons, the cover is durable and heavy as there have been cases of lightweight, precast, pre-stressed planks failing without warning. However, there is an argument for using treated timber because it can be seen to deteriorate.*

### Siting
All sites must be chosen with care.

**Access for maintenance**     Where a tanker will be used for de-sludging and cleaning there should be a vehicle access within 30m of the site. The access must be at a level where the work can be done without hazard to the building's occupants and without taking the contents through a dwelling or workplace. Access may be through an open covered space.

> *Tankers not only carry a limited length of hose, usually 30m, but they also rely on a vacuum to lift the contents and so cannot lift them more than 10m from one level to another.*

**Distance from a building**     No minimum has been laid down for the distance between an occupied building and a tank but 15m appears to be generally accepted.

> *Although tanks need not be covered, they can be if they are ventilated. They can then be sited nearer a building than 15m if the ventilating pipe outlets are sited further away. This could overcome any conflict between the needs of access and distance.*

**Contamination of water**     The choice of a site which will not lead to contamination of water must be governed by the circumstances, after taking into account that the construction should prevent leakage of the contents and the entry of subsoil water.

> *The main risk of contaminating water arises from the discharge of untreated or poor quality effluent. This can be avoided by regular maintenance; too many tanks are out of sight and out of mind.*

### Factory-made units
Increasing use is being made of package sewage treatment plants which can normally be buried in the ground, out of sight. These replace the septic tank, the settlement tank and the filter bed but still require regular maintenance, de-sludging and an outfall, and most also require an electricity supply.

Factory-made units will meet the requirements if they carry a British Board of Agrément (BBA) certificate and are installed in accordance with the certificate and the manufacturer's instructions.

> 🕮 *The units are generally of glass-reinforced plastics and light in weight, so par-ticular care has to be taken when installing them to prevent an empty unit from floating out of the ground if the water table is high.*

### Filtration system

A filtration system is intended to expose effluent to bacteria which, in the presence of air (aerobic action), will break down the matter which remains when it leaves the septic (anaerobic) tank.

The filtration system itself can consist either of a filter bed, down through which efflu-ent can percolate or, if space allows, a pattern of irrigation pipes, along which effluent can disperse over the ground.

If the level of the incoming foul-water drain is below the level of the outgoing effluent drain then a small pump can be introduced, where there is an electrical supply. The pump must be sited between the septic tank and the filtration system to ensure that, if a filter bed is being used, the filter media cannot become waterlogged or, if an irriga-tion system is being used, that it can be at ground surface level.

Either arrangement will discharge water clean enough to run into a watercourse, or soak into the ground. If the final disposal is to a watercourse or similar, the position of the outlet should be permanently and clearly marked.

> 🕮 *Both systems, be they filter bed or irrigation, need air in ample quantity if they are to work.*

### Filter beds

Filter beds may be constructed of masonry, concrete or glass-reinforced concrete. The brickwork should be at least 220mm thickness of engineering bricks laid in mortar (1:3 cement:sand). The *in situ* concrete should be at least 150mm thick (C/25/P mix).

### Irrigation systems

The normal irrigation system is a three-pronged or arrow-head formation of 75mm open-jointed clay pipes (field drains), laid near level in open ground and surrounded with gravel or ballast. The pipes have a total length of about 60m or more, depending on the nature of the ground: the less absorbent it is, the longer the pipework.

> 🕮 *To discourage access, and damage, to the system, it is prudent to enclose it with at least a lightweight fence, inspect it from time to time and remove vege-tation which could interfere with its working.*

## Alternative approach

The requirements can also be met by following the recommendations of BS 6297 (the relevant clauses are in Sections 1 and 2; clauses 6-11 of Section 4, and appendices). The code contains additional detailed information about design, construction and installa-tion of small sewage treatment works and cesspools, but specialist knowledge is advisable.

## F1.3 Cesspools

A cesspool can be expensive to build and the cost of frequent emptying and cleaning will be high. It would be unwise to share a cesspool with a neighbour. If you do build a cesspool, remember that the storage capacity below the inlet is what matters: you can decrease the depth by increasing the area. You might wish to do this if the water table is high or if you strike rock.

> 📖 A **cesspool** is a covered, watertight storage tank with an inlet but no outlet, and it has to be emptied regularly.

A cesspool will meet the requirements of the Building Regulations if it is:

- **designed** to have sufficient capacity to store the foul water from the building until it can be emptied;
- **constructed** so as to contain the contents and resist entry of subsoil water;
- **sited** so as not to prejudice health or contaminate water supplies, and be accessible for emptying.

### Design

The capacity below the inlet should be at least 18,000 litres (18m³).

> 📖 *The size given here is a minimum size and the local authority responsible for emptying should be consulted before a new cesspool is built, or the use of an existing one is increased.*

Cesspools should be covered, ventilated, and provided with access for inspection. Cesspools should also have no openings except for the inlet, the access for emptying and cleaning and ventilation.

### Construction

Cesspools should be constructed of masonry, concrete or glass-reinforced concrete. The brickwork should be at least 220mm thickness of engineering bricks laid in mortar (1:3 cement:sand). The *in situ* concrete should be at least 150mm thick (C/25/P mix).

Covers should be durable, non-ventilating and of suitable strength such as heavy concrete slabs. Cesspools should be provided with an access for emptying and cleaning. The access should have no dimension less than 600mm and be fitted with a lockable cover of durable quality, having regard to the corrosive nature of the contents. Where the depth is more than 1m, metal step-irons or a fixed ladder should be provided.

The earlier references made to sewage treatment in this section will apply here also to factory-made cesspools, siting, access, disposal, water contamination and the British Standard code of practice.

# F2  Rainwater disposal

## CHECKLIST
- ☐ Connection to a sewer or drain
- ☐ Soakaway
- ☐ Open outfall

## Requirements

The Building Act requires that:
- satisfactory provision must be made for the disposal of rainwater from the building (BA 21);

The Building Regulations require that:
- the rainwater outfall which is provided should be suitable (BR H3).

### Meeting the requirements

### F2.1 Connection to a sewer or drain

The connection may be made into a manhole on a rainwater or combined sewer or drain, or onto a length of pipe between manholes. For a connection into a manhole the drain should discharge over the channel and in the direction of flow. For a connection between manholes use a saddle (⇨ 4.2.1).

### F2.2 Soakaway

For many years, simple pits were used without question. Typically, they would have a diameter of 1m and a depth of 1.5m below the incoming drain – regardless of the level of the water table – and be filled with hardcore (broken brick or stone). No doubt, many are now clogged with the soil used to back-fill them to ground level but they served their purpose, or appeared to do so.

Today, a more calculated approach is sometimes adopted. First, a soakaway needs to be big enough. Second, it will be effective only if it is wholly above the water table. Perhaps the most practical course is to consult the local authority.

### Calculated capacity

You need to know the rate of inflow – rainfall rate, multiplied by area drained. You need to know also the the rate of outflow – the soil infiltration rate, or permeability of the ground. The rule is: clay bad; gravel good.

Both rainfall and infiltration rates can vary considerably in different parts of the country. For those who are interested in the calculation procedure that has been developed, it is set out with examples in the BRE Digest 365 (Sept 1991) and requires rainfall data – usually taken from a map – and permeability data, which can be taken only from site tests.

### Water table

Establish the high level of the water table, so that the soakaway can be constructed wholly above it. You will need a trial hole – say, 50mm in diameter – or some local knowledge. The normal shape for a soakaway is a cube but if the water table is high a trench shape may be more practical.

### Construction

This can be a traditional method: a simple pot filled with hardcore, to give about 30 per cent voids, to the top of the incoming drain and back-filled to ground level with soil.

Alternatively, it can be a chamber of precast concrete rings, to give 100 per cent voids, with a strong and durable cover. The cover can be set below ground level and back-filled with soil.

Several smaller soakaways, perhaps one for each downpipe, might be more convenient than one larger one.

### Siting

No minimum has been laid down for the distance between a building and a soakaway but 5m appears to have been generally accepted.

## F2.3 Open outfall

If the final disposal is to a watercourse or similar, the position of the outlet should be permanently and clearly marked.

# F3 Groundwater disposal

There is no requirement in the Building Act for a groundwater drainage system of the open outfall type.

## Open outfall

The requirements of The Building Regulations will be met if the final disposal is an open outlet to a watercourse or similar. The position of the outlet should be permanently and clearly marked.

# Appendix G
# Loft conversions

## INTRODUCTION

In this appendix the guidance is for:

G1 Site and drainage
G2 Foundations
G3 Walls
G4 Floors and stairs
G5 Roofs
G6 Finishes
G7 Piped services
G8 Wired services
G9 Fixtures and fittings
G10 Means of escape
G11 Heat loss

This section gives guidance on meeting the requirements when making an extra storey by converting the roof space into dwelling accommodation.

The meaning of basement, ground, first and second storey has been given earlier in *HomeBuilder* (⇨ Appendix C).

> 📖 A **habitable room** is one which is used or intended to be used for dwelling purposes. It includes any kitchen but not a bathroom. For ventilation purposes a habitable room does not include a room which is used solely as a kitchen.

A loft conversion is a material alteration and, in general, the requirements and the guidance on meeting them given earlier apply to a loft conversion. However, a loft conversion is treated as a special case and there are exceptions to the requirements and to the guidance. This section describes these exceptions.

## G1 Site and drainage

For guidance, you should refer to the requirements for drainage, especially where you intend to make any alterations to the foul-water or rainwater drainage systems below ground.

> 🗒 *It would be unusual if the systems were unable to take an increased flow but if you intend to discharge waste or foul water to an existing ventilation discharge stack, be sure it is suitable for the purpose.*

# G2 Foundations

The additional loads, if any, will be small and you will most probably find that the existing foundations will be adequate.

# G3 Walls

## Heat loss

For guidance, you should refer to the guidance given earlier regarding heat loss (⇨ 4.3).

## Openings

Remember that a roof which slopes steeper than 70 degrees above the horizontal is treated as though it is a wall – and that includes any openings in the roof. Openings in a roof which slopes 70 degrees or less are treated as parts of the roof.

> *The sides of a dormer window will also be treated as external walls if they slope steeper than 70 degrees.*

### External fire spread
Openings can be made within 1m of the boundary only if they are exempted openings (⇨ 4.3.3). The openings which can be made 1m or more from the boundary depend on the area of opening and the distance from the relevant boundary (⇨ 4.3.3).

### Means of escape
While a window is not acceptable as the means of escape from a second storey, it can provide a means of rescue from a second storey which is the result of a loft conversion (⇨ Diagram C–3).

# G4 Floors and stairs

### CHECKLIST
- [ ] New floor
- [ ] Existing floor
- [ ] Stairs

## G4.1 New floor

For guidance, you should refer to upper floors and stairs (⇨ 4.4).

### Structural support
You will probably find that the existing ceiling joists will not be suitable for use as floor joists. If this is the case, there are two possible ways of avoiding their replacement and damaging the ceiling below, by using binders and insertion.

**Binders**     It may be possible to strengthen the ceiling joists by picking them up with one or more binders laid directly on the joists (at right angles to them). If the binders can be supported on suitable walls, or by hangers fixed to the roof rafters, the joists can then be strapped to them. It may also be possible to incorporate the binder and hangers in the partition walls which you will probably need to form the new rooms.

**Insertion**If you cannot use binders, it might be possible to lay new floor joists between the ceiling joists (raising the floor level) and support these joists on suitable walls.

### *Fire resistance (collapse)*
The floor should have 30 minutes fire resistance (spread) – loadbearing, integrity and insulation when tested from below.

## G4.2 Existing floor

For guidance, you should refer to the requirements discussed earlier (⇨ 4.4.2) for floors and stairs and upper floors.

### *Structural support*
You only need to consider the existing floor if you will be placing loads on it that could exceed its loadbearing capacity.

### *Fire resistance (collapse)*

## G4.3 Stairs

Here we are concerned with new stairs.

### *New stairs*
For guidance, you should refer to the requirements discussed earlier (⇨ 4.4.3) for floors and stairs – but with the following exceptions.

**Headroom**　　　Where the roof does not allow enough space to achieve the height of 2m, the height in the centre of the stair may be reduced to 1.9m and against the wall to 1.8m (⇨ Diagram G–1).

**Spiral and helical stairs**　　　Stairs with goings less than those given in BS 5395 can be considered in conversion work where space is limited and the stair serves no more than one habitable room.

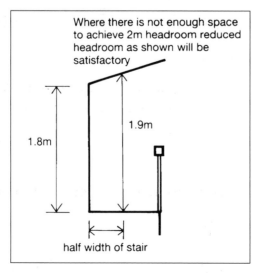

Where there is not enough space to achieve 2m headroom reduced headroom as shown will be satisfactory

1.9m

1.8m

half width of stair

*Diagram G–1:*
**Measurement – reduced headroom**

**Alternating stairs**    Designed specifically to save space, alternating stairs may be used where space is limited but only in straight flights and only to give access to one habitable room together with, if desired, a bathroom and/or WC. This WC must not be the only one in the house. The design is subject to certain limitations (⇨ Diagram G–2) and users rely for their reasonable safety on familiarity through regular use.

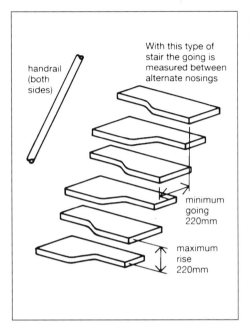

*Diagram G–2:*
**Alternating stairs**

With this type of stair the going is measured between alternate nosings

handrail (both sides)

minimum going 220mm

maximum rise 220mm

**Fixed ladders**    These ladders may be used for loft conversions but only where the space is (without alteration to the existing space) too limited to accommodate a stair and then only to give access to one habitable room. The ladder should have fixed handrails. Retractable ladders are not an acceptable means of escape.

> *This does not exclude the use of retractable ladders to give access to a roof space which is not a habitable room.*

# G5  Roofs

For guidance, you should refer to the guidance given for roofs (⇨ 4.5).

### Heat loss

For guidance, you should refer to the guidance given earlier (⇨ 4.5).

### Means of escape

While a window is not acceptable as the means of escape from a second storey it can provide a means of rescue from a second storey which is the result of a loft conversion.

# G6  Finishes

For guidance, you should refer to the guidance given for finishes (⇨ 4.6).

## G7   Piped services

For guidance, you should refer to the requirements discussed earlier (⇨ 4.7) for piped services.

> ✍ *If you intend to discharge waste or foul water to an existing ventilation discharge stack (soil vent pipe) be sure that it is suitable for the purpose.*

## G8   Wired services

For guidance, you should refer to the requirements discussed earlier (⇨ 4.8) for wired services.

## G9   Fixtures and fittings

For guidance, you should refer to the requirements discussed earlier (⇨ 4.9) for fixtures and fittings.

Position heat-producing appliances to suit.

## G10   Means of escape

There is no requirement to enclose the stairs but, if there is a basement, there may be additional requirements.

### One storey to two storeys

Each habitable room should **either** open directly to a hallway or stairway leading to the entrance or have a suitable outside door or opening window through which the occupants of the house can reach a place of safety.

### Two storeys to three storeys

For guidance when the roof space of a house with two storeys is being converted into a third storey with habitable rooms, refer to the earlier advice in *HomeBuilder* regarding the means of escape from houses with three storeys (⇨ Appendix C) – **unless** the following conditions will be satisfied:

- the work will not involve raising the roofline above the existing ridge level;
- the new storey will have no more than two habitable rooms; and
- the area of the new storey will be no more than 50m².

If the conditions will be satisfied, the **existing first floor** should usually have 30 minutes fire resistance but a **modified 30-minute standard** of fire resistance can be accepted for those parts of the floor which:

- separate only rooms, not circulation spaces; and
- if the rest of the guidance is followed.

Small openings and gaps should be suitably fire stopped.

> 📖 A **modified 30-minute standard** requires the loadbearing performance to
> be maintained for 30 minutes but requires the integrity and insulation
> performances to be maintained for only 15 minutes when the floor is tested
> from the underside (REI 30/15/15).

## Separation of the new storey

The new storey should be separated from the storey below by fire-resisting construction.

The new floor should have 30 minutes fire resistance.

## Stair enclosure

All doorways in the enclosure should be fitted with a door.

The **existing doors** to habitable rooms should be fitted with a self-closing device and **new doors** to habitable rooms should be fitted with self-closing fire doors. Any glazing in the enclosure – and in any doors in the enclosure except doors to bathrooms and WCs – should be fire resisting.

### Existing stair

The stairway in the existing storeys should be enclosed with fire-resisting construction and the enclosure should, **either**:

- extend to a final exit; **or**
- give access to at least two separated alternative routes (⇨ Diagram C–4(b)).

### New stair

This may be a continuation of the existing stair or it may be a separate stair. In either case it may be an alternating tread stair (⇨ Diagram G–2). The intention is to protect the people in the loft storey if a fire in the lower storeys could prevent them from reaching a final exit at ground-floor level.

If the new stair is a **continuation of the existing stair**, then the fire enclosure around the existing stair must be both continued upwards to separate the extended stairway from the loft space and fitted at the top level with a self-closing fire-resisting door to complete the separation (⇨ Diagram G–3).

*Diagram G–3:* **Protected stairway**

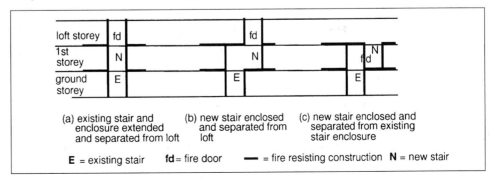

(a) existing stair and enclosure extended and separated from loft

(b) new stair enclosed and separated from loft

(c) new stair enclosed and separated from existing stair enclosure

**E** = existing stair    **fd** = fire door    ▬ = fire resisting construction    **N** = new stair

If the new stair is **not a continuation** of the existing stair and stairway enclosure, it must be provided with its own fire-resisting enclosure to separate it from the accommodation on the existing first storey. There are, then, two possibilities. **Either:**

1   The fire enclosure around the new stair must be both continued upwards to separate it from the loft space and fitted at the top level with a self-closing fire-resisting door (⇨ Diagram G–3). **Or:**

2   If the fire enclosure around the new stair is not continued upwards to separate it from the loft space it must be fitted at the bottom level with a self-closing fire-resisting door to separate it not only from the accommodation on the existing first storey but also from the enclosure around the existing stair (⇨ Diagram G–3).

# G11  Heat loss

A loft conversion is not a **material change of use** as the use of the building remains the same. However, the conversion will be a **material alteration** if it will result in the building not complying with one or more of the "relevant requirements" listed in Regulation 3(3) of the Building Regulations where previously it did so.

This listing includes Part A (structure), B1 (means of escape), B3 (internal fire spread - structure), B4 (external fire spread) of Schedule 1 and it is almost certain that one of these, and probably more than one, will be relevant.

As the alteration is a material alteration, **building work** must be carried out so that it complies with all the applicable requirements of Schedule 1. Also, it must be carried out so that, after it has been completed, **the building** complies with the requirements of Schedule 1 or, so far as it did not comply before, it is made no more unsatisfactory.

## What does this mean in practice?

You should take up any loft insulation you now have where it would be under the new rooms (you may be able to re-use it) and you should insulate:

•   the **existing walls** where they will be exposed to the new rooms;

•   the **new partitions** which separate the new rooms from any roof space areas which will remain;

•   the **roof** above the new rooms (or the new ceiling if you will have one);

•   the **roofs** over new dormer windows (if any).

For guidance refer to the earlier advice on conservation.

# Appendix H
# Relevant requirements

## INTRODUCTION

In this appendix the guidance is for:

H1 Material alteration
H2 Material change of use
H3 Controlled service or fitting

These are the requirements referred to in Section 1.2.


## H1  Material alteration

These are the **relevant requirements** which, if they would be adversely affected by an alteration, define it as a **material alteration**.

Following each requirement is an indication of :
*       the parts of the building to which it can apply;
*       where you will find the guidance to meeting the provisions in Part 4 and the Appendix.

### A Structure (structural support)

Loading (BR A1)
Ground movement (BR A2)
    4.1 Site: 4.1.5 Foundations; 4.1.6 Ground-supported floors
    4.3 Walls (except 4.3.4 and 4.3.7)
    4.4 Floors and stairs
    4.5 Roofs

### B Fire safety

Means of escape (BR B1)
    C Means of escape
    G Loft conversions
Internal fire spread – structure (BR B3)
    4.3.6 Internal walls – Fire resistance (collapse)
    4.4.2 Upper floors – Fire resistance (collapse)
External fire spread (BR B4)
    4.3.1 External walls – External fire spread
    4.5 Roofs – External fire spread
Access and facilities of the fire service (BR B5)
    4.1.2 Site and foundations – fire service access

# H2 Material change of use

These are the **relevant requirements** with which the building will have to comply if a change of use is defined as a material change of use. You will have to carry out whatever alterations are needed to make it comply in addition to any alterations which you may yourself choose to carry out. Following each requirement are the parts of the building to which it can apply and where, with one exception, you will find the guidance to meeting the provisions in Part 4 or the Appendix of *HomeBuilder*.

## B Fire safety

Means of escape (BR B1)
> C Means of escape

Internal fire spread – linings (BR B2)
> 4.6 Finishes – Walls and cladding

Internal fire spread – structure (BR B3)
> 4.3 Walls – fire resistance (collapse)
> 4.4 Floors and stairs – fire resistance (collapse)

External fire spread – roofs (BR B4[2])
> 4.5 Roofs – External fire spread

Access and facilities for the fire service (BR B5)
> 4.1.2 Site and foundations – fire service access

### *Resistance to the passage of sound*

Airborne sound (walls) (BR E1)
Airborne sound (floors and stairs) (BR E2)
Impact sound (floors and stairs) (BR E3)

## F Ventilation

Means of ventilation (BR F1)
> E: Ventilation

Condensation in roofs (BR F2)
> 4.5 Roofs

## G Hygiene

Sanitary conveniences and washing facilities (BR G1)
> 4.9.3 Fixtures and fittings – Sanitary appliances

Bathrooms (BR G2)
> 4.3.9 Fixtures and fittings – Sanitary appliances

## H Drainage and waste disposal

Solid waste storage (BR H4)
> 4.1.1 Site and foundations – Solid waste storage (access)
> 4.9.4 Fixtures and fittings – Solid waste storage (capacity)

## J Heat-producing appliances

Air supply (BR J1)
Discharge of products of combustion (BR J2)

Protection of building (BR J3)

4.9 Fixtures and fittings – Heat-producing appliances

## L Conservation of fuel and power

(BR L1)

4.1.6 Ground supported floors

4.3.1 External walls

4.3.5 Internal walls

4.4.1 Suspended ground floors

4.4.2 Upper floors

4.5 Roofs

4.7 Piped services – Water-services (heat loss)

4.9 Fixtures and fittings – Heat-producing appliances (controls)

D Energy conservation (heat losses through the fabric; heat losses through gaps in the fabric)

### Additional requirements

If the building will be used as a dwelling where previously it was not:

Resistance to weather and ground moisture (BR C4)

4.2 Foundations – Strip-foundations (moisture); Ground supported floors (moisture)

4.3 Walls (moisture)

4.4 Suspended ground floor (moisture);

4.5 Roofs (moisture)

Resistance to the passage of sound (BR E1-E3)

See Approved Document E

Resistance to the passage of sound (BR E1-E3)

# H3  Controlled service or fitting

These are the requirements which define a controlled service or fitting and with which new work must therefore comply.

G Hygiene

Sanitary conveniences and washing facilities (BR G1)

Bathrooms (BR G2)

4.9.3 Sanitary appliances

Hot water storage (BR G3)

4.7.3 Water services – Unvented hot-water storage systems

H Drainage and waste disposal

Foul water drainage system (BR H1)

4.2.1 Drainage – Foul water drainage

F1 Drainage disposal – Foul water

Cesspools, septic tanks and settlement tanks (BR H2)

F12 Sewage treatment – Cesspools

Rainwater drainage (BR H3)

4.2.2 Drainage – Rainwater drainage

F2 Drainage disposal – Rainwater

4.7.2 Piped services – Rainwater collection

Solid waste storage (BR H4)

4.1.1 Site and foundations – Solid waste storage (access)

4.9.4 Fixtures and fittings – Solid-waste storage (capacity)

J Heat-producing appliances

Air supply (BR J1)

Discharge of products of combustion (BR J2)

Protection of building (BR J3)

4.9 Fixtures and fittings – Heat-producing appliances

# Useful addresses

Ask your district council for the addresses of your planning, building control, highway and fire authorities. See your local telephone book, or Yellow Pages, for the addresses of your statutory water and sewage undertakers (usually both entered under "Water") and gas and electricity authorities.

The following lists those bodies and authorities mentioned in *HomeBuilder*.

Association of Corporate Approved Inspectors
    The Secretary
    Louisa House, 92/93 Edward Street
    Birmingham B1 2RE
    *Telephone:* 0121 233 8888

Association of Planning Supervisors
    16 Rutland Square
    Edinburgh EH1 2BE
    *Telephone:* 0131 221 9959

British Board of Agrément
    PO Box 195, Bucknalls Lane, Garston
    Watford WD2 7HG
    *Telephone:* 01923 670844

British Geological Survey
    Keyworth
    Nottingham NG12 5GG
    *Telephone:* 0115 936 3100

British Standards Institution (BSI)
    British Standards House, 389 Chiswick High Road
    London W4 4AL
    *Telephone:* 0181 996 9000

British Research Establishment (BRE)
    Garston
    Watford WD2 7JR
    *Telephone:* 01923 894040

Cadw
    Brunel House, 2 Fitzalan Road
    Cardiff CF2 1UY
    *Telephone:* 01222 500 200

Construction Industry Council
26 Store Street
London WC1E 7BT
*Telephone:* 0171 637 8692

Construction Industry Training Board
Bircham Newton
Kings Lynn
PE31 6RH
*Telephone:* 01485 577 577

Council of Registered Gas Installers (CORGI)
4 Elmwood, Chineham Business Park, Crockford Lane
Basingstoke
RG24 8WG
*Telephone:* 01256 372 300

English Heritage (officially the Historic Buildings and Monuments Commission for England)
23 Saville Row
London W1X 1AB
*Telephone:* 0171 973 3000

Environmental Agency
Guildbourne House, Chatsworth Road
Worthing
BN11 1LD
*Telephone:* 0645 333 111

Institute of Plumbing
64 Station Lane
Hornchurch
RM12 6NB
*Telephone:* 01708 472 791

Institution of Electrical Engineers (IEE)
Savoy Place
London WC2R 0BL
*Telephone:* 0171 240 1871

National House-Building Council
Buildmark House, Chiltern Avenue
Amersham
HP6 5AP
*Telephone:* 01494 434477

National Inspection Council for Electrical Installation Contracting (NICEIC)
Vintage House, 37 Albert Embankment
London SE1 7UJ

*Telephone:* 0171 582 7746

Oil Firing Technical Association for the Petroleum Industry
Century House, 100 High Street
Banstead
*Telephone:* 01737 373311

Royal Institute of British Architects (RIBA)
66 Portland Place
London W1N 4AD
*Telephone:* 0171 580 5533

Royal Institute of Chartered Surveyors (RICS)
12 Great George Street, Parliament Square
London SW1P 3AD
*Telephone:* 0171 222 7000

Royal Town Planning Institute
26 Portland Place
London W1N 4BE
*Telephone:* 0171 636 9107

Secretary of State for the Environment (Regions and Transport)
Building Regulations Division, Bressenden Place
London SW1E 5DU
*Telephone:* 0171 890 3000

Secretary of State for Wales (Welsh Office)
Rivers House, Plas-y-Afon, St Mellons Business Park, St Mellons
Cardiff CF3 0LT
*Telephone:* 01222 825111

WIMLAS Limited
St Peter's House, 6/8 High Street
Iver SL0 9NG
*Telephone:* 01753 737744